The Institute of Archaeology of the USSR Academy of Sciences, Moscow

The National Museum of Afghanistan, Kabul

THE GOLDEN HOARD
OF BACTRIA

From the Tillya-tepe Excavations
in Northern Afghanistan

By Victor Sarianidi

Harry N. Abrams, Inc., Publishers, New York

Aurora Art Publishers, Leningrad

Translated from the Russian by Arthur Shkarovsky-Raffé
Layout by Stanislav Malakhov
Photography by Leonid Bogdanov and Vladimir Terebenin

Library of Congress Cataloging in Publication Data

Sarianidi, V. I. (Viktor Ivanovich)
    The golden hoard of Bactria.

    1. Tillya-tepe Site (Afghanistan) 2. Goldwork—
Afghanistan. 3. Afghanistan—Antiquities. 4. Tombs—
Afghanistan. I. Title.
DS375.T54S27   1985   958'.101   84-14654
ISBN 0-8109-0987-1

Created by Aurora Art Publishers, Leningrad, for joint
publication of Aurora, Harry N. Abrams, Inc., New York,
and Baihaqi Publishers, Kabul

Printed and bound in Vienna, Austria

Contents

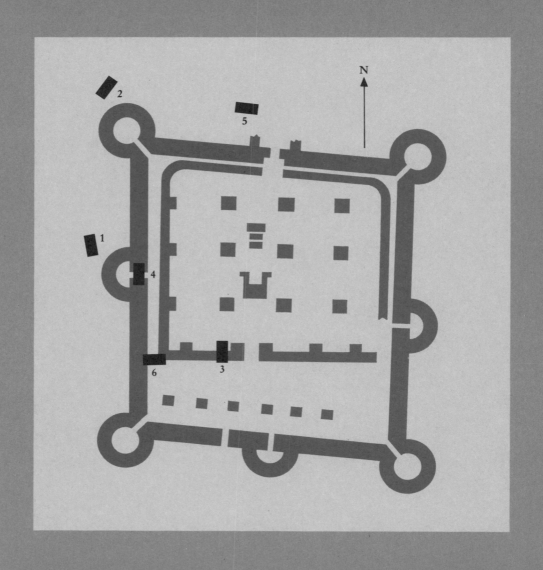

Plan of the Temple on the Tillya-tepe
Burials 1–6

THE STORY
OF THE EXCAVATION

It was the autumn of 1978. We of the field expedition came to Sheremetyevo International Airport outside Moscow to board the flight to Kabul. As we sat in the embarkation lounge listening to the multilingual babble all around, we could not help but wonder what the future season of fieldwork in Afghanistan held in store for us. We knew that we had months of hard work ahead. At the same time we could only marvel at the vicissitudes of life.

Indeed, our joint Afghan-Soviet Archaeological Expedition had been organized a mere ten years or so earlier. But what colossal changes this brief span had brought! We had started out in 1969, when a king was still on the throne, and proceeded after he had been deposed and a republic had been proclaimed. And now we were to go, once again, after the Revolution of 1978 had ushered into being the new Democratic Republic of Afghanistan. We had but a hazy picture of what would meet our eyes there. Yet there was one purpose that we had centered on: to keep the thread of continuity in our work unbroken. Although it was late autumn, we had to start the excavation of one of the ancient sites of archaeological interest.

We believed it best to pick a site in close proximity to some inhabited area, probably a town. Accordingly, we concentrated all of our field research on the ancient site atop Tillya-tepe, the "Golden Mound" that lies in the neighborhood of Shibarghan in Northern Afghanistan.

At the very outset of our project, ten years back, our eyes had been drawn to the majestic ruins of an ancient metropolis in this region, which the local Turkic-speaking inhabitants call Yemshi-tepe. Its tall, mighty walls pierced by several narrow gateways were fortified by defense towers and formed an impregnable ring of some two thousand feet (5 km) in diameter. Inside, in the northern section, stood the citadel, at whose foot were the remains of what had apparently been the palatial residence of the local ruler. Some fifty acres (20 ha) in area, this ancient city, indubitably a vast one for its time, comprised, along with the small villages of its sprawling suburbs, the administrative seat of the entire neighboring region, once part of the legendary empire of Bactria. The narrow strip of the Shibarghan oasis, which is sandwiched between the northern foothills of the Hindu Kush Mountains and the sandy deserts along the left-hand bank of the Amu Darya River, was in its day part of the fertile Bactrian plain.

Prior to the start of our expedition, no Bactrian sites of pre-antiquity were known,

Photography
in the Introduction
is by Vladimir Bury,
Vladimir Goncharov
and Alexander Shik

so our chances of immediately discovering one or several were very poor indeed. One could make out the flattened cones of ancient sites amidst the cotton fields filling the flat plain around Yemshi-tepe, but we knew that these sites had been populated in times of antiquity. As is usually the case, we guessed that the older sites lay further away, by the ruins looming almost right on the horizon. However, investigations there failed to produce anything new, merely indicating that these had been villages populated concurrently with Yemshi-tepe. Curiously enough, it turned out that what we sought lay but one-third of a mile (.5 km) away from the city's walls.

Climbing the slope of one more mound, we had not the slightest inkling of what lay in store for us. Overgrown with dry, brittle grass and weeds, this hillock—measuring about ten feet (3 m) in height and about 330 feet (100 m) in diameter—appeared to have no characteristics that would distinguish it from the others inspected before, being if anything even smaller in size. The reader can well imagine the surprised delight we felt, when we discovered atop this mound ancient

potsherds with painted ornamentation that the sun had bleached almost white. Nothing of this order had ever been found in Northern Afghanistan; potsherds of an identical nature were known only from the southern regions of Soviet Turkmenia, where they date to the end of the second millennium B.C. That artifacts of a similarly venerable vintage turned up here, almost at once, in what had once been Bactria, seemed incredible. A trial dig was initiated. The very first local peasant questioned as to what the site was called immediately and unthinkingly said: "Why, this is Tillya-tepe."

The intriguing, exciting ring of this name seemed to foretell some sensational find, yet day after day of digging produced nothing but more of the same unpretentious sherds, some not even ornamented. The small trench dug at the top of the mound, however, did bring to light the private houses of a rustic community dating back to the middle of the first millennium B.C.

The inclement December weather compelled us to interrupt our excavations of Tillya-tepe and await the next season. Back in Kabul by 1970, we readied ourselves for further digging, only to learn that while we had been away the asphalt highway being laid—over a period of several years—between the capital and Northern Afghanistan had reached Shibarghan. To lay the road its builders needed to throw up an embankment of earth. Although there were dozens of mounds along both sides of the prospective roadway, the builders, for some unfathomable reason, chose to dig up the Tillya-tepe mound. The huge excavator rhythmically burrowed into the soil; on one side we saw a line of empty dump trucks waiting, on the other, filled trucks scuttling away toward the site of the future highway. By the time we reached the spot, the destruction had assumed alarming proportions. In the place of what had once been a conical hillock was now a huge excavated bowl in the midst of which, swathed in eddying clouds of dust, the steel beam of the excavator swung unendingly to and fro. The potsherds splintered into thousands of fragments in the grip of the iron jaws of the excavator's scoop, while its massive treads completely flattened the walls of the ancient dwellings. Only thanks to our vigorous intervention was further destruction of this ancient site halted. Indeed, as we learned later, only a few yards were left of what today comprises Tillya-tepe's glory. We did not resume our own excavations until the following year, 1971, and even then conducted digging on a limited scale.

Over the next six years, until 1977, Tillya-tepe lay neglected by the side of the motorway between Akcha and Shibarghan, with only the half-filled-in pits and the sagging rim of the excavation serving as reminders of the heated arguments that had raged around it several years earlier. However, we had not written Tillya-tepe off in the plans of our expedition, and in the autumn of 1977 we resumed fieldwork there for the third time.

Half-gone and gripped in a stranglehold by the surrounding fields of cotton, the mound could still yield much information about the people who had once lived there. Having cleared away a small section of a cotton field with great difficulty and proceeding with our excavations, we uncovered the remains of a massive temple-like edifice that had been encircled by a defensive wall. Though tempted to investigate at least the overall floor plan and significance of this structure, we had to leave Afghanistan for home, as the winter of 1977 was near. Furthermore, to our regret, officials from the National Ministry of Information and Culture demanded that, before proceeding with further excavations, we attempt to restore a Moslem mosque, or medressah, which implied at least the temporary suspension of our work at Tillya-tepe.

Then came the Revolution of 1978. In power now were men espousing new ideas

and concepts as to what cooperation between neighboring countries should be like. As a result, in the autumn of that year our expedition set out for Kabul and thence to Shibarghan to complete our excavations of Tillya-tepe.

As work gathered momentum, the outline of an imposing edifice, a temple, whose collapsed ruins had at one time formed the mound, gradually took shape. This was a twenty-foot-tall platform constructed of oblong sun-dried mud bricks that rested atop a small, natural elevation. Almost a true square, it had along its outer perimeter a wall of similar mud bricks, with round towers at each corner and turrets in the middle of each side. Digging further, we soon disclosed within the walls the tops of brick columns. This seemed to be a happy beginning, full of promise. However, with the coming of November the weather worsened, and a raw, damp wind blew in drizzling clouds from the Amu Darya. Toward mid-month we were already thinking of calling off all further digging, especially after the incessant downpour of November 12, which forced us to cease operations by midday.

9

Besides the usual potsherds there was one find that day which, though claiming our attention, was not duly appreciated at the time. No wonder, as it consisted of the corroded fragments of iron bars from which iron nails protruded. One had been bent at a right angle and looked like a clamp that had held boards or planks together. Only later did we learn that it was from the coffin of our first "gold" burial site.

As it continued to pour the whole of the following day, November 13, digging was totally out of the question. Meanwhile, to open in Kabul on November 15 was an International Kushan Seminar. Fate so ordained that on that date—a bright, sunny day as it happened—Afghan and Soviet archaeologists made their now world-famous discovery. In the process of excavating the fort's western side one of the workmen turned up something on his spade that shot forth a yellow gleam. Very shortly after, we were all amazedly examining a small gold disk that lay among the clods of damp earth. Further digging made it clear that we had hit upon an ancient burial site rich in grave goods.

We then meticulously inspected the heap of earth that our workmen had turned over before November 13. Our labors were well rewarded. We discovered 164 gold plates, which had lain there all this time unwatched and unguarded. The local authorities were immediately apprised of the event and, very shortly after, armed guards were posted. On the next day it was decided to throw up a kind of shed over the site to protect the archaeologists and restorers.

Concurrent excavations of the temple resulted in the discovery of more burial sites. The fifth one was disclosed toward the end of the year, when we had just about finished clearing the third site and were intensively investigating the fourth.

Though we had only begun to clear the graves, rumors had spread far and wide that we had found a man of gold buried in a coffin of gold, as well as heavy gold ingots and pitchers stuffed with precious gems. Visitors poured in by foot and bicycle, on horse and donkey, in carriages and cars. There were days when one would see a whole fleet of cars and trucks of various makes and models parked in the vicinity. Soon a well-trodden path led from the road to Tillya-tepe. There came young and old, rich and poor, worker and schoolboy, office clerk and university student, alone and in groups. This all very much resembled a holy pilgrimage, with the curious flocking in from places as far away as Akcha, Andha, Mazar-i-Sharif, and Baglan. Even the big buses plying the Kabul–Shibarghan route would turn off the highway toward the digs. Yet, the citizens of Shibarghan were always in the forefront of the multitude. Indeed, in fine weather the activity provoked many to take pleasant strolls out in the country, and few ignored paying homage to the Golden Mound.

Meanwhile, we of the field expedition gradually worked out a novel but quite firm procedure of operation. Every day the archaeologists would submit the grave goods recovered to the chief, and an inventory would be drawn up. Next, the artifacts went to the restorers, who then passed them over, again via the chief, to be photographed using every type of color film. Each object was photographed several times from different angles. Also a hundred or so identical bits of plate had to be arranged and again photographed from diverse angles to provide a general notion of their appearance. That done, the objects would be returned to the chief who then submitted them to the special agent for the Institute of Archaeology of the Ministry of Information and Culture of the Democratic Republic of Afghanistan, to be registered in the official museum inventory.

Considering that we were engaged in simultaneously clearing two, if not three, graves, one will easily comprehend the difficulties we encountered. We soon realized that to adhere to the procedure described above, we would not have enough time to check each of the hundreds and thousands of items—many of which were thin gold plaques—against the inventory. Furthermore, the task of compiling a general catalogue loomed ahead, for which it would be necessary to examine at least the main finds once again. So, after some thought, we decided that all transfers of objects should rest solely on trust. And it should be emphasized that despite the fabulous abundance of gold objects, no artifacts, not even one the size of a penny, were lost or mislaid. At the end of each day the entire stock completely matched the inventory.

One must note that the members of our expedition were very uncomfortable. Indeed, after a whole day spent in a bleak and damp shaft grave some six feet or so down, all that the archaeologists could think of was the warmth and hot meal awaiting them in the evening. As a

rule, we had two members of the staff taking charge of each grave, and part of their job was to tick off, independently of one another, all the finds made during the day. Only when both counts tallied could they consider the job done.

Just imagine their numb fingers trying to separate the thin, identical plaques, which seemed obstinately to stick together, only to learn after a good half-hour spent counting that the total wouldn't tally! How frustrating! And while they had to start all over again, the other members of the expedition whose task for the day was done, sat and waited in trucks or cars for the results, silently cursing the gold and the graves and their doleful lot of having had to go and discover these "gold" burial sites! How much nicer it would be to deal with the usual type of archaeological artifact! After all, potsherds could lie around for weeks on end stacked and stored near the digs, and it wouldn't enter anyone's head that there was any need to keep a strict count of them, or—what's more—to mount guard over them. Gradually, we worked out by rule of thumb (so to speak) a system for our stocktaking; we would stack up the small plaques in heaps of five each, which enabled us to detect error more easily. Before leaving for the day, the archaeologists officially notified the senior officer of the posted guard.

However, before that was done the following operations had to be carried out. The flaps of the tent above the grave were drawn tight—or if a shed had been erected its door was

11

tightly secured—and the approaches to the graves were carpeted with tarpaulins, the ends of which overlapped the tent flaps or shed door. Next, a layer of soft earth was evenly shoveled on top of the tarpaulins and a special mark or device imprinted thereupon by the archaeologist supervising the excavation of the grave in question. On the following morning the senior guard officer and the supervising archaeologist would verify the imprinted mark and only then could the earth and the tarpaulins be removed and the tent flaps or shed door unfastened to allow the digging to be resumed. This procedure was faithfully repeated day after day. In fact, after the day was over we could not go back, unless we knew the appropriate password, as now the guards bore full responsibility for keeping everything intact. At the outset there were only a few guards, but after more graves were discovered, the entire area was wired for electricity, and trailers were brought in to house the now rather large detail mounting an around-the-clock guard.

We were running short of both time and funds for extensive digging, when suddenly we hit upon one more tomb, which obviously also required investigation. Indeed, we were still working on the goods of the fourth grave when the first layers of earth were removed from the top of the latest discovered—fifth—burial. We had only about a fortnight left on the schedule for the season.

It would, of course, have been easiest to save the fifth burial until the next field season—as we were advised to do. On the other hand, we could have suspended further digging around the temple altogether and employed the labor and funds thus released to search for and clear more "gold" burial sites, as that appeared to be far more efficient. However, the ethics and obligations of our calling made it essential for us to complete the job precisely at this moment, as beneath the temple's western side, a sixth burial site had just been discovered.

Toward the close-down of operations each day, we packed the grave goods of each site into separate crates that were reliably secured by heavy, massive padlocks. As I remember, it was early in the morning of a very ordinary day for the staff of our expedition, when all had gone out to the digs, except for myself. I wanted to investigate more thoroughly a fascinating crown uncovered amidst the grave goods in the third tomb. I opened the lid of the appropriate crate but could not find the object among the other artifacts. This did not cause me any particular worry, as I knew from experience that it might have been misplaced and put into one of the other crates. Indeed, how many visitors, ranging from officials of the Soviet Embassy to locals of varied standing and eminence, had begged to be shown some of the finds! I unlocked the other crates and gathered all that had been thus misplaced, but to my horror, I could not find the crown. I next rummaged through my desk, again to no avail. I sat down for a moment to collect my thoughts, and resolved, quite in keeping with the methods suggested by the best of fictional detectives, to inspect the room methodically, starting from the left-hand side.

Now I checked and rechecked all the crates and desks and even turned my sleeping bag inside out. I examined the contents of a small strongbox, where, in addition to our greatly depleted expedition funds, a number of small packets and matchboxes in which the smaller gold artifacts had been placed were kept. By now I was perspiring freely. This was no wonder, as all the finds were stored in my room, which was always securely locked when I was away, and I clearly remembered that after going through the hands of the restorers and photographers, the crown had been deposited in my hands again and had been duly registered.

After some respite I started searching my room once again, only now beginning from the right-hand side. Again, my efforts were futile. Now, a crown, as one will easily understand, is no bit of gold plate, no ring, that could be lost amidst the multitude of other objects. If, God forbid, it had been stolen, the other valuables would have likewise disappeared, I reasoned. But all the other artifacts were there. I searched again and again, high and low, but all to no point. Totally depressed, I wondered what would happen now!

My unsuspecting colleagues were, by now, wrapped in slumber, but I kept circulating around my room striking out at random, almost in a trance. Cursed be that gold! Opening up the crates, I stared at the gold objects stored within, looking with revulsion and repugnance at all that glittered and gleamed in the light of the electric lamp. Particularly revolting were the plentiful gold plaques that kept slipping out of my fingers when I again and again inspected the boxes in which they were kept. My life was over, I thought. And all because of this accursed gold, the cause of my misfortune!

The night was far gone when, for the umpteenth time, I opened the door of our strongbox and mechanically, merely to assure myself and allay my own conscience, rummaged through the matchboxes, which, naturally, could on no account hold such a large object as the missing crown. Not really understanding what I was doing, I took them all out, suddenly to discover the neatly folded and tied crown beneath. Only now did it occur to me that,

having registered and duly described the object, I had stowed it away for better safekeeping in the strongbox, where I would deposit most of the smaller objects received from the other graves. It was the jumble of packets and matchboxes that had blocked the crown from view. But, as they say, there's a silver lining in every cloud. This tragicomic ending made me wonder why the crown was not constructed in one solid piece, but could be dismantled. Could it be so that, considering the nomad's traditional way of life, the crown could be safely stowed away in a saddlebag, without fear of damaging it during long treks or military campaigns?

Time was running out, but affairs kept piling up. According to our scheme of operations, I was to leave for Kabul early and start passing over our finds to the National Museum. The rest of the staff was to complete investigations of burial sites 4 and 6 and to conserve the digs. In short, there was exactly one week before I had to go, and we were all out at the digs, each man performing his appropriate task, when from behind the tall heaps of cast-up earth, one of our archaeologists appeared and silently beckoned to me. When I approached he opened up his hand

13

to reveal bits of gold plate from another—the seventh—burial site! That was the last straw.

Indeed, our time was almost up, our funds were exhausted, and we ourselves were worn out after all the stresses and strains of virtually five months of arduous, intensive, and—the main thing—nerve-wracking labor. Plain, simple arithmetic showed that we needed at least six weeks on the average to explore but one burial site, but we had only a week left for everything. Despite the fact that the temptation to learn what the grave furnishings of the seventh site were like was heightened since the gold plaques glittering in the archaeologist's palm appeared to be of a quite novel order, duty summoned me to forego emotion for common sense. Our workmen were astonished when we told them to cover up the seventh site. Armed Afghan soldiers were posted on Tillya-tepe to guard the unrecovered treasures until the next field season.

In the early morning of February 8, 1979, we left Shibarghan in an army jeep for Mazar-i-Sharif. The idea was to pay the local governor a brief visit, acquire from him an exit permit, and, without further delay, head for Kabul. We reached Mazar-i-Sharif quickly enough, but events there unfolded in slow motion. It was the dinner break when we arrived, and the governor was out. When he reappeared promptly after his break had ended, we learned that before issuing us an exit permit he was required to inform the central authorities in Kabul. To tell the truth, it was a turbulent time, and we had to cross the Hindu Kush Mountains, where anything might happen— carrying, mind you, a veritable treasure trove of gold!

The governor telephoned Kabul, and after some time a categoric refusal to have us go by road came through. We were told that with our precious cargo we must go out to Kabul by air. There were no flights that day and so we had to spend the night in a hotel. Two armed guards were posted outside my hotel room and denied access to all, even our driver, while more guards were posted at the hotel entrance and also under cover nearby. One might think such precautions excessive, but, after all, the treasure in my room was worth millions of dollars.

Skies did not clear until the third day, and, under armed escort we finally drove out to the local airport. Soon a small plane landed. All its passengers were ordered out and into the airport building. While their flight documents were processed, we, with our precious cargo, were hurried onto the plane. Through the portholes we could see policemen frisking the bewildered passengers before letting them climb back on board.

After a few minutes aloft we found ourselves above the Hindu Kush range. Seeing this part of Afghanistan from the air instead of a car was entirely different. Mighty, craggy summits topped by white snowcaps and twinkling blue glaciers seemed to float by. Far below we could make out a deep, narrow gorge through which ran the silvery thread of a mountain stream; a tiny hamlet was comfortably ensconced on the incline. Closeted behind sheer crags, its only link with the outer world were some barely discernible mountain trails.

Finally, the mountains seemed to grow smaller and gentler, and more and more hamlets could now be glimpsed in the ravines. Eventually the town of Charikar loomed in an emerald patch in the foothills abutting the northern slopes of Hindu Kush. Later disembarking in Kabul's airport, we were met by officials from the Ministry of Information and Culture and a police squad that had arrived in two jeeps. Under armed escort, we were whisked with our treasures at top speed to the suburb of Darul Aman on the other side of the Afghan capital, where the country's National Museum is located.

Too tired to do anything more that day, we saw to it that the crates and the rooms into which they had been deposited were duly sealed. The next morning we turned up to hand over our finds. This was hard work. Each of our twenty thousand objects had to be measured and weighed with extreme accuracy, photographed once again, and again inventoried—and all in what one could really call "one hell of a rush," which naturally made for some unanticipated problems that took some time to correct.

On the day after we had initiated this most painstaking task, I received an apologetic telephone call in my hotel room toward evening, explaining that one of the crates was short a plastic bag of gold plaques. It seemed that the simplest solution would be to peek into one or another of the remaining crates, which could easily contain the supposedly missing plastic bag. However, to do so it was necessary to tear the paper sticker on the crate that bore the signatures of all five officials who had received the material when it was first deposited with the museum. In short, the crates could be opened only in the presence of all the members of the respective commission. And though all five were on the museum staff, on the day in question one was away and a second, sick. The five finally did meet and the missing bag was found. But before that happy eventuality occurred, some thirty-six hours had to elapse! I was assailed by all sorts of thoughts and doubts during this time—especially during the two almost sleepless nights,

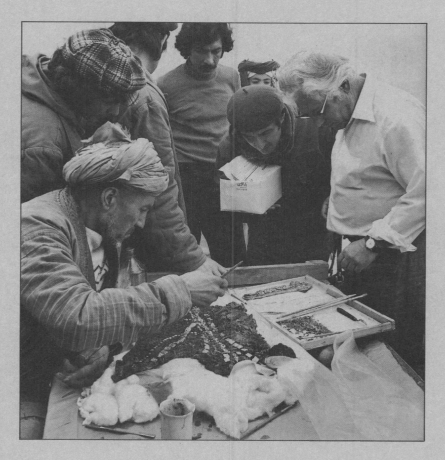

when everything always seems far more dramatic than in the light of day.

The episode just described is only one of the many that happened while we were handing the treasures of Tillya-tepe over to the museum staff. The staff slaved away from dawn until late in the night to complete the task. At last, we caught a glimmer of light at the end of the tunnel at the point when most of the finds were safely stowed away in the museum's strong rooms. Our visas were about to expire but, due to a two-day national holiday, we were not able to complete our assignment on time. I suggested surrendering the remainder of the treasures to the National Bank, but the Ministry of Information and Culture was dead set against that. Our airplane tickets for Moscow, where our families were so eagerly awaiting our return after nearly six long months away, were canceled and our visas renewed. Only after the holiday, after having handed over the entire collection of artifacts to the National Museum, were we finally allowed to leave aboard an Afghan Ariana flight to arrive in Moscow late at night.

We left Afghanistan in February, 1979. The very next month, however, brought trou-

15

ble. When leaving Tillya-tepe with the firm hope of returning several months later to uncover the seventh burial site and, possibly, chance upon still more graves, we had tried to prepare for every conceivable contingency. Thus, the authorities not only in Shibarghan but in Kabul itself had been duly apprised of our plans, armed guards had been posted to keep watch over the Golden Mound, and Shibarghan's governor had been placed in charge of all the excavations as they were when we left. Every precaution appeared to have been taken. But reality shattered all our high hopes.

The season of spring rains commenced shortly after our departure with the result that one of the ancient walls at the excavation site collapsed, baring a silver utensil of a type similar to objects encountered in the earlier excavations. The Ministry of Information and Culture was at once notified of the event and Inspector Muhamednaim Ajan of the Institute of Archaeology was sent out to review the situation. He took stock of the situation and correctly advised that the pit be immediately filled in, pending the resumption of digging. Unfortunately, that was not done.

The next spring there turned up in Kabul's shopping district gold ornaments highly reminiscent of those recovered from the Tillya-tepe burial sites. Moreover, one antique dealer asked the National Museum to grant him a permit to export and sell abroad a number of small gold ornaments and a silver Chinese mirror absolutely identical to artifacts recovered from the Tillya-tepe graves. In fact, the resemblance was so astounding that the museum staff sequestered the said articles. Several days later they decided to inspect the shop, only to learn that its proprietor had shuttered it up and had left the country.

At any rate, however much one may regret the lot of these treasures from the Golden Mound, one can only trust that future excavations will, beyond doubt, bring to light more masterpieces of Afghanistan's ancient art for the world to feast its eyes upon.

THE TILLYA-TEPE
NECROPOLIS

The legendary empire of Bactria has engaged the imagination of historians from the times of Greco-Roman antiquity to the present. Small wonder, considering the fact that as far back as in the second millennium B.C., a still largely enigmatic yet indubitably unique Eastern civilization flourished in the great Bactrian plain. Besides leaving an indelible imprint on all the subsequent historical and cultural development of this part of the ancient Eastern world, its traditions by far outlived its fame. Indeed, in the middle of the third century B.C. there arose in what are now Northern Afghanistan and the adjacent regions of Soviet Central Asia, the Greco-Bactrian Kingdom, whose ruling elite was composed of local Hellenized Bactrians and foreign Greek colonizers. The fusion of the cultures of these two nations largely set the pace for local cultural development, and there emerged what may be termed a Greco-Bactrian art.

We have only the meager information provided by historians of antiquity to go by as regards the formation of this state. What ensued next is a complete mystery, for there are virtually no written records from which to proceed. All that exists is faint mention that somewhere in the mid-second century B.C. the once opulent Greco-Bactrian Empire

crumbled under the force exerted by nomad tribes. Dominant among these were the Yüeh-Chih tribes, otherwise known as the Kushans, who hailed from Southern Siberia and the adjacent areas. In their whirlwind advance across the boundless Central Asian steppes, they reached the southern parts of what are today Uzbekistan and Tajikistan, and crossed the Amu Darya to settle on its left bank in what was Bactria proper. There they established several independent principalities. With time, they ceased to wander and adopted urban customs and an urban way of life. Some hundred years later the former nomads founded the Great Kushan Empire. However, what happened between the demise of the Greco-Bactrian Kingdom and the rise of the Kushan Empire is a blank spot in our historical record. It may now be partly filled in by the wealth of material yielded by the excavation of the Tillya-tepe necropolis. Indeed, the painstaking efforts of the joint Afghan-Soviet Expedition have, for the first time, enabled us to assess the overall cultural levels of this "dark age" in Bactria's history and to outline its place in the history and culture of the Middle East as the whole.

Despite the inclement weather spanning the rain-drenched autumn of 1978 and the bleak, snow-swept winter of 1979, both

17

Soviet and Afghan archaeologists demonstrated equal vigor and enthusiasm in excavating the Tillya-tepe necropolis. The Soviet members of the expedition included Victor Sarianidi, the chief, V. Bury, a restoration expert, and V. Yerofeyev, a mechanic, both from Moscow; T. Khojaniyazov from Turkmenia, R. Suleimanov and S. Khakimov from Uzbekistan, and U. Pulatov from Tajikistan. The Afghan party was represented by inspectors Abdul Habib Azami, Mohammad Asef Sharqi, Mohammad Aref Inayat, and Mohammad Ajan Naim, all of the Archaeology Institute staff.

The ruins excavated were of what had apparently been a temple of fire-worshipers which had been built toward the close of the second millennium B.C. With its central altar, it stood on a tall, twenty-foot-high brick platform. The shrine as such consisted of two column-lined halls, and was reliably protected by mighty defensive walls along its perimeter and fortified by towers at each corner. Evidently there had been an inhabited community at the foot of the temple. However, as nothing is known of the culture, or the origins or fate of the temple-builders, this will require further study.

Toward the middle of the first millennium B.C. the temple was extensively replanned. Yet, in the Achaemenian period (the sixth through fourth centuries B.C.) the shrine was still a most imposing and impressive structure, whose outer walls had been fortified by an additional mighty brick rampart. Toward the close of this period the building was destroyed in a conflagration, so that all the troops of Alexander the Great found here in the fourth century B.C. was a miserable village that had been built up on the temple ruins. As the mound was subsequently deserted, near the beginning of the first century A.D., the place was turned into a cemetery.

Judging by the richness of the grave goods excavated, this was the family cemetery of the rulers of one of the larger Kushan princedoms, possibly the richest and most influential of the five principalities mentioned in written records.

Though it has not been proved beyond doubt, it is highly probable that the city of Yemshi-tepe, which is next door to the Golden Mound, was adopted as residence, if not founded, by the invading Kushan nomads. In all likelihood, these were the early Kushans of the second or third generation of immigrants. That the long-deserted Golden Mound was adopted as a family necropolis is suggested by the following authenticated fact: all the graves were disposed in a place that was clearly visible—and thus well controlled—from the Yemshi-tepe citadel. However, the fantastic opulence of the grave goods most sharply contrasts with their external plainness; the graves themselves consist of vertical shafts with no markers on top, with the exception of the horse skull at the edge of the fourth site. This may possibly serve as indirect evidence of absolutely secret burials, the graves having been dug under cover of night. The coffins, which were constructed of wooden planking, stood on legs, but had no lids; they were wrapped in shrouds spangled with sewn-on gold and silver disks—with the exception of the fourth grave, in which the coffin was inserted into a leather case painted a bright crimson. The coffins were placed on the pit floors, the graves were boarded up, hides were draped over them, and soil was shoveled on top. Thus, the tombs were originally hollow; only with the passage of time did the weight of the earth on top cause the wooden superstructure to collapse, thereby protecting the graves until the present day.

All the tombs were intact, with the exception of the third, which had been ravaged by rodents in ancient times. Because of excessive dampness the skeletons were in a very poor state of preservation, and the facial bones had been crushed when the boards collapsed.

Interment evidently adhered to the following procedure. The dead were first garbed in sumptuous funerary attire, mostly worn on ceremonial occasions such as official audiences, religious rites, and the like. It was extremely difficult to reconstruct the attire, as virtually nothing was left of the cloth. The exact positions of the hundreds of ornamental plaques that had been sewn onto the garments in some degree enabled us to reconstruct the decoration of such parts of clothing as cuffs, sleeves, hems, and so on. However, an added complication was that the deceased were dressed in several garments—the third tomb revealed three pectoral clasps, one on top of the other, suggesting that there had been at least three different layers of clothing. As the cloth decayed the plaques collapsed on top of each other, and when the graves were laid bare, we found hundreds, if not thousands, of diverse plaques in what at first glance appeared a chaotic jumble. It required pains-taking analysis and careful clearing to reduce this seemingly hopeless mess to some definite system; we recorded not only the different types and forms of plaques but also their exact position and whether they faced up or down. We had to sketch several drawings of each layer and indicate on each by means of differ-ent symbols the different plaques and their position as we originally found them. This enabled us first to separate the sets of plaques of identical types, which allowed us to trace the outlines und subsequently the cut of the garments worn. Gradually the shape of the cuffs, sleeves, hems, edgings, and trimmings was revealed, which eventually presented us with a point of departure for approximately reconstructing the funerary attire.

Of great assistance in reconstructing the garments were extant relics of the monu-mental and applied arts of the ancient East, especially of neighboring Iran. In the carved stone reliefs of the imposing palace of Perse-polis, built in Achaemenian times, the types of garments commonly worn in this part of the ancient East in the middle of the first millennium B.C. were preserved for poster-ity. Further information about Achaemenian art is provided by the world-famous gold artifacts of what is known as the Amu Darya (Oxus) Treasure now in the British Museum, London. (Incidentally these artifacts were discovered in the second half of the nineteenth century only a few dozen miles away from Tillya-tepe, on the right bank of the Amu Darya [Oxus] River, in what is today Soviet Tajikistan.)

It is to be regretted, though, that we possess far less information as to the types of garb worn in the times of the Greco-Bactrian Kingdom, the period directly preceding the formation of the Tillya-tepe necropolis. However, what also greatly assisted our efforts to reconstruct the said garments were the images of the Kushan and Parthian kings struck on the coins they minted, plus the few extant stone effigies, which do provide some notion of what the formal dress of these potentates looked like.

SITE 1

The tomb structures, astonishingly simple in design, were all pits with rectangular floors sunk vertically into the mound. Although the layout of this pit was violated in the process of excava-tion, we were nevertheless able to reconstruct its approximate contour, and ascertained that the rectangle was about eight feet (2.5 m) long and four feet (1.3 m) wide. The grave itself had been dug on the mound's western slope, outside the defensive wall and was only some six and a half feet (2 m) below the top.

The coffin was secured by six iron clamps disposed in pairs on either side of head, wrists, and ankles. The clamps are nine and a half inches (24 cm) long, two inches (5 cm) wide, and about a quarter-inch (0.5–0.7 cm) thick; the nails used to hammer them into the planks were about three inches (7–8 cm) long, and their heads were less than a half-inch (up to 1.2 cm) in diameter.

The body lay fully extended on its back in the coffin, with its head pointing north.

According to a tentative anthropological analysis the remains are probably of a female between twenty-five and thirty-five years old.

Insofar as the bulk of the ornamental plaques were found between the shoulders and hips, evidently the upper parts of the garments worn were more profusely and richly decorated. Besides the sewn-on plaques, the gold threads of a decayed cloth were also uncovered; they were found exclusively beneath the vertebrae and nowhere else, from which it may be deduced that they are either from the shroud that lined the inside of the coffin, or, more likely, from a short cape or cloak. As the threads retained a wavelike form, one may presume that the weft threads had been of either wool or silk, which had completely rotted away before the grave was excavated.

The gold threads were disposed beneath the skeleton, in isolated multi-layered patches not in one unbroken pattern, thus indicating large ornamental designs. Considering that the gold threads had had a multitude of pearls on them and that the intricate designs they had thus created were edged with gold plaques, one may gain some notion of how dazzling a sight the funerary garments must have presented.

To judge by the holes at their corners, seven gold plaques with identical repoussé ornamentation that we have conventionally termed the "man with a dolphin" had been apparently sewn onto this gold-threaded cape or cloak (ill. 86). The representation of the dolphin is fairly realistic; however, the scales on its body indicate that the goldsmith had only a hazy notion of the creature. This implies that the plates themselves are of local Bactrian provenance. On the other hand, the subject matter undoubtedly has associations with Greco-Roman art, in which the representation of the dolphin holds a leading place. The man's legs, which have been transformed into writhing

snakes, are highly reminiscent of an analogous design on a carved ivory from the Kushan city of Begram.

Conspicuous amidst the plaques disposed on the skeleton's chest were large rosettes of six petals each that had retained their original arrangement; they had been sewn on in a checkerboard pattern in two rows, forming one broad band girding the chest and back. Behind, on the neck was a gold clasp in the shape of two massive convex cast disks that had a hook and loop that served to fasten the cloak (cat. 1.2). They had apparently shifted away from their original position—borne out by the fact that the lock of the pectoral chain worn round the neck happened to be in front and not at the nape of the neck.

One must note that the aforementioned rosettes found beneath the skeleton were positioned above the layer of gold threads and were from another garment, a robe, not the cloak. Stretching from the ornamental band toward the shoulders were straps comprised of three rows of different gold adornments, some triangular with minute granulation, others trifoliate and inset with turquoise, and the third, hemispherical in shape. There was also a small quantity of miniature gold bows having minute granulation and inset with turquoise, lapis lazuli, or garnet.

The stomacher was most likely embroidered with a large heart-shaped design comprised of a slender strip of barrel-shaped knobs of gold and paste. As for the massive, cast, five-lobed gold brooch inset with turquoise and pearls, to judge by its position—it was found beneath the jawbone—it must have been pinned to the front of the robe. The loose concertina-like sleeves were most sumptuously and opulently ornamented; they were enclosed in circular strands of gold scarab-like ornaments inset with turquoise and decorated with granulation, of double helices, of squarish plaques having an eye or flower design and further adorned with turquoise insets and repoussé rosettes, and of gold semicircles, which were found in particular abundance. The gold embroidery terminated at the cuffs in a severe, horizontal stripe comprised of several rows of scarab, cylindrical, and tube-like ornaments.

Plaques of another shape were likewise discovered, however in a haphazard, chaotic jumble that made it extremely difficult to ascertain where they exactly decorated the garments worn. Yet, apparently the small, round "face mask" plaques (ill. 29), with the representations on the obverse, had been sewn onto the shoulder fronts, as had been bow-shaped, round rosettes, and certain other kinds of plaques. To judge by the small number of hemispherical and conical plaques disposed alongside the lower limbs, they could have decorated long trousers worn tucked into the tops of soft boots.

Summing up, one may say that it is probable that the dead female was attired in a robe, the stomacher and sleeves of which were richly ornamented with diverse gold plaques of varied shape and design. The plaques uncovered at the foot of the skeleton decorated, if not the footwear, then most likely the lower hem of the robe, in which case it must be said that the upper parts of the garments were far more profusely and abundantly adorned than the lower, virtually unornamented, parts.

For the sake of comparison, we may address ourselves to the carved stone effigies of Parthian-Kushan times, more specifically, to the statue of a Hatra princess. She is depicted garbed in a puckered robe terminating below the knees, from beneath which descend other garments. Like the garment from the Tillya-tepe necropolis, the dress worn by this princess is adorned, for the most part, only at the top.

Though, regrettably, we do not know how female trousers were ornamented, we do know that the trousers men wore often had a long band of sewn-on round and cylindrical knobs or bosses in front that stretched from the waist down to the very bottom. According to Herodotus, Sarmatian women wore much the same dress as the men, for which reason we may presume that the female's trousers were spangled with gold plaques in much the same manner as

were those worn by men. If this was indeed so, the supposition is borne out by the grave goods uncovered in this burial.

We may reconstruct the female's garb as follows: a long robe with a richly ornamented stomacher, opulently adorned sleeves and puckered-up trousers that were tucked into the tops of boots or shoes. Thrown over her shoulders on top of the robe was an abbreviated cape or cloak embroidered with plates bearing the representation of a man with a dolphin and fastened by a clasp comprised of two massive disks. Besides the plaques, the jewelry also consisted of a brooch fastened to the stomacher in front or a pectoral chain.

Her hair was held in place by a pin with a gold finial decorated with pearls and dangling leaf-type adornments (ill. 18); attached to the lobe of her right ear was a massive gold earring or clip in the shape of a boat decorated with minute granulation (ill. 32).

The grave goods included the deceased's personal belongings, mostly toilet articles. These consisted of a round ivory compact containing a lump of caked white powder extremely reminiscent of the type of face powder in use today. There was a braided basket with a full assortment of cosmetics, namely splinters of black crystals, apparently antimony, a miniature round, lidded silver pot embellished with a finely etched plant design (ill. 146), iron pincers, tweezers with a wooden handle, a bone stick with sharpened ends, and finally, pink lumps of rouge and white lumps of ceruse.

What the small drumlike gold object was for is hard to say. At any rate, it is wonderfully worked and is inset with blood-red garnet, sky-blue turquoise, and mother-of-pearl possessing a gleaming finish.

Uncovered near the right shoulder was a pair of gold plaques designed in the shape of a flower with dangling gold disks. What these plaques served to ornament has not been clarified as yet.

Finally, a plain gold ring revealing strong signs of wear, embellished with a simple ornamental design of a circle and two almond-shaped bits, was worn on the little finger of the left hand. In contrast to the patently ceremonial dress, it appears ordinary and had most likely graced the wearer's finger throughout her lifetime.

SITE 2

The second grave, outside the temple's outer northern wall, is a rectangular shaft tomb almost ten feet (3.0 m) long and just over five feet (1.6 m) wide. Its floor is only six feet (2 m) down from the top of the mound. Careful vertical clearing disclosed a shallow layer of dark-brown wood dust arching inward from the edges of the pit to above the coffin—apparently the remains of the rotted superstructure. In all likelihood, the originally hollow grave had been roofed over with wooden planks whose ends could have rested on the recessed banks that, regrettably, were no longer in evidence when the grave was uncovered. Further, a thin layer of earth had probably been shoveled on top of the roof planking. With the passage of time the planking rotted away and the earth on top caved in to fill the grave and coffin. Evidently, after the cave-in it had filled up with mud, or may have been intentionally filled up and covered with turf, as, when excavation was initiated, no signs of any cave-in were manifest on top of the mound.

The coffin itself, about seven feet (2.2 m) long and about two feet (0.65 m) wide, stood on wooden legs, not right in the center of the grave floor but somewhat to one side so that it was two feet (0.6 m) away from the western wall and sixteen inches (0.4 m) away from the eastern side. The bier was built of broad, thick planks, the sides being fastened to the bottom by means of iron clamps that, bent at right angles, were massive iron bars about six inches (15–17 cm) long and about two inches (4–5 cm) wide. Iron nails were used to hammer in the clamps in pairs at the lower corners and singly in the middle of each end. Nails that had been driven vertically

into the side of the coffin's upper rim were intact. They could have been used to fasten the lid, but no traces of a lid have been discovered. It is quite likely that these nails were employed to secure the shroud in which the coffin had unquestionably been wrapped.

All that remained of the shroud were the gold and silver disks with which it had once been spangled, which were uncovered on a level with the coffin's upper edge, on the skeleton itself, and beneath the coffin. In places the coffin planking was found to have remnants of white gypsum plastering; at the head this two-inch-thick (5 cm) layer of plaster had retained the imprint of rotted wood inside, and a vertically sunk nail on top. The fact that the first gold plaques to be recovered, possibly from the shroud, were found on a level with the driven-in nails warrants the assumption that the coffin, together with its supporting legs, had stood no more than sixteen to twenty inches (40–50 cm) high.

When laid to rest the corpse was placed on its back, extended, with its head pointing north. The deceased has been tentatively identified by anthropological analysis as being a female between thirty and forty years old.

The deceased evidently wore a tiara or diadem of a conical shape, as may be deduced from the position of the gold plaques with which it had once been spangled. Two identical hairpins were found by her temples—one on each side—consisting of bronze shafts topped by gold heads. Her lower jaw was enclosed from temple to temple by a broad gold chin stay. This might have originally been ornamented with gold florets that by the time of excavation were found scattered alongside the stay. On either side of the skull were two-faced gold pendants that have been conventionally termed the "ruler and dragons." Around her neck was a necklace of large beads of gold and ivory. The neck opening of the gown had evidently been embroidered with barrel-shaped fluted gold beads, conspicuous amidst which were a pair of identical musician figurines that had been arranged on the right and left shoulders (ill. 59). Under the nape of the neck was a massive five-lobed brooch, while on the breast, apparently under a robe, was a round Chinese hand mirror (ill. 145). The robe had been secured high up on the breast by a pair of gold clasps depicting cupids astride dolphins. A gold figurine of the Kushan Aphrodite had been apparently sewn onto the stomacher of the dress (ill. 80).

The funerary garments had been spangled with a host of gold plaques. There were four rows, including some shaped as ram's heads, on the cuffs. Sewn on each sleeve slightly above the cuff were one miniature figurine of a fish made of paste, two scale models of a foot made of lapis lazuli, one gold scale model of a foot (the other was missing), two miniature scale models of a hand, and carved stone scale models of an ax and astragal. Her wrists were graced by gold bracelets embellished with sculptured figures of antelopes, while on her ankles were massive, cast, open-ended anklets with flared ends.

At her feet were a silver vessel and a braided basket containing an iron pickax and two Siberian-style daggers. On the outside the basket was decorated with six gold open-worked phalerae with centrally positioned rosettes. The gold pipe uncovered by her right hand was mostly likely a status symbol.

An analysis of the position of the sewn-on plaques that had once adorned the garments enabled us to visualize the funerary clothes as consisting presumably of the following: the deceased was garbed in a caftan-type dress, evidently with a neck opening; running down the middle of the front from neck to lower hem was a broad band of sewn-on hemispherical gold plaques that alternated with heart-shaped spangles inset with turquoise (ill. 100). Parallel to the band on either side were rows of large gold disks alternating with gold dividers, both inset with turquoise. Descending from the shoulders were more broad bands composed of gold sewn-on hemispherical and heart-shaped plaques; on the back of the collar were identical gold disks of a smaller size. The Kushan Aphrodite brooch

sewn on to the stomacher served as the pivot of the entire decorative design.

From the stone reliefs of Palmyra in Syria we know that a long caftan-type tunic with a neck opening was a common Parthian garment; moreover, a broad, decorative spangled band always ran unbroken, down from the neck hole to lower hem. A similar type of garment with a long, broad decorative band in front is likewise to be seen on the carved stone effigies of Kushan rulers, specifically on the statue of who is presumed to be Kanishka at Surkh Kotale, a shrine in Afghanistan.

A long robe was worn on top of the tunic—as indicated by the two rows of identical plates that ran down from the shoulders and terminated below the knee, that is, lower than the hem of the tunic. The plaques consist of two parts: a convex hemispherical shape contoured by minute knobs, and a miniature gold disk dangling from the former on gold wire. It would be only natural to presume that the decorative design of the spangles was not confined to these plaques alone. There were also other designs, possibly complex and with plant motifs; this is borne out by the more than fifteen hundred hemispherical gold plaques that were scattered in profusion on and around the bones.

The long robe that was worn over the caftan-type tunic was practically always worn by the Kushan aristocracy and was customarily fastened across the chest by paired clasps, as is shown by the aforementioned Kanishka statue from the Surkh Kotale shrine, which has two identical round clasps on the chest.

The sleeves of the robe ended in cuffs decorated in the following pattern: the top was embroidered with a ring of hemispherical plaques followed lower down by a row of pyramids, their apexes pointed upward, and then again another row of hemispherical plates. Next came the unquestionably main row of ram's heads facing in opposite directions, which had eyes of cornelian and ears and curled horns of turquoise (ill. 153). Nearer to the wrist, rows of hemispherical and pyramid-shaped plates

23

alternated in the same order as above, while at the bottom was a row of fluted hollow cylinders with loops attached to enable them to be sewn on. However, since above the cuffs the spangles are of a different type, the cuffs belonged to sleeves of the tunic, not of the robe.

As was noted earlier, two hairpins, each consisting of a bronze shaft pointed at one end and with the other capped by a gold finial were found by the temples (ill. 20). Each finial is disk-shaped with a conical projection in the middle of which is a tiny turquoise bead. Rising up from the conical projection are gold wires threaded with pearls and embellished with minute gold granules. Dangling on wires from this peculiar type of bud are disks and a large half-moon object to which are appended in turn freely dangling similar gold disks. The fact that the pin shafts were of bronze, not gold, suggests that when worn they were concealed by the hair.

Two identical gold "ruler and dragons" pendants that were evidently attached to the tiara are cast and two-sided, implying that their decorative design could be seen from either side (ills. 44–47). Both have rings on top by which they could be hooked. Each pendant bears the representation of a frontally facing male figure of a serene and dispassionate mien, with slanted, catlike eyes topped by thinly penciled brows. In the middle of his forehead lies a caste mark. His straight, slightly flared nose with its emphasized nostrils, his thin-lipped slit of a mouth, and his willful, jutting chin complement the overall imperious, stern visage. His head is capped by a crown from whose repoussé circlet with its slanted incisions rise stepped pyramids encrusted with turquoise and lapis lazuli.

Long coiffeur-curled hair descends from beneath the crown down either cheek. Apparently, a torque graces the neck; below it one can make out the neckhole of a blouse. Drawn on over the blouse is a short tunic, caught in a wasp waist by a sash, from beneath which folds spread out. The tunic, half-open on the chest, is tight-fitting; the puckered sleeves on the outstretched arms terminate in broad cuffs from which tightly

balled-up fists are thrust. A long, stylized garment akin to a billowing skirt, embellished with large, almond-shaped turquoise insets, descends from beneath the tunic; peeping out from beneath its hem are possibly the toes of footwear.

Sandwiching the central figure are identical fabulous creatures resembling flying dragons, richly encrusted with turquoise and garnet. Their horned, horselike visages, yawning, fanged jaws, well-modeled facial muscles and slanted ears compressed back in rage, demonstrate the manifestly aggressive and menacing image of these monsters. Their heavily curled horns are decorated with repoussé rings set crosswise, while their eyes are picked out by convex rhomboidal insets of translucent yellow cornelian. Their sinuous necks carry bristling manes formed of upright, bulging almond-shaped beads of turquoise; their small wings are encrusted with semiprecious gems, evidently to convey their plumage. Their short front paws, on which the hooves are designated by turquoise insets, rest on the ruler's balled-up fists. The bodies are unnaturally arched, and the hind paws are spread backward. Between them the winding tail coils to end beneath the body.

This episode depicting a king grappling with dragons is a favorite subject in the arts of ancient Asia Minor. Similar scenes are likewise to be found in Greek art and there, as in the Bactrian pendants, the monsters demonstrate a similar style of presentation and a similar iconographic posture, winged, horned and with their heads turned aside. They are all indicative of an Asiatic style and are most likely an echo of ancient Oriental, primarily Persian, influences. The garb of the king depicted on the Tillya-tepe pendants is a medley of the typically Scythian—as represented by the tunic secured by a left-hand fold and caught at the waist by a sash—and the Achaemenian—as represented by the skirt. Of special interest are the dragons with their contorted hindquarters, an element that is peculiar to the Siberian animal style. Winged horses were common in the arts of Asia Minor, including Achaemenian art; however, the horned horse is

24

rare and though such isolated samples are to be found in the Hellenized Orient, it is more characteristic of Altai art. Indeed, the most striking similarities to the winged and horned horse motif will be seen on a cap from the Issyk barrow in Kazakhstan, and the Karagalinka diadem from Northern Kirghizia, both in the Soviet Union. This motif was particularly common in the Sarmatian epoch, which is illustrated by the figurine of a winged horse from the Hermitage collection in Leningrad.

The annular, curl-tipped horns of the dragons disclose a marked stylistic affinity with the famous aigrette from the Amu Darya (Oxus) Treasure and the figurines on the gold Pasargadal bracelets. Even if the motif of the horned and winged horse was of nomadic origin, it was fully Bactrianized in the pendants discussed; on the whole, the representations are entirely within the range of motifs common to Asia Minor and demonstrate a fusion of Persian, Achaemenian, and Eurasian Scythian traditions.

As was already mentioned, the sculpted Kushan Aphrodite brooch served, as it were, as the focal point of the entire decorative design embellishing the front of the stomacher (ill. 80). The face, depicted in a three-quarters profile, is marked by broad cheekbones, a straight nose with no bridge, large almond-shaped eyes, fleshy cheeks, unexpressive lips, and a small but well-delineated chin. The headdress is either a turban-like affair or a tall conical hat with a bushy trimming. According to Herodotus, the Scythians wore pointed turbans to which the Kushan Aphrodite's headdress is reminiscent in some degree. However, it is quite possible that it is not a hat but a hairdo that is depicted on the brooch in question; her long locks, parted down the middle and swept upward, frame her face in a coil that is drawn into a tall chignon on the crown. From beneath this coil or turban, as the case may be, descend short-cropped locks that conceal her ears.

The female depicted has a stocky neck, tiny breasts crisscrossed by ribbons or perhaps straps with a central clasp, a tiny waist, and a round belly with a distinctly modeled navel. Her right arm is bent and rests on her thrust-out hip, and her left arm, with its bangles, rests on a column and holds a roundish object. Her hips are wrapped in a tightly rolled piece of cloth, part of which falls in folds and terminates in flounces. Outlined beneath is her slightly bent and thrust-out left leg, her foot being discernible beneath the hem. Her right leg is slightly thrust back, with only the toe peeping out from beneath the flounces. Wings with a distinctly modeled plumage spread out from behind her shoulders.

Disposed on either side of the figure are small columns with plinths and double-stepped capitals. One is topped by the tiny figure of a cupid which has a weakly modeled, schematic face, on which only the eyesockets, nose, and mouth are discernible. His locks are combed back, and his two arms are outstretched with the left clasping a bow with a tautly drawn string. Beneath the belly and between the legs there is a mound which presumably designates the male genitals, and finally, small wings protrude from the shoulder blades.

The iconographic posture of the seminude goddess and, primarily, the cupid, leave no doubt that the image takes after one of the most popular of the Greek deities, the goddess of love, Aphrodite. Indeed, the portrayal of a seminude Aphrodite with one arm resting on a column is a particular favorite in Hellenistic art, as may be gathered from the glyptics of the third and second centuries B.C. But how Bactrianized the Kushan Aphrodite is! In place of the ample proportions and the exquisite figure of the Greek goddess, we are presented with a short-legged matron with a distended, ugly belly and tiny breasts; further, the stern if not cruel face has nothing at all in common with the Greek prototype. No doubt the Bactrian craftsman, when discharging this commission for the Kushan nomads of yesteryore, depicted the ethnic type of queen of the local early-Kushan society. In other words, he gave form to that concept of female beauty that was peculiar to the then-sedentary former nomads who still firmly adhered to the traditions the Yüeh-Chih had brought with them from their homeland.

Apparently the long robe was fastened at the neck by a pair of identical figured clasps which depict a fish whose head is bedecked with a sumptuous tridental crest, thus demonstrating beyond doubt that the representation took after a dolphin (ill. 85). Seated astride the dolphin is a winged cupid. On the two parts of the clasp the cupids are presented in mirror image, with one given on the left-hand side, and the other on the right-hand side. The cupids wear wreaths on their heads from beneath which their hair falls in small curls to their neck. Their frozen faces, with their lips slightly distended in faint grins, with fleshy cheeks and large eyes, are far removed from the vivacious image of this harbinger of love from the Greco-Roman pantheon. Their necks are stocky and their bodies plump and crisscrossed with what are evidently straps that are conveyed by means of finely incised stripes. With one hand the cupids grasp the dolphin's crest; the other arms which are half-bent, rest on their knees and hold objects that possibly represent vessels. Their wrists and ankles are enclosed in slender repoussé circlets that apparently designate bracelets and anklets. Curved wings with clearly modeled plumage spread up from behind the backs.

As cupids riding dolphins are common enough in Greco-Roman glyptics and sculpture, this motif is unquestionably of Western origin. However, again it has been Bactrianized, indicated first by the cupid's bracelets and anklets, which attest to Hellenized Oriental influences emanating, for instance, from Gandhara, where anklets are not infrequently worn to this day.

Particularly striking are the massive bracelets gracing the wrists of the deceased, the ends of which depict antelopes in rapid flight (ills. 105, 107). The beasts display well-modeled hump-nosed muzzles with slightly flaring nostrils and half-open mouths with fleshy lips etched in relief. The fact that the bracelets show strong traces of wear leaves no doubt that they were constantly worn in their owner's lifetime.

Bracelets with sculptured representations of both real and fabulous animals are to be found in the Amu Darya (Oxus) Treasure which is on view in the British Museum in London, and in the collection of the Hermitage in Leningrad. Indeed, if we take the Hermitage possessions, we shall be faced with a closely related, if not identical, representation of contorted bodies and out-thrust hindquarters. Especially significant are the two gold-wire bracelets in the Hermitage collection that feature sculptured figures of antelopes whose fleshy-lipped mouths and laid-back ears and horns are directly analogous to the features of the beasts depicted on the Bactrian bracelets. We are faced with a stylistic, not to mention an iconographic, affinity, which warrants assuming that such bracelets were executed by the goldsmiths of most likely one Bactrian center.

Three rings were recovered. Two were worn on the left hand, one on the right. One of the two worn on the left hand has a large oval convex garnet or perhaps almandine, through which the setting can be glimpsed, surrounded by smaller inset semiprecious gems. The second ring (ill. 108) has a gold bezel on which a well-proportioned seated female figure is finely engraved. As the Greek name Athena is etched backward beneath it, this unquestionably indicates that the signet was used as a seal. However, the elongated face, with its huge nose above a sunken mouth and jutting chin, has nothing whatsoever in common with the classical beauty of this favorite Greek goddess, and most likely suggests a decline in Greco-Bactrian artistic tradition in local jewelry.

The third ring, worn on the right hand, is of hollowed gold set with an oval turquoise bezel upon which a seated female figure holding a shield in her right hand is engraved (ill. 109).

The females depicted on all three rings are conspicuous for their highly generalized faces, in sharp contrast to the painstakingly distinct modeling of their bodies and of their typically Greek clothing. Since as a rule jewelers copied the statues of deities set up in

26

public places, we may presume the representations on the rings to be copies of a rare type of seated Athena.

SITE 3

The third burial site was discovered almost on the very crest of the mound, sunk into the top of the dividing wall between the nine-columned and four-columned halls of the former temple. This oblong shaft of eight and a half by five feet (2.6 by 1.5 m) had been dug right into the mud brick wall. Its sides were absolutely vertical, with the exception of the eastern side, which sloped slightly down to the grave floor. No traces of plastering were unearthed.

Directly above the coffin a layer of dark-brown, powdery dust from the rotted wood in the shape of a truncated cone could be observed from the roof of the grave pit, where the recesses supporting the wooden planking had apparently been located as was the case in the second site. Over this layer was a layer of rotted brown hide, and under the whole pile lay decayed hides, these of a black coloring. Evidently the roof of the originally hollow grave had consisted of wooden planks across which black-painted hides had been stretched below and brown hides above. Most likely the hides had been spangled with the many gold disks we found, onto which loops or eyelets had been soldered; when the roof caved in, these disks had slithered down and had slipped through the tears in the hides into the coffin itself, where the excavators uncovered them. Finally, still observable on the grave floor were traces of the matting that had carpeted it, now completely decayed.

Note that only in this site did the gold disks possess soldered-on eyelets, in place of the ordinary edge perforations observed in the spangles recovered from the other graves excavated. Especially significant in this respect are the identical gold disks with soldered-on loops from the Kushan city of Begram; most likely they too came from ruined, if not looted, burial sites.

The oblong wooden coffin which was six feet seven inches (2 m) long, twenty-five and a half inches (0.65 m) wide, and about sixteen to twenty inches (0.4–0.5 m) high still had iron clamps bent at right angles at each corner. These clamps, which averaged a length of five to six inches (13–15 cm) and a width of two inches (5 cm), had been used to secure the side and end boards of the coffin. We also found straight strips of iron up to six inches (15 cm) long and about two inches (5–7 cm) wide, of which three pairs each had been nailed into each side of the coffin to fasten them to the bottom of the coffin. Finally, as had been the case in the second grave, three iron nails had been hammered in along the top rim of the coffin's western side. While they may have been used to nail a lid down, no traces of such a lid were uncovered. From this it may be inferred—as in the case of the second tomb—that the nails had been employed to secure the shroud in which the coffin had been wrapped.

Some direct archaeological evidence warrants the assumption that the coffin had rested on legs or other supports some four to six inches (10–15 cm) above the floor. However, no traces of such legs or supports were discovered, which is quite understandable, considering the ravages inflicted by burrowing rodents. However, there is no reason to question their once having been there, as the excavators established with complete veracity that, whereas the right foot of the deceased lay on the grave floor, the left had been four to six inches (10–15 cm) higher, thus serving to indicate how high the bottom of the coffin had once been.

Working from the heavily damaged remains one may only presume that the body of the deceased had been placed in the coffin on its back, extended, with its head pointing north. According to tentative anthropological analysis, the deceased person was a female between eighteen and twenty-five years old. Further confirmation is provided by the artifacts unearthed, which include many adornments but absolutely no weapons of any kind.

27

Since the third grave was ravaged by rodents, most of the smaller funerary adornments and offerings that had been inside the coffin had shifted away from their original positions. A gold vessel had been placed under the head of the deceased. At the bottom of the vessel lay the side section and one other section of a five-part crown or coronet; rodents had shifted the other sections. Also at the bottom of the vessel were several pendants with repoussé lion faces plus a five-petaled rosette; the second of the pair was unearthed by the side of the coffin.

By the neck was a massive torque that had not been disturbed. Within the torque were separate portions of a necklace with two conical clasps that had initially been at the nape of the neck; one of these clasps was in situ, the other of the pair was extracted from a rodent's burrow. Also discovered here was a gold chin stay of a type identical to that unearthed in the second tomb. Apparently there had been a hairpin to the left of the skull; another had shifted down to the breast (ill. 19). Both had most likely been attached at the temples—as was the case in other undisturbed burial sites.

Partly obscured by the torque was a heavy silver Chinese mirror beneath which three gold clasps lay undisturbed on top of one another. This indicated that there had been at least three layers of garments. The deceased had apparently worn on her wrists—the radial bones were missing—massive bracelets with flared ends; similar pieces graced the ankles—the shinbones were intact. In the same place near the feet, undisturbed, lay identical shoe buckles and gold sandal soles. Found by the left foot was a silver vessel with a few fragments of the cloth that had once covered it.

In view of the fact that the lower part of the skeleton was in a relatively good state of preservation, the sewn-on plaques were found to have retained their initial position; they traced an even line between the two feet, evidently indicating where the spangled hem of the robe had been. A silver Parthian coin was unearthed by the hipbones, which, judging by its position, had

been clenched in the deceased's fist. All the other numerous adornments, including the more massive pieces, had shifted away from their initial positions. Note should be taken, though, of the plain and well-worn gold ring of a peculiar ornamental design similar to the ring discovered in the first site. This may indirectly indicate a certain kinship between the buried in the Tillya-tepe necropolis.

The funerary offerings found outside the coffin included three ceramic vessels by the head, and, at the feet, a small silver utensil, beneath which lay a gold Roman coin and a signet ring engraved with a representation of a man by an altar. Also outside the coffin, at one of the corners was a second mirror with an ivory handle in a poor state of preservation and next to it a scattered heap of tiny fragments of black crystals that seemed to be antimony. Standing on the mirror was a small earthenware vessel, clearly for the toilet. Discovered nearby were three silver vials, underneath one lay a small silver utensil with an inscription in Greek.

The pair of hairpins consist of silver shafts with repoussé gold heads of an intricately shaped design: large twelve-petaled rosettes nestling within which are two smaller six-petaled rosettes and one of five petals. The rosettes with curl-tipped petals on Greco-Bactrian phalerae are of a kindred style—with the exception that on the hairpins the petals' tips do not curl up.

Note that the half-moon plate, from whose tips and middle gold leaflets dangle, is reminiscent of the design of the hairpins unearthed in the first and second burial sites.

Again the deceased was buried with temple pendants, of which only one has been found. Its design consists of two identical protomas (foreparts) of horses turned in opposite directions (ills. 40, 41). The heads are represented in profile with well-marked nostrils, half-open mouths, and eyesockets of which only one of the original garnet insets remains. The manes and pricked ears are ornamented with almond-shaped turquoise insets. The forward-thrusting legs of one of these half-figures have retained the turquoise hooves; the flank and body are likewise decorated with oval turquoise insets. On the whole, the pendant has been clumsily crafted, which is indicated by the unnaturally short legs of the animals and their formalized posture. One is hard put to say with any degree of certainty whence the craftsman borrowed the motif, as it was quite common in Greco-Bactrian art; yet still earlier such protomas of two horses facing in opposite directions were encountered in Persian Luristan bronzes.

We again found, as in the second burial, a pair of hollow cast gold clasps with an open-worked high-relief design representing cupids astride dolphin-like fish (ill. 87). Though their designs are practically identical, on one of the pair the cupid is depicted head-on, on the other, from the back.

The fish are represented in profile with relief-worked gills and round eyes—white insets with centrally positioned points serving as pupils—well-marked on the large heads, which also carry sumptuous crests inlaid with well-polished, strongly convex turquoise beads; the fins and tails are also inset with turquoise, with the tails separated from the bodies by decorative half-moons; the scales consist of semicircular cloisons filled with paste.

The front-facing cupid has a broad-boned face with a large, fleshy nose, thick, sensual lips, and folds in the puffed and flabby cheeks. His tiny, deeply set eyes have clearly marked lids, and his forehead slants back to the hair, which is conveyed by small impressions. His neck is stocky, his broad shoulders face forward, and his right, strongly bent arm with bracelets around the wrist touches his head, while his left arm stretches forward and rests on the crest on the head of the fish. His weakly defined waist descends into abnormally fat hips and a round belly with a clearly marked navel; beneath the belly a mound probably symbolizes the male genitals, and the legs with their anklets end in distinctly modeled feet.

The head of the cupid on the other clasp, who is depicted from the back, is presented almost in profile and is crowned with a short-curled mop of hair. The face is lightly oval in form and has a straight, fine nose, almond-shaped eyes with round pupils that peep out from beneath slightly arched brows; his plump lips are half open, and his cheeks are puffy. His shoulder blades are well in evidence on his muscular back, and as with the first of the pair of clasps his right arm is strongly bent, a massive bracelet gracing his wrist. His hand touches his head, while his left arm stretches out and rests on the dolphin's crest. His hips are thick and plump, and his legs, adorned with anklets, end in feet with distinctly modeled toes.

Representations of cupids gamboling on the backs of dolphins amidst the waves were great favorites in Roman art; suffice to recall the famous statues of Venus at whose feet one will often see a cupid astride a dolphin—not infrequently in the same iconographic posture, with one hand touching his head and the other grasping the dolphin's crest.

But whereas the earlier imitations of these Greek mythological personages still retain a close affinity with the original, in the late Hellenistic period they are far removed from the prototype. This point is illustrated by the clasps in question on which the lively, mischievous boy-god of love is pictured as an aging, waddling cynic. Further, in place of dolphins we see here the types of fish with which Asia's rivers—specifically the Amu Darya (Oxus), Bactria's main waterway—teemed. The clasps were undoubtedly made by local Bactrian goldsmiths, who had almost completely forgotten how dolphins—just recently so popular in Greco-Bactrian art, as is shown by the statues embellishing the stone terraces of the fountain in the Greco-Bactrian city of Ai Hanoum in Northern Afghanistan—were depicted, let alone what they really look like.

Unearthed in addition to these clasps were another two pairs, one atop the other. While the first pair of clasps is small and rather ordinary, oval, and embellished with minute gold granules along the edges, the second buckles are undoubtedly of particular interest (ills. 81–84). They are comprised of two large open-worked plates joined by a pair of hooks on one and a pair of eyelets or loops on the other. The design is identical on the two, the representation on one being the mirror image of the other. It consists of the figure of a warrior disposed between columns or trees with dragons at his feet.

The warrior's head is presented in three-quarters profile; the straight nose, knitted brows, half-open mouth, and well-delineated jutting chin serve to convey the image of a man steeled in the wars. He wears a helmet whose gadrooned edge is embellished with scrollwork; on top are four cloisons in the plate with the hooks and three in the plate with the loops that may probably have been intended to hold semi-precious stones. A horn with a sharp point juts up from between these cloisons; a long plume curls up from the top of the helmet, which is held in place by a strap that passes under the warrior's chin; from beneath it long, wavy hair straggles down to his shoulders and frames his face. His muscular body is enclosed in a cuirass and draped in a softly flowing robe or mantle with folds, the ends of which are thrown over his left arm to descend smoothly from the elbow almost right down to his feet. On one shoulder the mantle is buckled by a clasp in the form of a half-moon, while below the chest it has been caught up by a tightly knotted belt. The second, bandolier-type, belt crisscrosses the abdomen and holds the suspended sword.

The warrior's hips are draped down to the knees by a puckered kilt that appears to consist of three parts; the upper two are conveyed by means of broad bands broken up into rectangles that softly descend and dangle between the legs; the lower third terminates in wide folds and from beneath them the muscular legs with their well-marked knees are seen. On his feet the warrior wears sandals with a strap inserted between his big and second toe. The sandal thongs girding his legs are quite distinct. Beneath his knee and halfway down his

calf the straps are tightly secured by hemi-spherical buckles.

His left forearm is enclosed in a broad band broken up into rectangles; the arm is bent at almost a right angle, his hand is raised and clasps the staff of a long lance. Discernible behind his hip is a sword handle with a pommel shaped like an eagle's head with a curved, vulpine beak. The handle touches the bent elbow over which the mantle is thrown, its folds serving as the backdrop. His other arm is concealed behind a round shield whose rim is decorated with a design of elongated rectangles; the central section of the shield is composed of broad bands with circles in the middle.

As was noted earlier, the warrior stands between two columns or trees at whose feet are two identical small dragons in blatantly menacing poses. Each possesses a slender, sinuous body with an abbreviated tail coiled into a ring; each paw has three claws. Their flanks have comma-type cloisons that were possibly to serve for gem insets. Their front paws, on which the long, curl-tipped claws are unsheathed, rest on their bent hindquarters; the outline of the forequarters is emphasized at the bottom by small, slanted incisions conveying the cropped fur. Short wings with small, round indentations at the joints spread out from the upper half of their strained, muscular spines; their heads, which sit on contorted necks with the similar bones brought out in relief, are turned back. The grinning, fanged jaws are capped by a row of sharp spikes; the entire menacing image is complemented by the wrinkled nose with vulpine nostrils. Perched atop the trees are birds, possibly eagles. Their eyes are emphasized by spikes presented in relief, and their wings are folded. The entire design rests on a straight, broad band composed of three ornamental strips of rectangles, lozenges, and semi-ovals.

The warrior is fully accoutred in the typical Greco-Roman manner, with the exception of his helmet, which somewhat differs from the classical type. This is especially true of the meandering plume, which is closest to the plume on the crest of the Macedonian-type helmet worn by the Greco-Bactrian king Eucratides.

It will be enough to recall the warriors on the rhytons of Parthian Nisa in Southern Turkmenia, who, it is contended, personify the god of war, Ares, to illustrate their affinities with the warriors on the above clasps. Yet, some details would seem to indicate that it is not Ares, but his Persian counterpart, Veretragna, who is depicted, which appears more likely. This assumption is also supported by the representation of the dragons—absolutely uncharacteristic of Greco-Roman art—while, it has definite parallels in Scythian, and especially Altai, art. It is precisely the presence of such fantastic creatures with grinning jaws and evilly wrinkled visages that is probably the salient feature of the style in which the artifacts from the celebrated Pazyryk barrows are executed. True, in the Altai finds the griffin possesses a bird's beak, while in the Tillya-tepe clasp the dragons have the heads of beasts. However, the Pazyryk finds include representations of grinning-jawed animal visages, which implies that the dragons depicted on the clasps here may well demonstrate the typified image of a fantastic creature that was once common in Altai nomad tribal mythology. One might add that the comma-type indentations on the flanks of the dragons are extremely reminiscent of the similar details to be observed on works of Eurasian art.

One more pair of clasps was unearthed, these cast in the shape of lyres; unlike the other clasps described, they had only loops or eyelets, instead of hooks and eyelets, which points to the existence of some additional fastening material. Since one of the pair lay next to the aforementioned clasps on the deceased's breast, there is no doubt that they were used as clasps, too.

Although in this third burial site what was presumed to be a necklace was found broken, with some portions discovered in rodent burrows, the shape of the beads plus the cone-type clasps warrants the assumption that these pieces had indeed comprised one whole necklace ini-

tially. There were three types of beads. Some were large and smooth; others were round and hollow and were completely covered with minute granulation which seemed to create an open-worked webbing; the third were of white earthenware girdled by tiny gold bands sandwiching a chain of triangles inlaid with turquoise (ill. 61). The pair of cone-shaped clasps into which the ends of the bead-threaded strings had been inserted were ornamented with both soldered-on granules and indented designs of rows of triangles; the clasps were heavily worn.

Found in various spots were four identical medallions, which rodents had quite obviously moved away from their original positions (ill. 38). Centrally portrayed on each was a bust of a human figure; executed in rounded relief was the head with broad cheeks, a straight slender nose, lips with a smile hovering in their corners, and a jutting chin. The hair is parted down the middle in such a manner as to have two horizontal rolls framing the forehead. Long shoulder-length locks frame the face. Visible in rather low relief around the neck is a kind of torque with flared ends, like the actual artifact unearthed in this tomb. Two folds of a robe descending from shoulder to waist are faintly delineated. The full-breasted figure is enclosed in a circle of faintly curved, slightly indented rectangles, and a chain of minute granules rims the whole medallion.

Soldered to the medallion's reverse is a thin, flat, round plate, to which in turn are soldered four eyelets jutting out in different directions. Braided gold wires ending in disks and leaflets dangle from the medallion. The smugly complacent face with its sarcastic smile apparently served to convey the secular image of a member of the ruling elite. Indeed, the round, moon-shaped face, with its slightly slanted, almond-shaped eyes beneath widespread arched brows, is most likely representative of a local Bactrian ethnic type.

One of the three rings found has retained an inset vitreous mass, but the image it once carried can hardly be made out due to the strong

31

iridescence. The second is embellished with a flat, oval bezel of some blue stone, presumably turquoise, bearing the representation of a man standing by an altar (ill. 111).

The figure itself is presented facing front, with its slightly tilted head in a three-quarters turn. The barely discernible bearded face is crowned with a wreath or a sumptuous headdress with two spreading ribbons, and the muscular body is seminude. On the shoulder is a round clasp from which a mantle descends in soft folds to wrap the thighs down to the knees. Both arms are bare; one hand rests on a long wand with a round pommel whose upper part is entwined with ribbons, and the other hand is lowered and presumably holds a spray or ear of grain—unless it depicts flames from the altar. The man's calves are entwined by circular stripes apparently imitating the thongs of footwear. One leg is straight, with the foot turned out, and the other is slightly bent; a straight horizontal line denotes the ground beneath the feet. On one side of the figure is a column with a double plinth and a capital, the shaft of which is enclosed by a half-moon in the middle. On the other side is a small pear-shaped altar on a platform, its upper part likewise enclosed by a half-moon with two dots below. Considering that goldsmiths and jewelers used to portray deities or heroes, one may presume that we are faced here with a design that is associated with the popular motif of a hero presenting a votive offering for the figure radiates a sense of confidence and grandeur. As is the case with the carved gems, the jeweler concentrated on the figure, just faintly limning the face.

One comparison that may be cited is a Roman cameo that shows a naked man pouring a libation onto an altar; in his right hand he holds two ears of grain; three more are depicted above the altar. It is thought that the statue of the harvest god, holding a patera and ears of grain in his hands that once stood in Rome is the prototype for this scene.

The third signet ring from this site also had a flat, oval inset of a bluish stone, probably turquoise, rimmed with minute granulation. It is engraved with a female figure in profile. Capping the faintly marked face is what is apparently a narrow-brimmed helmet. Her body is garbed in a short tunic gathered in at the waist; from behind her shoulders spread wings that curl at the tips. One arm is raised and holds a round wreath, the other is thrust forward and rests on a staff. From beneath the tunic a long bell-shaped skirt falls to the ground and is articulated by deeply incised vertical lines toward the hem. The wings and wreath would seem to suggest that this is Nike, the goddes of victory. However, the staff would appear to conflict with the classical representation of this Greek mythological personage so popular in the Asiatic East. Indeed, in place of the queenly goddess, we are faced with a bent figure leaning heavily on the staff she holds. This is most likely explained as a medley of imported Greek traditions and local Bactrian imagery, plus the emergence of syncretic deities. In this connection one might cite the representation on a Greco-Roman cameo of a winged female deity, who holds either a staff or an oar in her left hand. She was defined as a syncretic goddess, the fusion of Victory, Fortuna, and Nemesis.

Also unearthed in this tomb was an intaglio carved from a semi-translucent light-brown scaraboid, bored along its longitudinal axis to take a string or thong. Carved in incised relief on the flat side is an effigy of the humped Indian ox, the zebu; the animal's small head crowned with a crescent of coiled horns is depicted. Its powerful body and straight limbs are shown in motion, but there is no tail. This may possibly be of an earlier Greco-Bactrian, if not Achaemenian, origin.

Of particular interest is the cast-gold oval with four eyelets for fastening on its left side. The obverse carries an incised representation of a forward-facing female figure with her head in profile. The head is capped by a narrow-brimmed helmet, and her facial features are barely discernible. The full-bosomed body is garbed in a light and short tunic, caught by a belt right beneath her breasts and terminating in

32

straight folds that follow the lines of the hips. From beneath the tunic a longer robe flows down in soft folds outlining thighs and legs; the toes of shoes peep out from beneath the hem.

One arm is concealed behind a massive, round shield embellished with designs in relief in the shape of rings and convex circles with centrally positioned rosettes. Her other arm, with bracelets gracing the forearm and wrist, is thrust forward, and her hand is clenched. Thrown over this arm is a cloak, whose folds arch down to the knees and then rise up again to cross the opposite shoulder and descend from behind the shield. Placed on a slant in front of the figure is a spear, whose tip is hidden behind the shield. In front, at the base, is a Greek inscription, the reverse of the name Athena. Gold-mounted carved gems were worn as pendants from the wrist or waist; in his day Aristophanes scoffed at contemporary men of fashion, who decked themselves out in carved gems as if they were trinkets.

The unique gold shoe soles, indicative of a heelless type of footwear, are of exceptional interest. To judge by their jagged edges, both were cut by hand from a thin sheet of gold and have perforations at the toe and heel by which they were lashed to the shoes being worn. We may deduce from this that some two thousand years ago a heelless type of footwear was common in Bactria, which, it is true, may not have been the only style used.

Discovered in roughly the same position on the inner side of the shoe soles were two identical gold buckles shaped as small cast rings. From one edge jutted a short prong in the form of a mushroom; one side of it was worn down, evidently due to the narrow leather straps that had been passed through the ring. Lying next to each ring was a tiny gold object in the form of a cast hemispherical plaque with an oblong loop on the back for fastening.

Meanwhile, on the outer side of the soles we found one more pair of identical oblong cast-gold buckles with perforations in the middle. One end was rounded, and the other, with its prongs, was heavily worn. Near one of these buckles was a hemispherical plaque with a loop for fastening, of the same type as described above. It was also worn from frequent use. Rodents had most likely shifted the second buckle away from its original position. That shoe buckles were in use was already known from carved stone statues, such as Kanishka from Mathura; the heelless high boots depicted there are lashed at the ankles by straps that are fastened by means of buckles.

The third burial site produced the one and only comb unearthed (ill. 142). Made of ivory, it is covered on both sides with finely incised designs. However, the design is relatively easily discernible only on one side: a centrally positioned male figure that is slightly turned. He has a melon-shaped, probably shaven head with an elongated face on which the straight nose overshadows the small mouth; spreading arched brows highlight his almond-shaped eyes. His neck is long and sinuous, and he is garbed in a tight-fitting blouse with a neck opening; the blouse is tucked into trousers. In its style of execution the comb is reminiscent of the one recovered from the North Bactrian community of Dalverzin-tepe, and especially so of the carved ivories from Begram; all the artifacts were most likely imported from India, which had ivory in abundance.

The numerous fragments of round, ivory receptacles, which probably served a role in cosmetics, feature a patchily preserved ornamentation of incised or protruding circles. Jammed in the neck of a small pear-shaped silver utensil, which itself serves as an accessory for the toilet, was a fragment of a bronze shaft most likely broken off a cosmetic spatula.

Judging by the remnants unearthed, the third site contained at least seven round-bellied silver vials with long, tapering necks and out-turned lips. One other hemispherical vessel of inferior oxidized silver was quite different; its rim carried a high-grade silver fillet in relief ornamented with a chainlike design of impressed half-moons. This object could have possessed a lid, like a similar vessel recovered from the fifth

33

burial site. Note should likewise be taken of a small earthenware cosmetics vessel in the shape of a hemispherical cup with a handle, whose bottom has a distinct base plate embellished with a plain scratched design.

In all likelihood the iron handle found belongs to some toilet article. Embellished with two gold tubes at the ends, it is richly inlaid with triangles, semi-ovals, and heart shapes of turquoise and lapis lazuli that comprise one overall ornamental design. It also bears traces of a blade.

Other finds include two small, lidded gold pots presumably for holding cosmetics. The larger of the two is cylindrical in shape and is embellished with a repoussé ornamental band, the design of which is repeated on the lid. The second, smaller object is cast in the form of a bellied pot whose shoulders have two soldered-on loops through which a braided chain fastened to the handle of the flat lid is passed.

Among the funerary offerings recovered are three ceramic vessels. The largest, a two-handled, wide-necked jug, has a round body and flat bottom; one handle bears the imprint of a stamp—a bust of a person. The second vessel, also two-handled, is much smaller and has a full-bellied body and a broad, flat bottom. The third is a tall, slender cone-shaped goblet on a short stem; inside and outside it is covered by a thick, dark-brown slip.

The highly polished oval and convex carved stone pendants are set in gold fittings with two loops along the longitudinal axis that would enable them to be suspended from a thong or string. They are of ordinary pietra dura, with, in one case, an iron inset. Another type of pendant consists of small cylinders carved from turquoise or lapis lazuli set in small gold mounts—some of which are of a fancy toothed shape—and have a loop on top from which they could be suspended. On some specimens there were two sets of loops, one on either end of the pendant. We likewise recovered round, oblong, square, and lozenge-shaped pendants, all set in gold mounts with loops from which they could be suspended. There were even a few rare, hardly worked

stones enclosed in knotted strips of gold with loops at the top. Mention should likewise be made of the recovered faceted and mordanted cylindrical beads of cornelian probably of Indian origin, as well as smaller beads and strings of bored beads carved from river pebbles of diverse colors.

The two mirrors we found are of different provenance. One carries a circular legend inscribed with Chinese characters. The other has a massive ivory handle ornamented with a plain scratched design (ill. 144). The obverse is smooth, but the reverse is edged with a raised rim embellished with barely marked bosses and with a cone-shaped prunt in the middle. It bears an affinity to a round mirror having an identical ivory handle that is from Taxila.

Two coins were recovered from the third tomb. One is of gold and bears the bust in profile of the wreath-crowned Roman emperor Tiberius. On the reverse is an enthroned, sumptuously draped female figure holding a spray and scepter. Coins of this order were minted in the Roman Empire in the city of Lugdunum in Gaul, between A.D. 16 and 21. The Tillya-tepe coin is the first case of such a coin to be found not merely in Afghanistan, but in contiguous Central Asia.

The second coin is silver and has on the obverse the stamped, bearded head of a ruler in profile wearing a diadem. Depicted on the reverse is a seated archer holding a bow in his right, outstretched hand; an inscription in Greek runs around the rim. The coin was minted by the Parthian king Mithridates II, who ruled between 123 and 88 B.C.

Proceeding from the later Roman coin we may presume the third tomb to date from the first century A.D.

SITE 4

The fourth burial site was sunk into the crest of the temple's wall so far that only a minor portion jutted out from beneath the wall's inner face where a gold disk was recovered in the clearing process. We were thus in an ideal position to initiate excavation from the top, right above the burial. We obtained evidence of the shape of the grave pit after we had removed the top twelve to sixteen inches (30–40 cm) of turf, beneath which a horse's skull and shank bones were revealed by the northern end of the grave: the first and—so far—only evidence of a funerary wake.

This rectangular shaft grave, whose corners were slightly rounded, was about nine feet (2.7 m) long and about four feet (1.3 m) wide. Its floor lay at a depth of almost six feet (1.8 m) from the top of the mound. Inside, the grave was packed with earth, in the upper layers of which the remnants of wooden scaffolding were encountered. These were hollow pipes filled with the dark-brown, powdery dust of rotted laths. Judging by their configuration, it may be presumed that the grave pit had been roofed over by a wooden trellis whose transverse strips, disposed at spaces of about four inches (10 cm), had been held in place by five longitudinally placed laths, one in the middle and two each at either side. The traces of the longitudinal laths were far more distinct and frequent than of the transverse ones. The trellis had, in all likelihood, been supported by recessed banks at the upper edges of the grave pit, which were unfortunately not distinctly in evidence when the excavation was undertaken. A braided mat had been placed on the trellis after which earth was shoveled in on top. The traces of the matting consisted of thin layers of white, powdery dust bearing the imprint of braiding, especially on the coffin and around it on the grave floor, onto which scraps of the matting had fallen when the roof caved in under the weight of the earth above. Traces of decayed hide or leather were also evident on the grave floor.

The oblong wooden coffin was about seven feet (2.2 m) long, two feet four inches (0.7 m) wide, and about two feet five inches (0.75 m) deep and had been raised by legs at each of the four corners to a height of six inches (15 cm) from the grave floor. The sides of the coffin were secured to its bottom by means of iron clamps bent at right angles in much the same fashion as in the other tombs described, with one difference: this coffin was additionally held together by long strips of iron that ran along the bottom and partly up its sides. The coffin was lined with and wrapped in hides painted with a meandering design in white and black on a red ground. The leather sheath was likewise spangled with gold disks and numerous hemispherical plaques. It is difficult to say with certainty whether the coffin had a lid or not; although some insignificant traces of powdery wood dust were discovered above the coffin, their origin is still rather obscure.

Again, as in the previous graves six massive iron nails had been hammered into the upper edge of the sides of the coffin, one each at the corners and another two in the middle. The nails had either held the lid down or, which is more likely, the leather shroud.

The body lay flat on its back, with its head pointing north. According to tentative anthropological analysis and judging by the specific assortment of funerary offerings, the deceased was a male about thirty years old.

The deceased, who was six and a half feet (2 m) tall, lay with his head on a small cushion that had been placed at the bottom of a gold phiale carrying an inscription in Greek. Attached to the side of this bowl were a gold scale model of a tree and a figurine of an ibex, which was found some distance away on the grave floor. Attached to the vessel's upper tip and suspended over the deceased's forehead, these objects, as status symbols akin to a diadem or crown, were indicative of the deceased's high social standing. Other tokens of rank were the two gold chin stays, the gold pectoral with its centrally positioned cameo, and the gold braided belt with its nine round plaques.

A long sword and a dagger, both sheathed in gold-plated scabbards, were found on the body's left side. On the right side was another dagger with an ivory hilt. Placed at the foot was what was apparently a bridle embellished with gold phalerae and arched plaques with repoussé designs executed in the Siberian animal style. Note the probably deliberate placing on either side of the deceased of two identical assortments of objects, namely, a dagger in a golden scabbard, a gold pipe-tip, and the arched plaques. Disposed by the ankles were identical footwear sets, each comprising a round buckle, which has been tentatively dubbed the "dragon's chariot," and an engraved rectangular plate. Gold bracelets graced the ankles.

Also recovered from the coffin were thousands of gold spangles from the funerary attire, an Indian gold coin, and a glass intaglio bearing the representation of three warriors.

At the head of the coffin, but outside of it, were a small, folding leather-upholstered iron klismos (chair), two bows, and two gold-mounted quivers filled with iron arrowheads (ill. 156); one of the quivers possessed a silver lid in the form of a truncated cone that was ornamented with a finely incised design (ill. 155). From the fact that the grave pit contained a horse's skull and bones, one may deduce that it was a noble warrior—who still adhered to the nomadic traditions of his forefathers—who was interred in this fourth tomb.

By analyzing the ornamentation we were able to reconstruct the garments that the deceased wore. The tunic folded over onto the left side; its hem, front, cuffs, and back were richly spangled with gold plaques of diverse form and shape. On the back the plaques ran down the middle in a straight line, from the end of which another two lines of plaques slanted up toward the shoulders. The tunic was tightly caught at the waist by a gold belt from beneath which a kilt descended to the feet. On the whole, this garb is strikingly similar to the costume worn by the ruler depicted on the "ruler and dragons" head pendants from the second burial.

On the one hand, the tunic, often folded over on the left, was probably the typical dress of the nomad, as is indicated by objects of the visual arts recovered in Southern Russia. On the other hand, long, kiltlike robes drape the stately figures of the Achaemenid kings. In our opinion, the funerary attire in the fourth burial comprised a costume that was simultaneously typically nomadic (as is evidenced by the tunic) and Persian (as is evidenced by the skirt), a costume in which deceased representatives of a then-newly emergent ruling dynasty were garbed.

The massive cast-gold vessel that corresponds to the typical shape of the Greek phiale is especially interesting (ills. 138, 139). From the bottom of this object grooves fan out, broadening toward the top. The Greek inscription on the rim designates the vessel's overall weight in staters. Since a stater was equivalent to just over one-half an ounce (15.5–15.6 g), the inscription, deciphered, stands for forty-one staters, about twenty-one ounces (638 g).

As was noted earlier, attached to the bowl's rim was a gold scale model of a tree (ill. 121). It has a long trunk of rectangular cross section bulging out toward its foot, which rests on a stand of four petals set crosswise. Each petal is perforated in the middle to enable the entire affair to be securely fastened, which indicates that this object undoubtedly had a second purpose. The trunk terminates on top in a six-petaled rosette; gold disks dangle on thin gold wires from the tip of each petal. Sinuous branches spread out from the trunk in all four directions and disks also dangle on wires from their tips. Some wires are embellished in the middle by small threaded pearls which possibly imitate fruit.

The hollow gold figurine of the ibex (ills. 112–120) found nearby had evidently also been attached to the rim of the bowl by some resinous adhesive. The tiny rings in which the animal's hooves end show that the object was employed for some other purpose during interment, especially since a hollow tube juts forth from between the horns. Some additional details may have been inserted or some libation poured through this tube—which, however, seems much less likely.

The scale model of the tree and the gold figurine of the ibex had most probably been incorporated into a ceremonial headdress akin to a diadem or crown. It bears the closest affinity to the celebrated gold diadem from the Khokhlach barrow (the Novocherkassk Treasure) that once adorned the head of a Sarmatian princess. Disposed along this diadem's upper rim are representations of trees with sinuous branches from which leaves droop, birds, deer with spreading antlers, and ibexes. We have here an overall compositional analogy, as is shown not only by an identical choice of subject matter such as trees and ibexes, but also by such purely technical elements as the tiny pillars (Khokhlach) or rings (Tillya-tepe) in which the legs of the animals terminate. The famous collection of Peter I on view in the Hermitage in Leningrad boasts similar gold scale models of trees with similar branches of wire and leaflike disks dangling from them. Moreover, in one such case the trunk is akin to that of the Tillya-tepe tree, being rectangular, not round, in cross section and terminating in a similarly perforated stand. The quite warranted theory that such models of trees with scattered figurines of birds and beasts could be parts of intricate compositions like the one embellishing the Novocherkassk diadem has been suggested.

As the animals on the Novocherkassk diadem are presented in a rather schematic fashion, one has the impression that they are clumsily executed copies of artistically superior originals. If this is the case, one may imagine that in Bactria itself there existed diadems of a highly intricate compositional design, which were then copied by local goldsmiths and jewelers. Indeed, the magnificently executed figurine of the ibex from this fourth burial site sharply contrasts in style to the bulk of adornments recovered from the Tillya-tepe necropolis and, in all likelihood, adheres to the realistic traditions of earlier Greco-Bactrian art, times, incidentally, when local potentates wore diadems, not crowns. It is quite conceivable that the diadem in question, incorporating, aside from other parts, the scale model of the tree and the figurine of the ibex, was produced precisely during the period we have in

mind. Captured as a trophy by the Kushan conquerors, the diadem could have been divided as booty between the leaders of the invading forces. Finally, some two or three generations later, the new rulers of the emergent Kushan Empire, as if to emphasize by such symbols their inheritance of authority from the basileis of the Greco-Bactrian Kingdom, could have deposited such prestigious trophies in the graves of the first Kushan rulers.

The Scythians held gold bowls or phiales in special esteem, a point confirmed by Herodotus in his celebrated account of the origin of these nomad hordes. In it he mentions a bowl, as well as a plow, a yoke, and an ax. So, it is quite likely that the gold bowls recovered from the Bactrian tombs were placed there not by chance, but in accordance with the Scythian custom of depositing vessels of gold in their graves, a custom described by Herodotus.

The pectoral gracing the neck of the interred warrior prince is as exciting (ills. 68, 69). Consisting of an interlacing of gold wires, it is embellished in the middle by a cameo, carved from a hard stone comprised of two layers, white and brown. Executed in this classical cameo color combination is a bust of a man, with his head presented in profile, turned to the left. His nose is short and straight, his eyes are deeply set, and their round pupils are conspicuously delineated; his lips are poutingly full. He wears a Macedonian round-topped helmet with a broad ribbon tied around the narrow brim, from beneath which his hair falls down to his neck, partly concealing his ears in the process.

This is without a doubt a portrait, although one created during the earlier Greco-Bactrian period. Confirmation of this conclusion is provided by the realistic manner of bringing out the individual features of a person who actually existed, plus a type of helmet that is identical with those that the Bactrian kings wore. The helmet has an affinity with the one worn by the Greco-Bactrian king Eucratides that has a band running around it and knotted into a bow on the side. Since this detail is to be observed on the cameo in question, it may imply that the person portrayed was of the royal house that once ruled the Greco-Bactrian Kingdom. It must be noted that the pectoral was fastened by means of a small gold pin that was passed through a loop and then bent back. It would be appropriate to recall in this connection the gold pectoral from Northern Bactria with a similar fastening and a mounted inset gemstone with a representation of Hercules, which may have also been employed for some other purpose.

The gold braided belt with nine plates that was recovered from the fourth tomb is thus far unique amidst the Kushan artifacts found (ills. 88–97). All the plates bear one identical design, that of a woman astride a lion. Depicted in the middle is the beast in profile and in motion; its mane is tangled and its ears are pricked up. Its snarling visage, tongue hanging from between the cavernous jaws, is turned toward the viewer. Its muscular front paws beneath its massive chest have unsheathed claws, and its left paw is placed in front of its right leg. The body of the animal is draped in a rectangular saddlecloth that carries a design edged with a band consisting of circlets and has long tassles dangling from its corners. Across the cloth is a strap tightly girdled around the lion's belly; its left hip and hind leg are thrust forward, and its tail is coiled beneath its belly.

The woman straddling the lion is shown with a face that has regular yet sharp, if not cruel, features; her hairdo is rather intricate, with her hair parted down the middle, swept upward, and knotted into a chignon at the nape of her neck. A fillet encircles her forehead. Her neck, which is encircled by a torque, and her arms are bare; her breasts are draped in soft folds, and her waist is caught by a belt from beneath which a short skirt ending above the knee descends in vertical folds. Her right arm is bent at the elbow and lies on the lion's neck. Her left arm, with a bracelet around the wrist, rests on her knee, and her hand holds a typically Greek two-handled ornamented vessel. Her legs are spread wide apart; the thongs of her sandals are laced up to mid-calf.

Excavations of the Issyk barrow in Soviet Kazakhstan disclosed that back in the fourth century B.C. the nomads roaming these territories girdled their tunics with articulated gold belts. For this reason we may presume this belt recovered from the fourth tomb to be illustrative of nomad customs that hark back to still earlier traditions adhered to in Asia Minor, traditions that persisted up to the times of the Parthian and Kushan Kingdoms. Pertinent evidence is furnished by the braided belts embellished with large medallions that are to be seen on the carved stone reliefs in the Parthian city of Khatra and, more specifically, by the plates on the belt depicted on one of the Kushan statues of Mathura, on which horsemen are executed in high relief. It is noteworthy that neither Kushan, Parthian, nor Bactrian belts had special buckles with a rigid fastening, but were secured by means of soft straps.

In Greek mythology only the goddess Cybele is portrayed accompanied by lions or, now and again, riding a lion. Thus the female figure represented on the plates of the Tillya-tepe belt is but a borrowing integrated into the image of an Asia Minor deity. In Parthia, as well as, most likely, in Bactria, the Cybele cult was far less popular than that of the goddess Nani or Nanai. At the same time more direct parallels exist, firstly a Kushan intaglio portraying a goddess holding a bowl and straddling a lion.

The fourth was the only grave in which ceremonial weapons were found. The iron dagger recovered has a gold-mounted haft and is sheathed in a gold-mounted scabbard (ills. 157–161). Both haft and scabbard are inlaid and ornamented in repoussé with scenes of the mauling of animals. Represented on the scabbard is a row of five fantastic beasts in profile. First on the right is a winged and beaked carnivore with deeply inset eyes, its ears folded back. Its body is presented in a writhing posture; its sharp claws are withdrawn beneath its belly, under which its tail with its turquoise-inset tip coils to emerge behind its back. Gripped in its beak is the paw of the creature up in front. This is a winged dragon with a serpentine, writhing body and a huge head with a long tongue between its gaping fanged jaws. Its wrinkled, upturned nostrils end in an inset turquoise bead, spiraling horns crown its low brow, and its ears are flattened back. From beneath its neck a small beard straggles. A repoussé-worked crest runs down its spine from head to tail, and turquoise-inlaid wings spread out from its back. Its hindquarters—with their stretched-out talons and long sinuous tail—are contorted and presented from the back.

The next creature in the row has pricked-up ears between short, twisted horns, a long contorted neck, a winged body, and a tail coiled beneath its belly. Three of its paws are depicted; a hind one is gripped in the jaws of the dragon behind. Its wings and neck are richly inlaid with turquoise. It, in turn, has sunk its fangs into the creature in front, which possesses a curved beak topped by a short horn. Its round, deeply set eyes with their massive brows are overshadowed by the forward-jutting ears. Its long, serpentine neck bears a low crest; the finely incised line below evidently serves to convey the impression of tangled fur; small wings spread out from behind its back, and its tail is coiled beneath the body.

The creature in the rear is also a winged beast, manifestly feline. Its head, with its snarling face and laid-back ears, is turned back, and wings fan out from its back. Its long tail is coiled beneath its belly, and its talons are inlaid with turquoise. The beast behind has sunk its beak into this one's shank.

Though this image ends the scene carried by the scabbard, the composition is continued on the dagger's haft. Depicted here is a creature similar to the third in the row on the scabbard. It is biting the haunches of the creature in front, its ears stand up, and its small, spiraling horns are bent back. Its long neck with its raised crest and folds of skin below is twisted; its winged body is inlaid with turquoise. Its talons are presented in motion; sandwiched between them is the long tail, which goes under the belly and then rises up

onto its back, terminating in a loop with a turquoise inset. Like the rear beast on the scabbard, the creature in front is snarling, with its face turned back. The forequarters are stretched out, and the hindquarters are twisted around and shown from the back, with the paws spread apart and up. Between the paws is the tip of the coiled tail, embellished with a round turquoise inset. The creature behind is mauling this one's right paw.

Meanwhile, depicted on the pommel is a bear cub with parted paws and a stubby tail. Its small head has upward-jutting turquoise-inlaid ears, and its eyes are small and somnolent. The nostrils of its long nose are well delineated; in its mouth the animal holds a vine with clusters of grapes.

The reverse of the haft is completely covered with a repoussé plant design in the shape of small palmettes whose tips twirl out.

The motif depicting beasts of prey, including fantastic creatures savaging ungulates, is possibly most common in the art of what is known as the Scytho-Sarmatian animal style.

The gold plating of the second scabbard is again ornamented with a repoussé-executed episode of two fantastic dragon-like creatures engaged in combat (ills. 162–166). Presented from the back on the broader upper part, where the dagger grip is visible, is a creature with the head of a wolf that is turned to one side. The viciously scowling visage with its malevolent jaws, its puckered, protruding nose picked out by a turquoise bead, and its round, madly rolling eyes beneath menacingly knitted brows is crowned with spreading antlers tipped by round turquoise beads; its long ears are likewise inlaid with bulging turquoise insets. A wedge-shaped beard covers its chin, and a thornlike knob protrudes from its upper jaw. Its long, sinuous neck carries a low crest, soft folds of skin fan out from beneath its neck and continue down its belly, and small wings are folded along its muscular back. Its massive three-taloned paws with unsheathed claws reach forward. The lower portion of its body is contorted and presented in

39

profile; its taut legs are shown in motion, the right beneath the belly and the left partly engulfed in the mouth of the second dragon. The long, turquoise-inlaid tail passes between its feet, coils far down on top the back and finally terminates in a ring.

The second monster possesses a small and elegant serpent head, with faintly delineated nostrils and small eyes, and forward-thrusting ears picked out by turquoise insets and set between a low wavy crest running back down its neck. The three-taloned front legs, likewise inlaid with turquoise, also have unsheathed claws and are thrust out. Small wings, again inlaid with turquoise, are folded back along its broad, knobby, sinewy spine. Its long body, whose ribs seem to bulge beneath the smoothly stretched skin, snakes along; the powerful, resilient hindquarters are shown in profile and in motion, the left leg brought up beneath the belly and the right leg placed far back. Its long, turquoise-inlaid tail softly coils around the right hind paw and ends in a tasseled tip embellished with three turquoise insets.

Each of the ribs of the scabbard is embellished with a magnificent mouflon's head, with triangular perforations in the middle of each forehead.

As this scene is unique, never seen before on any other artifact, the affinities it shares with the Pazyryk barrow finds are of exceptional value. Deserving of mention here are the carved wooden mounts of a horse harness that depict raised figures of snow leopards, whose limbs are seen in profile but whose bodies are shown from above. Again, as in the case of the Tillya-tepe objects, the front paws with their three claws are stretched out forward, while one of the hind limbs is thrust beneath the belly and the other is thrown back. Also the writhing, coiled tails are articulated in both cases—by slanted incisions on the Pazyryk finds and by oblong turquoise insets on the Tillya-tepe scabbard. We are confronted here with a stylistic, even iconographic, affinity, further confirmed by the raised shoulder muscles that are conveyed by comma-like protuberances

on the wooden mounts and by almond-shaped turquoise beads on the gold sheath.

Also meaningful are clear, and by no means accidental, stylistical details such as the small spike on the pug nose, the small chin, and the three-taloned paws, which if not totally identical to, resemble the artifacts from the Siberian collection at the Hermitage in Leningrad. Indeed, the resemblance is very striking, pointing to the obvious connection between the origins of the aforementioned objects. The strong modeling of the taut muscles of the dragons on the Bactrian scabbard is in keeping with the ancient Eastern—or more exactly Assyrian—style where, incidentally, one should seek the source of the objects in question. Yet the antlered wolf head is more likely representative of the art of the northern forests zone and thus indicates the many-faceted character of the formation of the Scytho-Sarmatian animal style.

The scabbard is of an intricate design. The carved ivory hilt of the one-edged iron blade, inserted at either end in two gold fittings, could be thrust almost fully into the sheath in such a manner that only the very top was visible. Attached to the bronze mount on the scabbard's back was a leather sheath into which two other smaller, double-edged blades could be thrust with their points facing one another. The hilts of these smaller daggers are also of carved ivory, bearing a design of grape vines and what must be a lion's head with open jaws. The hilt tops were inserted into gold end-casings inlaid with garnets in the middle. However, unlike the one-edged blade, the pair of smaller daggers functioned not as offensive weapon but as status symbols, which is illustrated by the richly ornamented hilts that are bigger than the blades themselves.

Such three-dagger sets in one sheath have not been encountered before. The only similar objects are the dagger-and-knife sets with scabbards from tombs in Mongolia and Tuva dating back to the fifth through third centuries B.C. One could also probably note a resemblance to the twin-dagger scabbards—in which the blades are sheathed parallel to one another—of the Uzbeks, known as the *koshpichaks.* The ceremonial specimens of the *koshpichaks* such as those from the opulent collection of the Emirs of Bukhara were studded with a host of precious gems.

Discovered between the deceased's ankles were round, open-worked, cast shoe buckles, one each on either side (ill. 124). They are absolutely identical, with the outer raised rim inlaid with two rows of large protruding almond-shaped turquoise beads. As they run toward one another in a kind of herringbone pattern, only a narrow strip of gold is visible in between. The projecting prong on the rim's edge is mushroom-shaped; its shaft shows signs of wear from the straps used to secure the buckle.

The roundel within the raised rim bears the representation of a canopied chariot. Its wheels are inlaid with turquoise. The ballooning canopy is embellished along the top with tiny, almond-shaped turquoise bead insets interspersed with miniature convex gold lozenges, and along the hem with a broad band articulated by oblong recesses. The canopy is affixed to two upright bamboo rods attached to the chariot, of which the side facing the viewer is decorated with a finely executed ornamental design consisting on one of the buckles of vertical stripes and raised circlets and on the other of tiny lozenges marked by a central dot. The edges of the chariot are inlaid with turquoise insets. As the entire design shows, the buckles were additionally embossed after casting.

Depicted within the chariot is a man wearing a long robe. His head is thrown back, his narrow face has high cheekbones and slanted eyes, a small nose with distended nostrils, and a half-open, well-delineated mouth. His short pigtail is raised, and at the nape of his neck the short hairs are conveyed by means of small slanted incisions.

The mandarin collar encircling his neck is embellished with turquoise insets. His torso is draped in a robe that falls in folds and has long, billowing sleeves, of which the cuffs are likewise inlaid with turquoise. Worn across his chest from shoulder to waist is a broad sash ornamented with oblong turquoise inlays. One arm is hidden, the other holds the reins managing the winged lion-like creatures harnessed to the vehicle. These beasts are depicted in a heraldic posture, each with one paw raised. Their snarling faces reflect a wickedly angry impatience. Their narrow eye-slits are inlaid with turquoise and cornelian, and their ears, rising from bulging foreheads, are folded back and embellished with turquoise insets. The long, low-lying crests that start between their ears are encrusted with minute oblong turquoise beads and are intended to represent manes on the distorted necks.

The stumpy, front three-taloned paws stand straight; steeply curved wings that are coiled at the tips and are inlaid with turquoise sprout from their shoulders. Their muscular chests are crisscrossed by straps carrying turquoise inlays; traces intersect the wings at the base. These barrel-chested beasts with their indrawn bellies are depicted resting on their hindquarters. Their abbreviated coiled tails are decorated with slanted incisions.

A noteworthy point is that the eyes of the beasts are inlaid in the same manner as those of the antelopes on the bracelets from the second burial site; tiny turquoise beads have been set in the corners to denote the whites, and similarly small beads of yellowish cornelian represent the pupils, which bears out the assumption made that these bracelets and the shoe buckles are of identical provenance, most likely from somewhere in Bactria.

Chariots, including canopied carriages, have long been known in the East, as far back as in the times of ancient Assyria. However, there are several details, specifically the awning at the back of the canopy, that sets these carriages apart from the Bactrian exemplars. Some Chinese chariots that date back to the ninth century B.C. bear the closest resemblance—and are virtually identical at times—to these. In fact, the representation on the buckle compares particularly well with the chariots that have mushroom-like canopies attached by long poles that are depicted on grave bricks and reliefs of the Han dynasty. We have here a sufficiently definite link indicating the Far Eastern prototypes of the Bactrian representations. The affinity is even more convincing when one takes into consideration the type of garment worn—the free-flowing robe with its mandarin collar and wide sleeves—which directly corresponds to garb worn in Mongolia, and partly China, since times immemorial.

Though the indicated affinities would appear obvious, there is one essential reservation that must be made. Chinese chariots are always depicted as being drawn by horses, which is a salient feature of the national art tradition. But the buckles in question manifest a striking difference in that here the chariot is drawn by lion-like griffins, which may indicate a Bactrian reinterpretation of the imported motif. This is even more true of the technique noted of inlaying the eyes of these fantastic creatures; characteristic of local goldsmithing, it leaves not a shadow of a doubt that they are of typically Bactrian provenance.

Found near the buckles were identical objects of gold in the shape of five-petaled rosettes inlaid with turquoise, that judging by the loops on the back had been sewn onto the footwear. Discovered alongside were plaques depicting a panther and having at one end a transverse prong as fastener (ill. 98). The representation on the obverse of a stealthily creeping winged carnivore akin to a snow leopard or panther, but with unnaturally contorted hindquarters, is both stylistically and compositionally similar to the images on artifacts executed in the Siberian animal style and on the carved horn bow stick of a saddle bow and the belt mounts from the Altai mountains.

In this tomb there was one more plaque, depicting a winged dragon (ill. 98). Its jaws gape, its nose is turned up, and its eyes stare wide open beneath the bulging ridges of eyebrows. Its horns are short, its ears long, and a beard coils out from beneath its neck. Its writhing body

rests on bent paws, and its tail is coiled beneath the belly. This iconographic posture, as well as the very image of the dragon, bears an amazingly close similarity to the raised representation of the mauling episode on the scabbard found in this same tomb. However, of undoubted interest is the representation of a dragon similar in iconographic type and style that is to be seen on the gold Karagalinka diadem from Northern Kirghizia in the USSR. Apparently, Bactrian craftsmen had developed by that period canonical representations of fantastic creatures of the indicated type of menacing winged, serpentine dragon that had a definite semantic meaning in local legend and mythology; they repeated them time and again in their work, commanding a steady sale throughout neighboring regions.

The round shoe buckles enjoy a direct affinity with the clasp that fastens the long billowing trousers of King Kanishka at the ankle as depicted on the stone effigy from Surkh Kotale.

Further data are furnished by the reliefs in Palmyra, Syria, portraying Parthian kings, who, like their Kushan counterparts, were of nomadic origin. Again their feet are shod in low, heelless boots that are secured at the ankles by round buckles with freely descending straps; in one such case these boots are held in place by a dual system of thongs. All this shows that there existed numerous ways of securing footwear by special thongs, some with gold-tipped ends, that would be passed under the arch of the foot over onto the instep, where they crossed to be fastened at the ankles by one or several buckles.

Ceremonial horse trappings were encountered exclusively in this fourth burial site. Discovered by the hipbones of the deceased were six almost round gold phalerae, three by the side of each of the afore-described daggers. They were all cast in high relief in the form of fantastic creatures coiled into an almost perfect circle. Three carry an identical design representing a resting eagle-griffin with its head nestled on its breast (ills. 149, 150). All three have retained a fragment of thick leather within, held tightly in

42

place by a strip of gold. The outer side bears signs of heavy wear, which leaves no doubt that the phalerae had originally been designed to hold the various straps of the harness.

Another two phalerae, also identical, were designed in the shape of a feline carnivore frenziedly gnawing its own paw (ills. 151, 152). Both disclosed heavy signs of wear, even to a point where one developed a cavity; there were within traces of a leather strap, however, without fastening prongs.

Finally, the last of the six was hemispherical in form and shaped as a winged beast biting its own tail (ill. 148). There were within remains of a leather strap tightly secured in place by means of a gold prong; meanwhile the outer side bore heavy signs of wear, especially near the tail.

The fact that these six phalerae were found not above, but below the waist, even lower down than the daggers, invokes memories of the typically nomadic funerary ritual, that of depositing in the grave together with the deceased the reins of his favorite horse; more often than not such objects would be found at the feet of the dead. Similar round phalerae, shaped as beasts curled in a circle, are to be seen in the earlier-mentioned Siberian collection kept at the Hermitage in Leningrad. Other similar objects have been unearthed within what is now Soviet territory in barrows along the Pontine shores and likewise in the semi-demolished barrow on the outskirts of the Ukrainian city of Zaporozhye.

It is quite likely that several more gold objects whose designation is still not clear served to decorate the horse trappings. Thus, discovered between the deceased's hip and the dagger, which partly obscured it from view, was a curved gold plaque depicting a panther savaging an antelope that had been brought down into the ground (ill. 123). The antelope's small, hump-nosed head with its splayed nostrils lies on the ground; it has long ears and small, elegantly coiled horns. Its legs, with their conspicuous hooves, are thrust beneath the massive, straining body and its abbreviated tail is bent down. Judging by some of the details, firstly the hump-nosed muzzle, it is a saiga, that typical denizen of the steppes of Kazakhstan and the Altai region. Representations of similar saiga heads are to be found on the Altai Scythian artifacts unearthed from the now-famous Pazyryk barrows. A large carnivore, either a snow leopard or a panther, is mauling the antelope. Its sleek, catlike body with its in-drawn belly and rippling muscles writhes as its powerful claws cruelly rip apart the haunches of its defenseless victim. The ears are laid back along the top of its head, and the visage is marked by a snarling grimace, distended nostrils, and lynxlike slanted eye-slits. Wings with curled tips spread out from the nape of the neck; the bulging muscles of the fore- and hindquarters are inlaid with turquoise.

This piece bears an extremely close affinity to the bone or wooden pendants of the saddle straps from the Pazyryk barrows with their carved zoomorphic representations. Indeed, like the Altai pendants, the Bactrian plaques possess perforations by which they may be securely fastened to the strap—which leaves no doubt that they had a similar, if not identical, purpose. Depicted on this gold plaque is an extremely common motif related to the Scythian animal style, that of a beast of prey, often with wings, savaging an ungulate.

The obverse of the second, crescent-shaped plaque found carries the raised representation of a horse being mauled by two predators (ill. 122). The drooping head of the horse, with its heavy mane, mouth gaping in panic-stricken fright, heaving nostrils, and laid-back ears, is turned aside. One front leg and both hind limbs are bent and its tail is curled beneath its belly. The fantastic, winged carnivores savaging the horse are shown from the back with contorted hindquarters. One of the two has sunk its teeth into the horse's flank; the other is biting its neck. These monsters' distended nostrils bespeak fury and their protruding eyeballs, a mad rage. Their ears are laid back, their bodies writhe catlike, their claws are unsheathed, and their tails are

43

curled beneath their bellies. Their tautly straining muscles ripple, accentuated by the turquoise
insets. Though the presented motif of beasts
savaging their victim is one that was extremely
popular in Scytho-Sarmatian art, the compositional scheme described has not been encountered before—which only indicates how truly
endless were the variations on this ever-present
theme of the animal style.

Found beneath the left arm of the deceased in the fourth tomb was a time-darkened,
oval artificial gem, which, in full accord with the
accoutrements of the buried warrior, depicted
three fighters who are apparently engaged in
drawing lots.

The bearded warrior on the left is presented standing in profile. He wears a war
helmet with a tall crest. Most of his body is
concealed behind a round shield, from beneath
which a short tunic descends in folds that barely
cover his thighs. His right leg is straight, the left
slightly bent; a short sword swings his right hip.
The centrally positioned warrior, who also
wears a helmet, is bending down. His right
downward-held arm is concealed from view,
and his left arm holds an amphora. Behind him
we can make out the muscular body of the third
man, who is half-naked. Both of his arms are
held down, with the right hand clenching a tall
shield; his head, turned in profile, is crowned by
a tall helmet. Inserted between the three figures is
an upright fluted pillar, topped by the effigy of
an eagle with outspread wings.

A similar scene may be seen on an Italic
carved gem. However, there appears to be a still
more striking resemblance between it and a
gemstone from the Hermitage collection in
Leningrad, on which the scene and the iconogra-
phy are virtually identical with the Bactrian
artifact described in the previous paragraph. It is
believed that the episode portrays the Heraclidae, who upon their return to Peloponnesus,
erected an altar to Zeus and then drew lots to see
which city each should possess (ill. 71).

Discovered in this fourth tomb was but
one gold coin; its obverse has embossed

upon it a male figure resting on the Wheel of
Dharma and also carries an inscription in the old
Indian language (ill. 131). The reverse depicts a
lion with upraised paw and carries the inscription "as fearless as a lion." The coin is unique and
will not be found in any numismatic catalogue in
the world. King Agathocles from the Greco-
Bactrian city of Ai Khanoum is known to have
minted a similar type of coin; further, the lion
was often portrayed on coins struck by the kings
of ancient India and the Sakas. Evidently, the
coin is of a type struck during the transitional
stage between the Indo-Greek and Kushan
epochs, and most likely is of the first century
A.D., when the warrior in the fourth tomb was
apparently interred.

SITE 5

The fifth burial site was discovered on the
southern side of the hill within the masonry of
the defensive rampart of Achaemenian times.
The rectangular grave pit was presumably almost
seven feet (2.05–2.10 m) long and about thirty-
one inches (0.8 m) wide; its floor was about five
and one-half feet (1.65 m) down from the surface
of the mound. Inside, the pit was filled with
earth; at fifteen and a half inches (0.4 m) up from
the grave floor the excavators discovered
remnants of wood dust, evidently from the roof,
as had also been the case in the other burial sites.

However, in this fifth tomb the deceased
person was apparently laid to rest not in a coffin,
as in the previously described sites but in a
hollowed-out tree trunk about six and one-half
feet (2.0 m) long and twenty-six inches (0.65 m)
wide. This assumption would appear to be
warranted as the usual iron clamps were not
found here. Nor was there any trace of a lid. The
hollowed-out log was wrapped in a shroud
possibly in several layers—shown by the fact
that silver sewn-on disks and plaques in the form
of vine leaves were unearthed not only on top of
the log but also beneath it. Most likely they were
attached to the shroud, as was the case in the
other sites.

Again, as in the previous tombs, the remains indicated that the body had been placed on its back with its limbs extended. Its head did not face northward, however, but westward. According to tentative anthropological data and judging by the assortment of artifacts unearthed, the grave held a female between fifteen and twenty years of age.

This tomb yielded the least number of objects among those thus far cleared. In conformity with the local rite, a gold band hugged the chin, modest clips with turquoise inlays adorned the ears (ill. 33), the bosom was bedecked with a sewn-on pectoral, a bracelet with gemstone insets graced the left wrist, and there were gold anklets on both legs. Found by the right hip were a handled mirror and the remains of gold-and-pearl embroidered cloth, while a braided basket, a small vessel of silver, and an iron hook were discovered by the right wrist. Disposed parallel to the right forearm was a long silver pipe holding the remains of rotted wood—apparently a scepter or wand.

Unearthed at the head of the coffin were beads of cornelian, pendants of diverse shape and form, including astragals, the miniature figurine of a lion, an intaglio depicting a griffin, and a silver plaque with an inlaid gemstone portraying Nike, the winged goddess of victory, in flight. At its foot was a large vessel cast of an inferior grade of silver. The complete absence of any of the sewn-on plaques on the garments of the type found in all the other Tillya-tepe graves uncovered was significant. Only a small quantity of pearls had been used to embroider the deceased's funeral attire; evidently this fact points to the buried girl's low social standing or birth in comparison with the others interred in the Tillya-tepe necropolis.

The most conspicuous of all the adornments unearthed in the fifth tomb is the peculiar type of pectoral that had been sewn onto the front of the bodice (ills. 64, 65). It consists of two types of quadripartite pendants, one having garnet or turquoise insets, the other having flat dividers in the shape of jointed crescents. Since it was not only threaded together, but also stitched on around the neck opening, this pectoral represents a highly original type of jewelry. A similar type of necklace composed of alternating round pendants and dividers was common in Taxila (now in Bangladesh).

The bracelet discovered on the left wrist of the deceased is of a rather unusual shape, not encountered elsewhere thus far in the Tillya-tepe necropolis (ills. 102, 103). It is expandable, as it is contrived of thin gold wire, whose spiraling ends coil onto one another. Although this type of bracelet has been found in Taxila, and also in Parthian Majidi-Suleyman and North Bactrian Dalverzin-tepe, only the Tillya-tepe object is additionally embellished with seven inset fittings.

Special note should be paid to the intaglio, a pendant of milky translucent chalcedony engraved with the representation of a winged griffin (ill. 74). The monster has a long and sinuous neck bearing a crest and a small head with a cavernous beaked jaw. The barrel-chested body with its in-drawn belly is slightly bent, the long muscular, taloned paws are shown in motion, the slender tail is coiled at the tip, and the wings consist of large feathers rendered in marked detail. Since the edge had broken off long ago, this may be the reason that the pendant was placed among the grave goods.

The pulsating representation of the racing griffin is not consonant with the overall artistic style of the Tillya-tepe ornaments unearthed. It is quite likely that the intaglio was carved by a Greco-Bactrian jeweler; exactly the same type of eagle-griffin, down to the smallest detail, is to be found on objects from earlier Scythian barrows excavated in the south of what is today the European USSR. This representation was drawn upon to embellish the magnificent gold gorytuses, or bowcases, which experts have defined as artwork in the Greco-Persian style. One might add that this definition reflects the protracted, and as yet unconsummated, discussions raging around the actual origin of the representation of the eagle-griffin, prototypes of

45

which are to be witnessed in both Persia in the East and Greece in the West. It must likewise be noted that the chalcedony intaglio pendant with the carved figure of a griffin comprises but one of the few masterpieces of Hellenistic artwork unearthed in the Tillya-tepe necropolis.

Preserved on the round miniature silver plaque inlaid with a green gemstone is the finely engraved representation of the winged goddess of victory, Nike, in flight (ill. 72). The figure is shown in profile. The goddess wears a helmet; her face, however, is sketchy with no attempt at detail. One outstretched arm holds a round wreath from which long ribbons droop; her other arm apparently bears a palm branch that lies on her shoulder. The goddess is garbed in floor-length garments falling in folds. The plumage of her wings is distinct. The representation bears a strong similarity to that on the brass signet ring recovered from the Tulkhar burial in Northern Bactria. There the goddess is depicted with her outstretched left arm holding a wreath from which long ribbon ends droop; her right arm is not shown.

Unearthed on the mirror (ill. 143), which has a silver flared handle stand, is a fragment of a textile embroidered with gold thread and pearls in such a manner as to create a plant motif. This may possibly be the remnant of the case in which the mirror was kept. If that supposition is true, then the Tillya-tepe mirror possesses a close affinity to a similar silver mirror with a flared handle from the second Pazyryk burial, which had been enclosed in a leopard skin case.

Unlike the shrouds or wrappings in the other tombs, that of the fifth burial site was not spangled with round gold disks, but with silver ornaments in the form of vine leaves.

SITE 6

The last—sixth—tomb excavated was discovered in the western outer corridor of the former temple. As the grave was in a good state of preservation, we were able to clarify all the details of how it had been arranged. It was established that at the outset a pit about ten feet (3 m) long and eight feet (2.5 m) wide had been dug, but that at just over three feet (about 1 m) down, the diggers had made the pit about eight feet (2.5 m) long and four feet (1.2 m) wide, leaving recessed banks along the perimeter. They then dug about three more feet (1 m) down, which thus added up to a total depth of about six and a half feet (about 2 m). After the coffin was deposited on the grave floor, a wooden structure was set up over it in such a manner that its ends lay firmly on the recessed banks skirting the pit. A dark brown layer of wood dust descending from the edge of the recessed banks to the coffin was distinctly evident; duplicated above it was another layer of dust that comprised the remains of a mat. Apparently, as had been the case in the fourth tomb, a wooden trellis supported by the recessed earth had been placed across the coffin and was covered over with mats. The earth removed in the process of digging had been shoveled in on top of the mats and trellis.

The coffin proper was constructed of planks. Its sides were secured to the bottom by means of iron clamps and nails—three pairs each along the sides and two pairs at the head and foot. The following fact is of special interest: on the longer sides the clamps were secured to the bottom by two nails and to the wall by one, while at the head and foot the clamps were fastened to the bottom by one nail and to the walls by two. The coffin was oblong in form— about six-and-a-half feet (2 m) long, twenty inches (0.5 m) wide, and about sixteen inches (0.4 m) high. It rested not on the grave floor but on mud brick mounts which elevated the coffin by about eight inches (0.2 m) from the floor. The excavators, however, found the skeleton on the tomb's floor, onto which it had slithered after the bottom of the coffin rotted away. The side walls, as was already stated, rested on mud brick supports that had been placed flat at the corners, and on the edges beneath the longer sides. (It is quite likely that there had been similar brick supports in the third burial site, although this was something that we failed to establish due to the grave's poor state of preservation.) No traces of a coffin lid were discovered; evidently, it had been covered with a shroud bespangled with gold and silver disks. In the process of clearing we found the disks for the most part along the sides of the coffin and within; apparently, mainly the central panel of the shroud had been embellished.

The body was discovered lying on its back in an extended position, again with its head pointed westward—a position, although the same as in the fifth tomb, was different from that in most of the Tillya-tepe burial sites. It has been established through a tentative anthropological examination and on the basis of the assortment of grave goods unearthed that a female between twenty-five and thirty years of age was interred in the sixth tomb.

In this site the head of the deceased, with its tall crown, lay on a shallow silver vessel. Clips in the shape of winged cupids were worn in her ears, and identical hairpins were found by both temples (ill. 16). Dangling from the crown was a pair of temple pendants carrying a representation of the goddess Anahita surrounded by birds, beasts, and fish. The woman's chin was encompassed by a gold stay, and a necklace was worn around her neck. Discovered amidst the thousands of gold spangles on her bosom was the gold figurine of a winged goddess that has conventionally been dubbed the Bactrian Aphrodite. Beneath her neck was a pair of massive clasps depicting an amorous scene from the Dionysian cult cycle. It is possible that her arms lay above the shroud. Her right arm held a gold scepter, while her left fist grasped a gold Parthian coin. One more Parthian coin, this one of silver, was found in her mouth. A round Chinese mirror lay on her bosom, and at her feet were a large silver vessel and another mirror with an ivory handle. Again, as was the case in the third burial site, there were small lumps of minerals that we conventionally termed anti-

mony, ceruse, and rouge; also found were toothed wheels of mica japanned with a black lacquer (small ornaments of mica of an identical type were found on her forehead and cheekbones). The feet of the deceased had apparently been shod in footwear embellished with small gold plaques.

Outside the coffin, by its head, was a braided basket containing a small ceramic pot, and miniature knives and tweezers of iron. Also found were three glass pots with the stone-hard remains of some grey mass, in all likelihood cosmetics.

We can imagine the dead woman to have been garbed as follows before burial. The neck opening of her long robe was trimmed with a chain of gold spangles; fastened on its back were large gold disks encrusted with turquoise insets separated from one another by dividers. Crossing the breast from the shoulders were four bands of stitched-on adornments: a narrow one of tiny gold tubes from which trident-shaped pendants dangled, a second composed of twelve rectangular convex plaques joined by strands of pearls, and two more bands of round plaques with "wings." All four ended in a pear-shaped mount which, in turn, terminated in the stitched-on figurine of the Bactrian Aphrodite. Thus, the richly ornamented bodice comprised the focal point of the entire garment; while the lower part could have been adorned with intersecting strands of gold spangles. One may definitely state that the hem was trimmed with an even series of round plaques.

It is possible that a long cloak with tight-fitting tall cuffs embroidered with several encircling rows of plaques was worn over the robe. The cloak could have been secured on the bosom by the clasps depicting the amorous scene. A folded shawl had probably been deposited by her right shoulder, as a cluster of plaques was found there.

The crown worn on her head is composed of a fillet cut out of sheet gold that encircled her forehead and to which five palmettes were attached, all designed as stylized trees with a horizontal strip to denote the ground. The trees themselves are presented with trunks from which spreading branches terminate in pointed leaves (ills. 12–15).

Perched atop each tree is a pair of tiny birds, each with miniature heads on upstretched necks and outspread wings. Attached to the back of the trees are the same type of six-petaled florets; they have turquoise beads in a frame of granules, also to be seen on the fillet forming the base of the crown. There are six florets on each tree—two on the lowest branches and two on the upper branches, one in the center, and the sixth at the very top. Attached to the petals by gold wire are dangling disks. Small tubes have been soldered to the fillet and the base of the palmettes for the purpose of locking the entire affair together.

All five palmettes are of an identical design, except for the central piece from either end of whose horizontal strip there rise two heavily stylized, sinuous trunks. Their boughs, beneath the palmette, form a ring into which a whorled rosette has ben inserted; meanwhile the upper boughs entwine into a sharp-pointed leaf. On the back the palmette is embellished with nine six-petaled florets with centrally positioned pearls; again disks dangle from the tips of the petals as in the case of the other palmettes, the sole difference being that a disk, not a floret, is attached to the top.

Greco-Bactrian, Seleucid, Parthian, and, subsequently, Kushan rulers did not wear crowns but narrow fillet-diadems. The headgear of Parthian noblewomen consisted of a veil and narrow tiara, totally unlike the Tillya-tepe crown. On the other hand, representations of trees with birds perched on their boughs will be found on the ceremonial headdresses of Scythian and Sarmatian kings, and—note—of Scythian queens, with the prevalent decorative motif being that of leaves, flowers, and palmettes, not infrequently together with birds.

Representations of trees upon which birds are seated ornament the headdress of a noble warrior that was recovered from the Issyk barrow; gold leaflets together with a unique gold diadem were found in a tomb on the bank of the Karagalinka River in the north of the Soviet Republic of Kirghizia. In the times of the Han dynasty crowns carrying representations of trees and birds were recorded even in Korea; moreover, the affinity with the Bactrian specimens is so strong that it may indicate a strong influence emanating eastward from Bactria.

The pair of identical earring clips recovered from this tomb are most exciting indeed (ill. 36). They are cast in the form of ellipses with open ends, one of which flares and is embellished with a superimposed fluted rosette, while the other is in the shape of a winged cupid. The cupid's head is hollow and the upper part of his forehead is pierced with a perforation in the form of a crescent. His face is broad, his nose short, his eyes small, and his lips compressed. His stocky neck rests on broad shoulders. His arms are held down and his hands seemed balled into fists. His plump body sports a rounded belly with a dot for the navel, and his short, chubby legs are bent at the knee. Short wings sprout from his shoulder blades.

It should be noted that earrings with figurines of cupids were rather common in Greco-Roman jewelry. However, nothing with a perforated forehead crescent is known; quite obviously this detail has a meaning of its own, reflecting the lunar symbolism with its millennia-old traditions so popular in the Orient.

The aforementioned necklace consisted of ten hollow beads and was fastened by two conical clasps, whose facets were further embellished with soldered-on granules and turquoise-inlaid, five-petaled rosettes (ills. 66, 67).

Note that representations of neck ornaments are frequently encountered in Kushan art, especially on coins, upon which necklaces comprised of large round beads are to be seen amidst the jewelry of numerous kings, starting with Kanishka.

The pair of temple pendants recovered are rectangular, open-worked plaques embossed in high relief with the centrally positioned figure of a standing female (ills. 48–50). She wears a

48

diadem, a circlet with an embossed design of ovals. In front her hair has been tucked within the diadem; at the sides it falls upon her shoulders. Her face is round and plump, her eyes are small, and her nose is straight. Her neck is stubby. The nipples on her cup-shaped breasts are picked out in relief, and her bosom is crisscrossed by straps having a round buckle where they meet. Bracelets grace her forearms; her left arm clasps a round object, possibly a pomegranate, to her bosom; the right is bent at the elbow and raised. Bracelets are worn around her wrists. Above her shoulder are heart-shaped turquoise insets that may represent wings, although that has yet to be established. Her waist is faintly marked, her hips are round and fleshy, and beneath her belly the genital area, covered with small incisions, is picked out in relief. The figure is naked, except for long folds draped across from the right hip to the left knee, outlining the legs beneath; the tips of sandals can be glimpsed beneath the closely tucked hem.

The female figure is sandwiched between two upturned fantastic monsters with the heads of either wolves or dogs and gaping jaws; their finlike forequarters press against the woman's hips. Their manes are picked out by turquoise inlays. In place of hindquarters the animals have bunches of leaves caught by a ribbon—unless these are fishtails. The entire scene is mounted on a straight band inlaid with large semi-ovals of turquoise that terminates on either side in fish heads with staring eyes, wide-open mouths, and turquoise-inlaid front fins. The turquoise inlays above the heads may serve to imitate dolphin crests.

The scene is flanked by two upright "columns," actually cloisons filled with a black paste; a horizontal band encrusted with small turquoise lozenges runs along above the head of the female figure and terminates at either end in representations of full-faced birds whose bodies are in profile. Their eyes and rapacious beaks are distinctly modeled; the tips of their folded wings, of which the plumage is conveyed by means of small incisions, are raised. Climaxing

the entire composition on top is a four-petaled rosette with turquoise inlays.

Portrayed on the pendants is the East Persian Great Goddess Anahita, not swathed in garments but half-nude in conformity with Hellenized aesthetic taste. The Great Goddess ruled the skies, the world of animals and plants, and the waters. This is implied respectively by the birds by her head, the fantastic beasts, the pomegranate, and the fish at her feet.

Another exciting object is the statuette of the Bactrian Aphrodite (ill. 99). She possesses a high-domed forehead with a caste mark in the middle; almond-shaped eyes in which the pupils are pronounced beneath long arched brows; a narrow, straight nose with finely modeled nostrils; pouting, bee-stung lips; and a rounded chin. Her wavy hair, which is parted down the middle, has been tucked in beneath a tightly bound fillet ornamented with rows of circlets disposed on a slant, instead of falling down over her ears. Folds crease her plump neck and her nipples stand out on her full breasts. Her right arm, graced by two rows of bracelets on her forearm and three more on the wrist, is placed akimbo, while the left, with two bracelets on the forearm, is bent at the elbow and rests on a column of which the capital is denoted by a turquoise inlay. Softly folding garments are draped across her hips in such a manner as to leave the genital area exposed; one end is thrown across her left wrist. Well outlined beneath the drapery are her two legs; the left one juts forward while the right one is straight. Gently curved wings with clearly defined plumage sprout from her shoulder blades.

Though this is the same iconographic image that was represented on the brooch from the second tomb, the style is totally different. Indeed, the pensive, charming face invokes Hellenistic associations. The posture of the goddess in both of the recovered Tillya-tepe objects and especially the column arouse recollections of the sculptures of Aphrodite as executed by the Greco-Roman masters of Crete and Alexandria. It is quite possible that the Bactrian figure conveys the canon of female beauty peculiar to East Persian and especially Bactrian society. Though both representations are basically identical and are most likely of the same deity, some details differ. Thus, for example, in one case the hair has been braided around the fillet so as to frame the face in a broad roll; in the other it has been tucked in beneath the fillet. The Bactrian Aphrodite probably possesses a typically Greek hairdo common throughout the Hellenized Orient.

The unique pair of clasps pinning the cloak at the deceased's throat are undoubtedly deserving of the closest attention (ills. 77–79). They depict mirror images of the same scene. A huge fantastic monster dominates, with its lion-like face on which its nose with its conspicuously delineated nostrils is wrinkled in frenzied rage. Its tongue juts far out from its cavernous jaws. The menacing posture is accentuated by its enormous, rolling eyes beneath the beetling brows and by its pricked-up ears, from which a tangled beard snakes down and forward. A crenellated crest inlaid with turquoise runs along its sinuous neck. Its powerful body rests on three paws, each with three talons; the fourth is raised and touches the beard. Thrown over the creature's back is a saddlecloth, also encrusted with turquoise, and trimmed with tassels offset by turquoise inlays. The long tail curls between the legs and terminates in a turquoise-inset tassel.

Riding the beast are a woman and a man. The woman has inclined her wreathed head toward her partner. She has a straight and slender nose, large eyes, generous lips, and an oval-shaped chin. Her hair, parted evenly down the middle, falls in curling braids upon her bosom. Her hip-length tunic, whose round neck opening is split in front, is embellished with round cloisons and is belted at the waist. The wide, straight skirt is hemmed with turquoise-inset oblongs. Her one visible leg—the woman is seated astride the beast—is shod in a calf-length sandal held by a strap with an oblong buckle. Three leaflets lie from mid-calf to foot. Her one visible arm is clothed in a long sleeve, and in it

she holds a two-handled vessel; the other arm evidently embraces the man's shoulders.

The man is seated sidesaddle with both legs facing the viewer. His head, which is turned slightly toward his partner, is bound by a fillet or diadem in the form of a twisted roll inset with turquoise in the middle. His hair is also evenly parted down the middle and descends to his shoulders from beneath the fillet. He also has a straight nose and generous lips, and his eyes are almond-shaped. His long robe, with a plain opening for the neck, falls down to lie on the knees in semicircular folds; meanwhile the hem is stretched straight from calf to calf and is ornamented in the middle with an oblong cloison filled with a black paste. The edge of an undergarment peeps out from beneath the hem in softly slanted folds, and visible beneath it are the pointed, curled-up tips of boots. With one arm he embraces his companion around her shoulders; the other caresses her full bosom.

To be glimpsed behind the male figure is the representation of the goddess of victory, Nike, who appears to be bestowing her blessings upon the amorous couple. She is depicted in flight, with long, turquoise-encrusted wings spread up and out from behind her back. Her hair has been brushed into a roll that frames the head in a semicircle, and her two braids are knotted into a chignon. The goddess wears a long, flowing tunic belted high up beneath the bosom. In front it is slitted on a slant to reveal her naked, anklet-graced leg. Covering her hips is a short, heavily pleated kilt. Her right forearm is bedecked with two bracelets, and around her wrist she wears a third one; in her hand she holds a wreath; the left arm is similarly adorned with bracelets and in that hand she carries a long palm branch. The fact that on the pair of clasps, one of which is a mirror reflection of the other, the goddess is depicted holding a wreath in her right hand and a branch in the left may be by no means fortuitous.

Portrayed in front and at the feet of the fantastic monster is the reclining figure of Silenus. His face is coarse and bearded, his pug nose is fleshy, and his eyeballs protrude from beneath his deliberately tangled brows. His hair is likewise in unruly disorder, and his animal-like ears jut out. He is garbed in a goatskin cloak reaching down to the knees, which is caught at the waist by a kind of cummerbund. He has lifted himself up from the ground with a staff he clasps in one hand; in the other hand he holds a rhyton in the form of a horned goat's head, which he offers to the woman. Though his figure is more expressive than those of the other personages, one must necessarily note its unnaturally abbreviated upright arm without the slightest hint of an elbow—apparently due to the jeweler's mistake in allotting too little space when composing the entire scene.

What is this intricate, patently thematic composition supposed to imply? The fact that the amorous couple is accompanied by Silenus, bosom friend of Dionysus, quite definitely indicates that an episode from the Dionysian rites is represented. The assumption that indigenous Dionysian cults existed throughout the Hellenized Orient, including Bactria, where winegrowing was practiced from times immemorial is fully warranted. In Bactria the Dionysian festivals that marked the end of laborious tillage and the arrival of autumn leisure were accompanied by drunken orgies with riotous songs and dances. However, the manner in which the Bactrian gold clasps adorned with the aforedescribed Dionysian scene were executed is truly far removed from the very lively Hellenistic trend. Only the face of Silenus recalls to some degree the profound realism of Greco-Bactrian art; as for the other personages, their representation is static and their faces frozen.

Deserving of notice among the host of Greco-Bactrian presentations of Dionysus is one showing the wine god seated in a chariot and embracing Ariadne with one arm and offering her a cluster of grapes with the other. Meanwhile the chariot, drawn by a pair of carnivores, most likely panthers, rumbles along amidst an ecstatic group of dancing maenads, horned and goat-footed fauns, and satyrs.

Representations of the triumph of Dionysus coupled with Ariadne in a chariot drawn by two panthers will likewise be seen executed in relief on Roman sarcophagi and in Greco-Roman stone carvings. The difference between these compositions and the one depicted on the Tillya-tepe clasps is only that whereas on the reliefs Dionysus and Ariadne are shown seated in a chariot, on the clasps they are portrayed riding a fabulous beast. However, even this semantically insignificant difference finds its explanation in Roman art in which there exist representations of Bacchus and Faunus riding a feline animal, apparently a panther. Most noteworthy is the fact that, as in the case of the fantastic beast portrayed on the Bactrian clasps, the panther is enlarged out of all proportion to its riders, and is depicted with a snarling visage, menacingly knitted brows, and a muscular body with cruel talons. Also significant are such stylistic details as the sawtooth mane and especially the curled beard of the monster on the Tillya-tepe artifact, which bear a close resemblance to those of the characters of Greek myths. Further, if one also takes into consideration the reclining satyr on the ground offering Dionysus a bowl, plus Nike holding a wreath and a palm branch, blessing the wine god, and Ariadne in the chariot, the interpretation of the scene depicted on the Bactrian object as being from the Dionysian mysteries presents the sole possible solution. There is every reason to believe that the fabulous beast on the clasp comprises a syncretic image harking back, in the final analysis, to Greco-Roman prototypes. In effect, merely the three-taloned paws, the saddlecloth, and, for that matter, the overall manner of execution indicate a local Bactrianized interpretation of a typically Greek scene.

In Greco-Roman art Silenus was portrayed more often than not as a jovial elder possessing a meticulously coiffed beard: hence, he is in sharp contrast to the Silenus on the Bactrian clasp where he has the coarse features of a commoner with tangled beard, a fleshy pug nose, bushy eyebrows, and a bulging forehead.

In this respect the Bactrian representation displays a closer affinity with the Persian iconographic type of a bald-headed, tangled-bearded personage with a dome-shaped skull. Yet the fact that on the clasp Silenus is depicted holding a staff invokes recollections of that rare variant that only Greco-Roman art is known to have.

Dionysian scenes in which the usual cast of personages is accompanied by the goddess Nike, as in the case on the Bactrian clasps, are encountered even less often. One such instance is on a silver dish which is believed to have originated in Bukhara and which is now preserved in London; the fact that it indubitably represents the winged Nike bestowing her benediction upon the Dionysian scene again points to a local Hellenistic interpretation of this popular episode.

One should not feel put out by the Bactrian clasps depicting Dionysus wearing female attire, for that kind of costume was common in Oriental Asiatic art.

The deceased's wrists were graced with a pair of identical cast gold bracelets whose ends are shaped like the heads of fabulous lion-like creatures (ills. 104, 106). The animal's brows are knitted into a menacing frown, its eyes seem to squint in rage, its nose is wrinkled, and its fanged jaws are half-open. Its laid-back ears and abbreviated, slightly twisted horns are encrusted with turquoise. On one of the bracelets a lapis-lazuli lozenge-shaped inset serves as a divider between the horns. The heads are hollow and are embellished at the base with a raised ring inset with almond-shaped turquoise beads.

These creatures belong to the category of lion-headed griffins foreparts of which adorn the bracelets from the Amu Darya (Oxus) Treasure preserved at the British Museum in London, and also the torque and clasps from the Hermitage collection in Leningrad. Representations of horned, snarling lion heads most likely originated in Asia Minor, more specifically, in Eastern Persia, as can be gleaned from the Persepolis sculptures. Indeed, it is clear that the lion-griffin is most probably a metamorphosed Assyrian cherub—which is illustrated, for instance, by Persian engraved gemstones. If we add that the terminals of gold bracelets from Taxila are also shaped as lion heads with a double border around their necks, this will once again emphasize their stylistic affinity with the Bactrian jeweler's art.

Found slipped over the middle finger on the left hand was a small signet ring inset with a dark cherry-red stone, presumably a garnet (ill. 110). The deeply incised profile of a human head is engraved in it. The hair is parted into neat curls, caught at the forehead by a fillet, beneath which locks descend over the ears or are trimmed into bangs across the forehead. The nose is straight and pointed, the eyes are small, and the thin lips are compressed. Evidently this is a portrait of a real person.

When the dead woman was laid to rest, a silver coin was inserted into her mouth—quite in keeping with the Greek ritual of interment, as the coin was intended to symbolize the fee to Charon for ferrying the dead person across the Styx to Hades (ill. 129). Depicted on the obverse is the embossed bust of a bearded king wearing a diadem that is knotted at the nape of the neck with long, flowing ribbons. To one side the coin has been counterstamped with the design of a miniature helmeted warrior enclosed in a dotted circle. The reverse carries the figure of an enthroned archer and a Greek legend that tells us that the coin was initially struck during the reign of the Parthian King Phraates IV (38–32 B.C.).

The countermark, which is of particular interest, was impressed during the reign of Sapaleisis, a nomad Yüeh-Chih tribal chieftain, who ruled Bactria before the rise of the Great Kushan Empire. Note that the counterstamp was neatly added so as not to damage the portrait of the reigning Parthian ruler, which, as experts contend, indicates a certain degree of dependence of local potentates upon their Parthian neighbors.

Clasped in the deceased's left hand was one more coin, this one of gold (ill. 128). The obverse depicts the profile of a bearded king with finely etched features, a slightly aquiline nose, deep-seated eyes, and fullish lips; he wears a round tiara. In the empty field behind his head is a heavily worn countermark in the shape of a miniature full-faced head. The reverse bears the image of an enthroned archer holding a bow, and along the rim runs a Greek inscription mentioning a Parthian king. No numismatic catalogue in the world reproduces anything like it, from which it may be deduced that this gold Parthian coin is unique.

SUMMARY

The entire collection of artifacts recovered from the Golden Mound outside Shibarghan, which numbers some twenty thousand pieces, may be broken down into several distinct categories.

The first and smallest group includes Greco-Bactrian objects seized as booty by the Kushan conquerors. Among these are the figurine of an ibex (Cat. no. 4.3) executed in the finest realistic traditions of Greek art; the cameo presenting a human profile that adorns a pectoral (Cat. no. 4.10), the chalcedony intaglio with its representation of a griffin (Cat. no. 5.8), and the phiale (Cat. no. 4.31). We could likewise include in this category the few imported objects such as the Chinese mirrors (Cat. no. 2.34; Cat. no. 3.70; Cat. no. 6.31), the Roman and Indian coins (Cat. no. 3.47; Cat. no. 4.25), the Italic gemstone (Cat. no. 4.27), and the ivory comb (Cat. no. 3.56).

Objects executed in the Greco-Roman style whose exact provenance has not been established, but which are presumably of local origin, comprise a second group. This includes signet rings with representations of gods and goddesses and especially with the name of Athena in Greek (Cat. nos. 2.1 and 2.2; Cat. nos. 3.60 and 3.78), cosmetic vessels (Cat. no. 3.41), and an intaglio (Cat. no. 5.10).

The largest group comprises items of local Bactrian manufacture that reflect diverse cultural and historical styles and traditions. The most noteworthy sub-category here incorporates objects revealing Hellenistic cultural traditions, however heavily reworked, such as the "cupids riding dolphins" breast clasps (Cat. no. 2.5; Cat. no. 3.2), the temple pendants depicting the Great Goddess Anahita amidst animals (Cat. no. 6.4), the gold belt with Cybele riding a lion (Cat. no. 4.2), the earring clips in the shape of cupids with pierced crescent symbols on their foreheads (Cat. no. 6.5), the Bactrian Aphrodite (Cat. no. 6.3), and the clasps carrying the Dionysian scene (Cat. no. 6.2).

The fourth group incorporates pieces reflecting a mixture of Greco-Roman and Siberian-Altai influences, such as the clasps depicting the gods Ares and Veretragna (Cat. no. 3.1), the ruler and dragons pendants (Cat. no. 2.7), the Kushan Aphrodite figurine (Cat. no. 2.6), the "dragons chariot" buckles (Cat. no. 4.1), the dagger sheaths (Cat. nos. 4.8 and 4.9), and what are presumably figurines of musicians (Cat. no. 2.29).

Objects that are typical of the Scytho-Sarmatian animal style comprise the fifth group, which includes phalerae (Cat. nos. 4.5, 4.6 and 4.7), plaques depicting the mauling of an antelope and a horse (Cat. nos. 4.35 and 4.36), and plaques portraying panthers with contorted hindquarters (Cat. no. 4.4).

The sixth and last group consists of artifacts that reveal profoundly local East Persian, or rather Old Bactrian, traditions harking back to the Bronze Age. They include the "goddess amidst animals" pendants (Cat. no. 6.4), the tree with birds perched on its boughs from the crown (Cat. no. 6.1), and bracelets with sculptured figures of animals (Cat. no. 2.4; Cat. no. 6.15). The same traditions are observed in one or another way in many objects relating to the afore-listed groups such as the winged Aphrodite (Cat. no. 2.6; Cat. no. 6.3), the motif of a hero engaged in combat with animals (Cat. no. 2.7), the mistress of the animal world riding a lion (Cat. no. 4.2), and the lunar symbols (Cat. no. 6.5). All such motifs and scenes have pronounced prototypes on Bactrian Bronze Age seals of the second millennium B.C.

This brief survey of Tillya-tepe jewelry incontrovertibly proves that Bactria had its own center of goldsmithing with its own established traditions harking back to the Bronze Age. Many motifs and scenes from Bactrian Bronze Age objets d'art, reflecting the richly populated mythology of people living in this part of the world as far back as in the second millennium B.C., are manifest—albeit in a reworked and reinterpreted state—in many of the treasures recovered from the Tillya-tepe necropolis. Local Bactrian jewelers were already producing items of a high artistic level, as is borne out by the gold and silver artifacts retrieved from plundered Bactrian burials.

The Amu Darya (Oxus) Treasure tends to demonstrate the following chronology as regards the rise and development of a local center of goldsmithing. As concerns the origin of the Treasure, one may indicate the quite palpable stylistic continuity displayed by some of the items with Persian Achaemenian art on the one hand and with the Golden Mound Treasure on the other. Currently the Persepolis Garden Pavilion Treasure furnishes additional evidence of the links between Achaemenian and Bactrian jewelry of the middle of the first millennium B.C. The Tillya-tepe collection not only brings these traditions up to the start of the first century A.D., but also documents the local provenance of the items incorporated, indicating that they adhered to local, well-established traditions. Apparently, there co-existed alongside metropolitan centers of Achaemenian "empire art," such provincial centers as that in Bactria. However, despite their adherence to profoundly local traditions, the art of all these regional centers was groomed to the overall "empire style" of the "metropolitan" art of Achaemenian Persia.

The chronological gap between the Amu Darya (Oxus) Treasure and the Tillya-tepe collection has now been filled in by the Takhti Sanghi Temple Treasure recovered in Southern Tajikistan (See: B. Litvinsky and I. Pichikian,

"Archaeological Discoveries in South Tajikistan," *The Bulletin of the USSR Academy of Sciences*, 1980, no. 7, in Russian), which leaves no doubt as to the existence of a specific Bactrian center of goldsmithing. Moreover, M. Rostovtsev's hypothesis as to the Persian provenance of the Hermitage's Siberian collection is not only shored up by the Tillya-tepe artifacts, but also supports the assumption that the Bactrian center was most likely the place where most of the Siberian collection was produced.

The jewelry from the Tillya-tepe necropolis unquestionably belongs to goldware of a dynastic school of debased Hellenistic art. In place of the vivacious Greco-Bactrian art with its elegance of form and realistic vitality, we observe here the new trend of inanimate, petrified form, hieratic, static personages and scenes, arch-stylization and an inordinate fondness for polychrome inlays. Such are the salient features of the decadent early Kushan art of the start of the first century A.D.

What was actually responsible for the overall inferior artistic level of the objects recovered from the Golden Mound? In the first place, this was most likely due to the low aesthetic tastes of the clientele for whom they were made. The Kushans, former nomads who then ruled Bactria, had only a very general notion of the Hellenistic cultural achievement. Their aesthetic tastes and requirements still lagged far behind their social status as rulers of such a highly cultured land as Bactria. In a barbaric search for splendor they bespangled ceremonial costumes with hundreds, if not thousands, of sparkling, tinkling gold pendants, leaving not one scrap of space unornamented. Bactria's gifted goldsmiths were obliged to cater to the aesthetically inferior tastes of their new, uncouth rulers.

Present research has indicated that Oriental and Greek art really began to come together some two hundred years after the demise of Greece's authority in the East, when the Kushan Kingdom first emerged. However, the Tillya-tepe finds shed new light on this. It was usually thought that this artistic synthesis had been fostered by the interaction of three factors, notably, the art of the Greek colonists, local Bactrian art and, finally, nomad art. But whereas before the third factor had been seen as insignificant, today one may definitely state that the nomad art of the steppes made an important contribution by virtue of its dynamic though conventionalized lines and its naiveté of expression. It was precisely these features that enlivened, at the start of the first century A.D., both the millennia-old traditions of Bactrian art and the academic dryness of later Hellenistic art. It may be suggested that nomad art served to catalyze the interaction of the two old—Greek and Bactrian—art trends with their richness of tradition, their well-established choice of form and theme, and their refined allegorical symbolism.

1
Eight-lobed rosettes. Cat. no. 4.12

2 ⇒
Sewn-on tubes. Cat. no. 4.11

3 ⇒
Hemispherical plaques with raised rims.
Cat. no. 4.20

62

Artifacts in black and white are reproduced in actual size

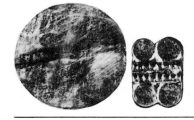

4
Disks. Cat. no. 4.15

Artifacts in black and white are reproduced in actual size

5
"Butterfly" plaques. Cat. no. 4.16

65

6
Square plaques with hearts design.
Cat. no. 4.13

7
Four-petaled rosettes. Cat. no. 3.14

8
"Volute" plaques. Cat. no. 3.27

9
"Volute" plaques. Cat. no. 1.19

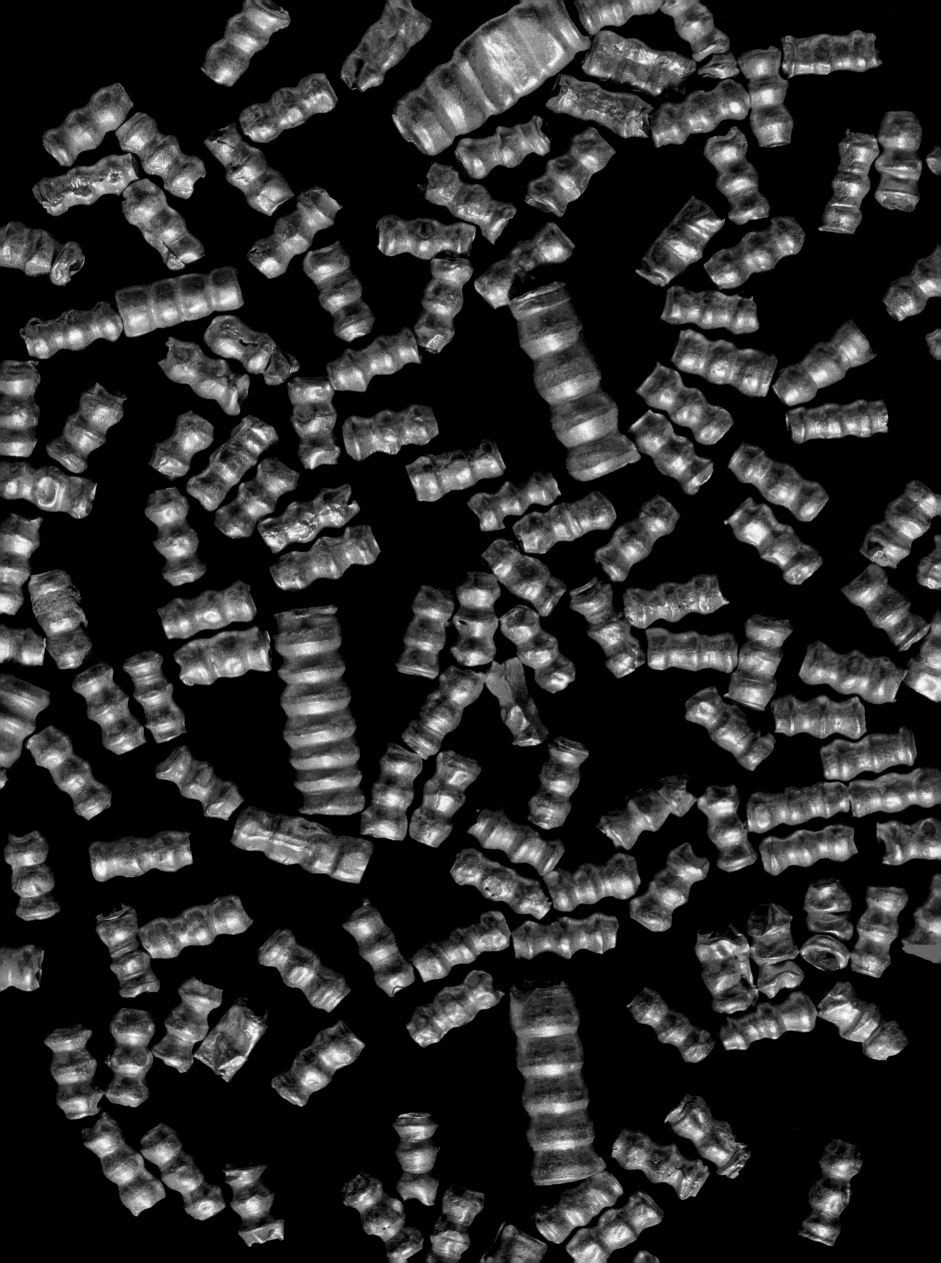

10
Ribbed tubes. Cat. no. 6.25

11
"Steering wheel" plaques. Cat. no. 2.12

12
Crown. Detail. Cat. no. 6.1

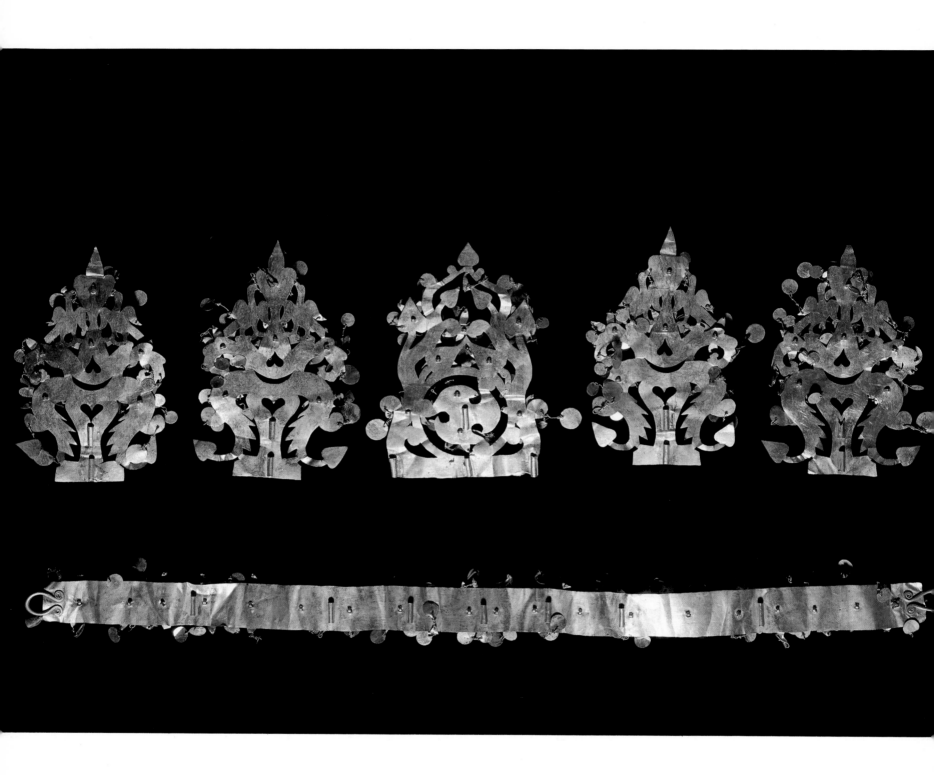

13
Crown. Reverse. Cat. no. 6.1

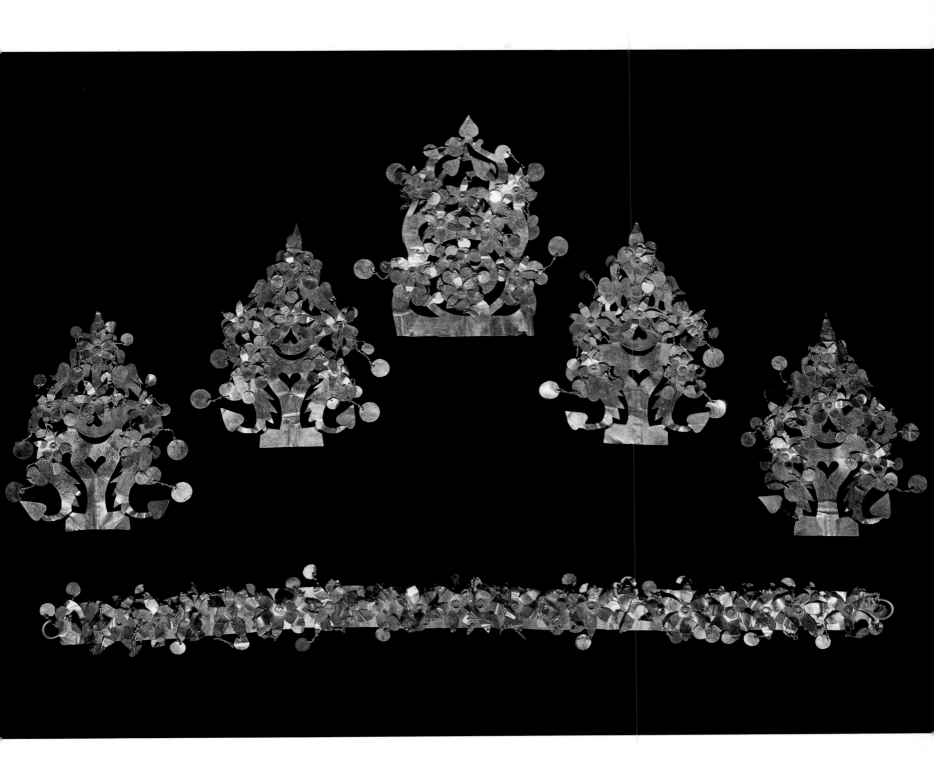

Crown. Obverse. Cat. no. 6.1

Crown. Cat. no. 6.1

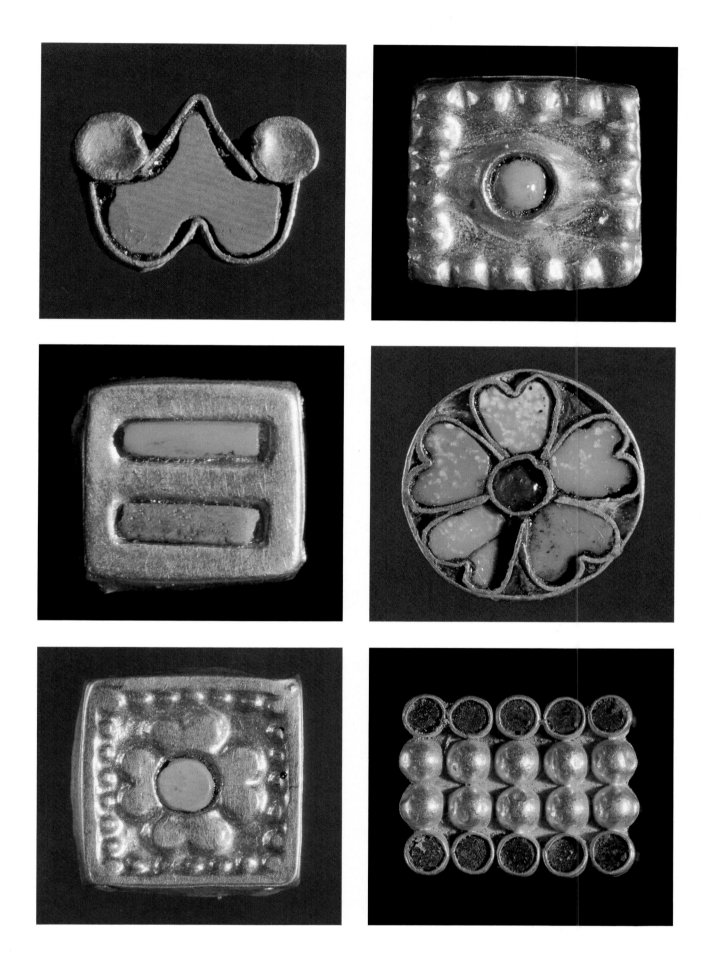

22
Triangular plaques. Cat. no. 1.9

23
Trident-shaped plaques with circlets. Cat. no. 3.11

24
"Eye-pupil" plaque. Cat. no. 1.14

25
Plaques with elongated insets. Cat. no. 1.16

26
"Floret" plaque. Cat. no. 1.12

27
Plaques with flowers. Cat. no. 1.15

28
Oblong plaques. Cat. no. 6.26

84

29
"Face mask" plaques. Cat. no. 1.13

30
Square plaques with central circlets.
Cat. no. 4.14

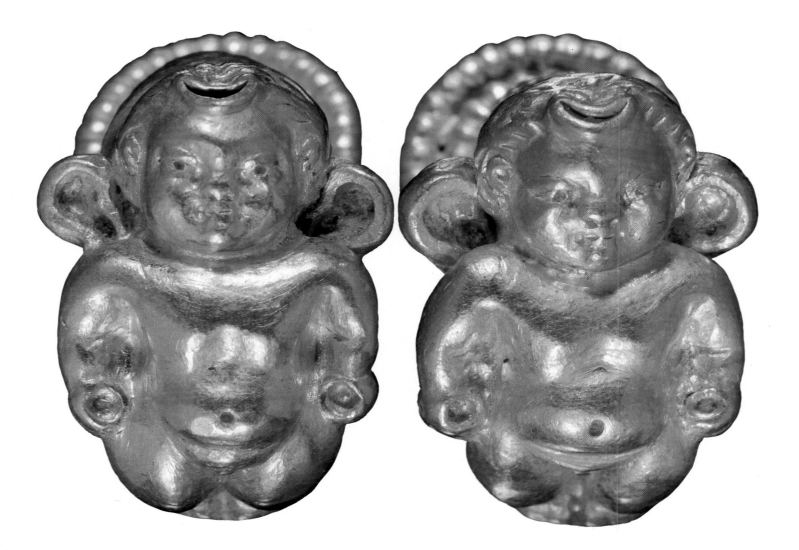

35
Scarab-type plaques. Cat. no. 1.20

36
Earring clips with representations of cupids.
Cat. no. 6.5

37
Cinquefoil plaques. Cat. no. 4.22

38
Medallions with busts. Cat. no. 3.15

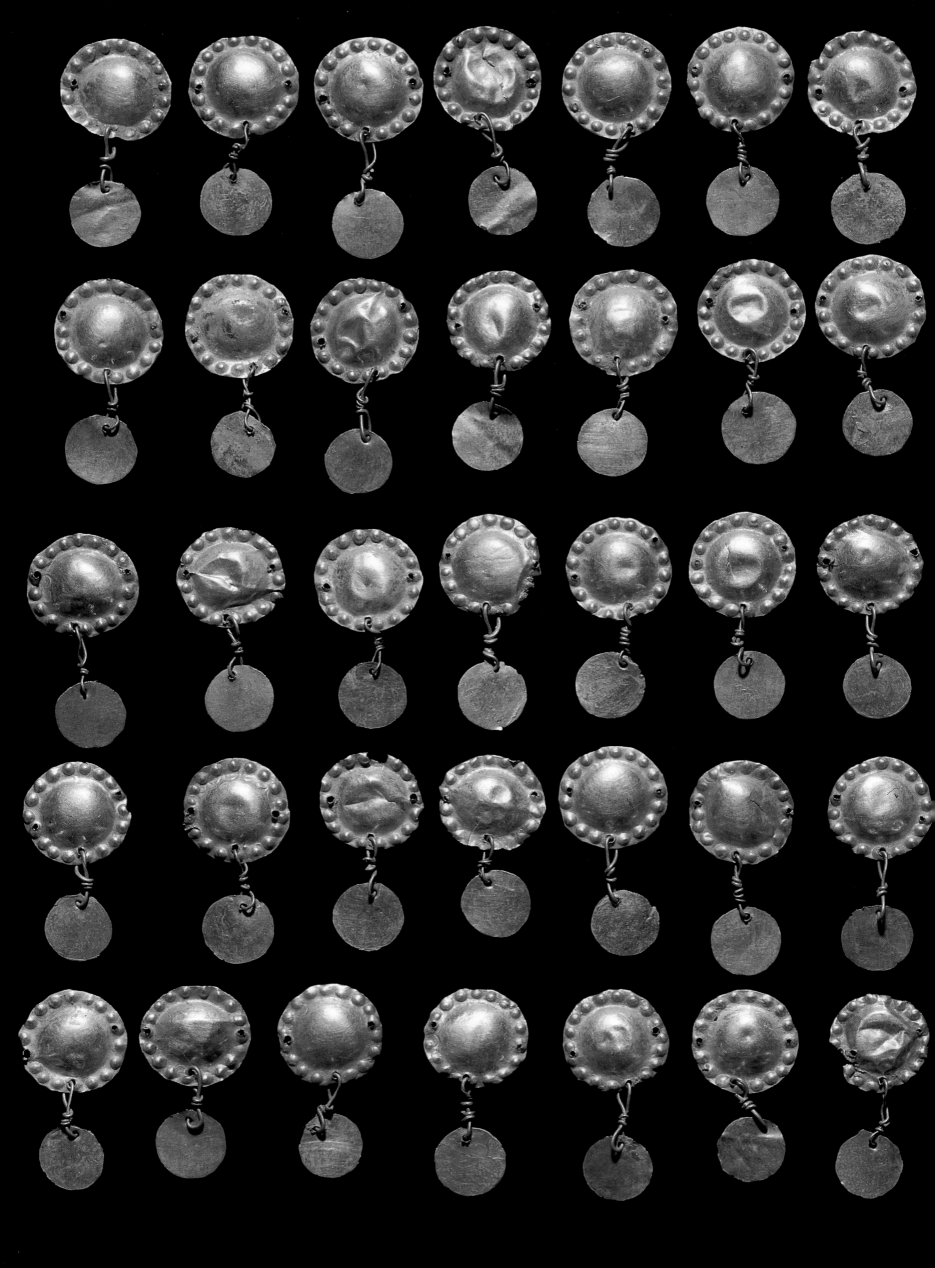

39
Large pendants with attached disks.
Cat. no. 2.24

40, 41 ⇒
Temple pendant with protomas of a horse.
Cat. no. 3.50

42
"Dual axhead" plaques. Cat. no. 2.11

43
Five-lobed brooch. Cat. no. 1.4

98

44
"Ruler and dragons" pendant. Cat. no. 2.7

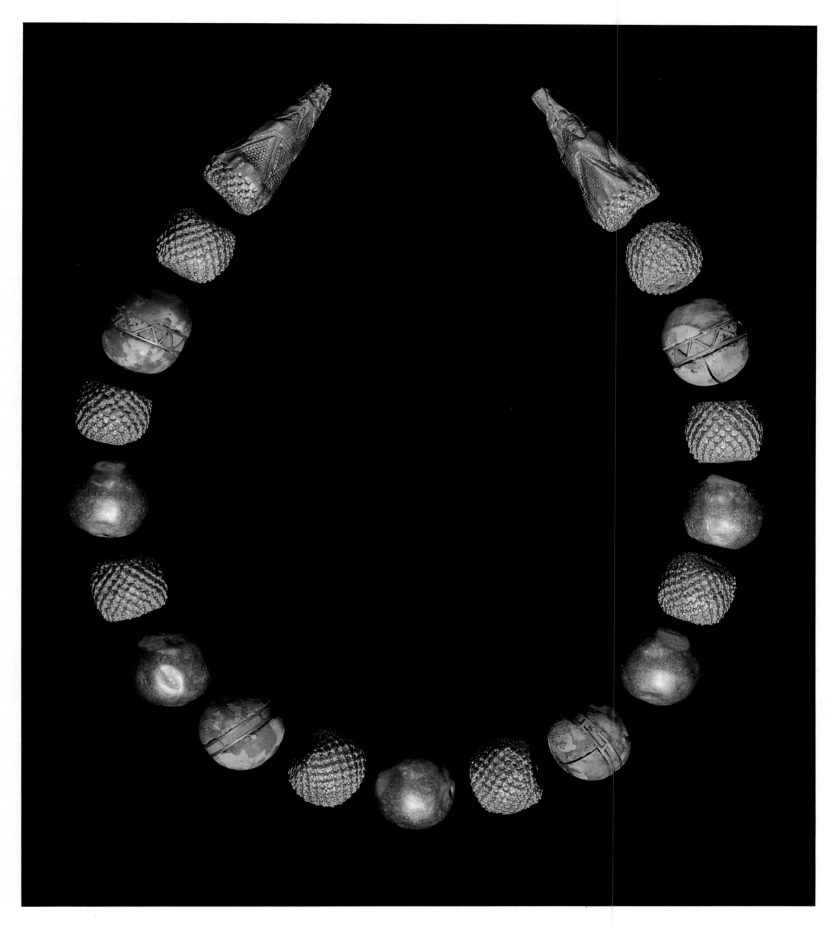

60
Small composite plaques. Cat. no. 2.20

61
Rimmed beads. Cat. no. 3.72

62
Large composite plaques. Cat. no. 2.19

63
Banded beads. Cat. no. 2.30

64, 65 →
Necklace. Cat. no. 5.3

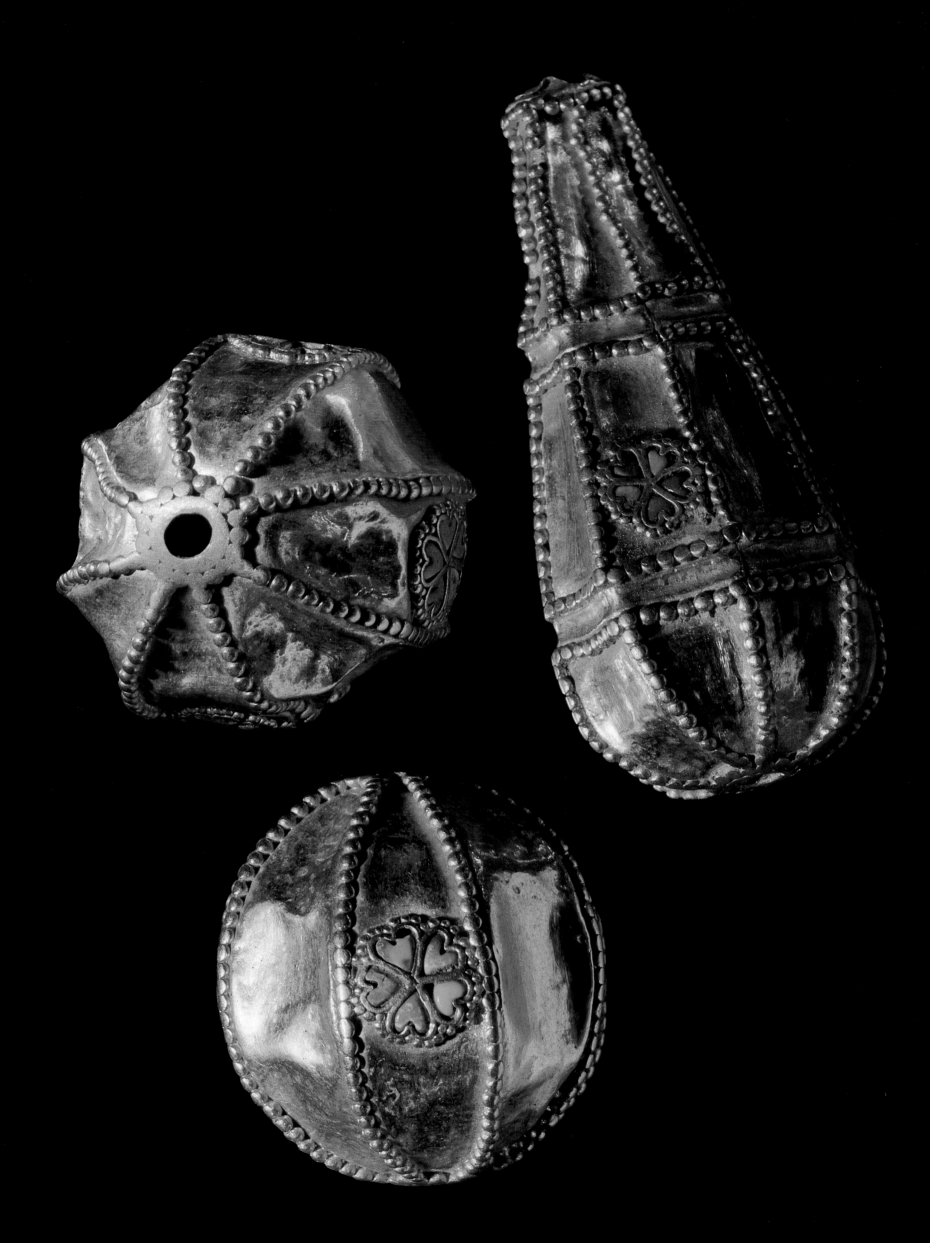

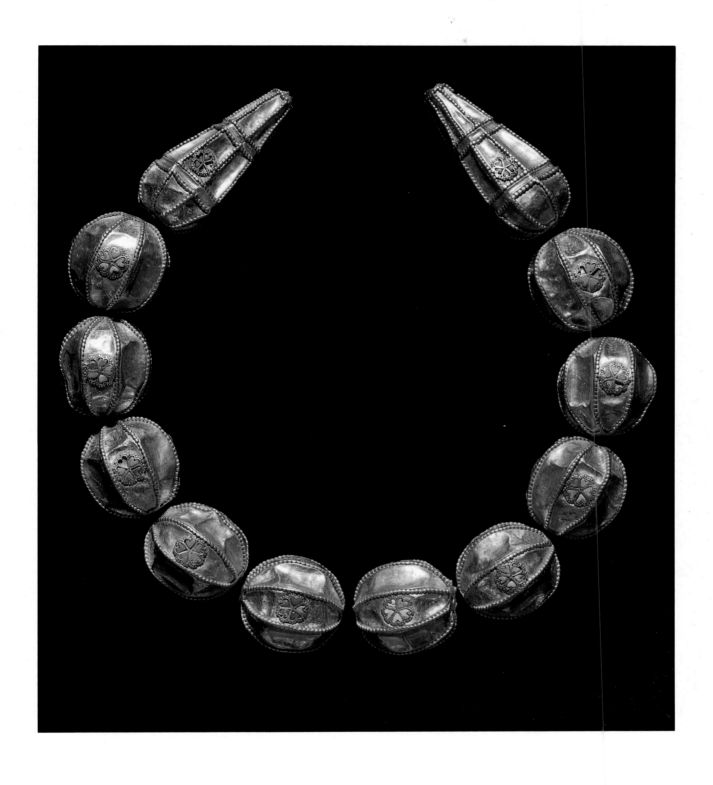

66, 67
Necklace of gold beads. Cat. no. 6.20

122

68, 69
Pectoral with cameo. Cat. no. 4.10

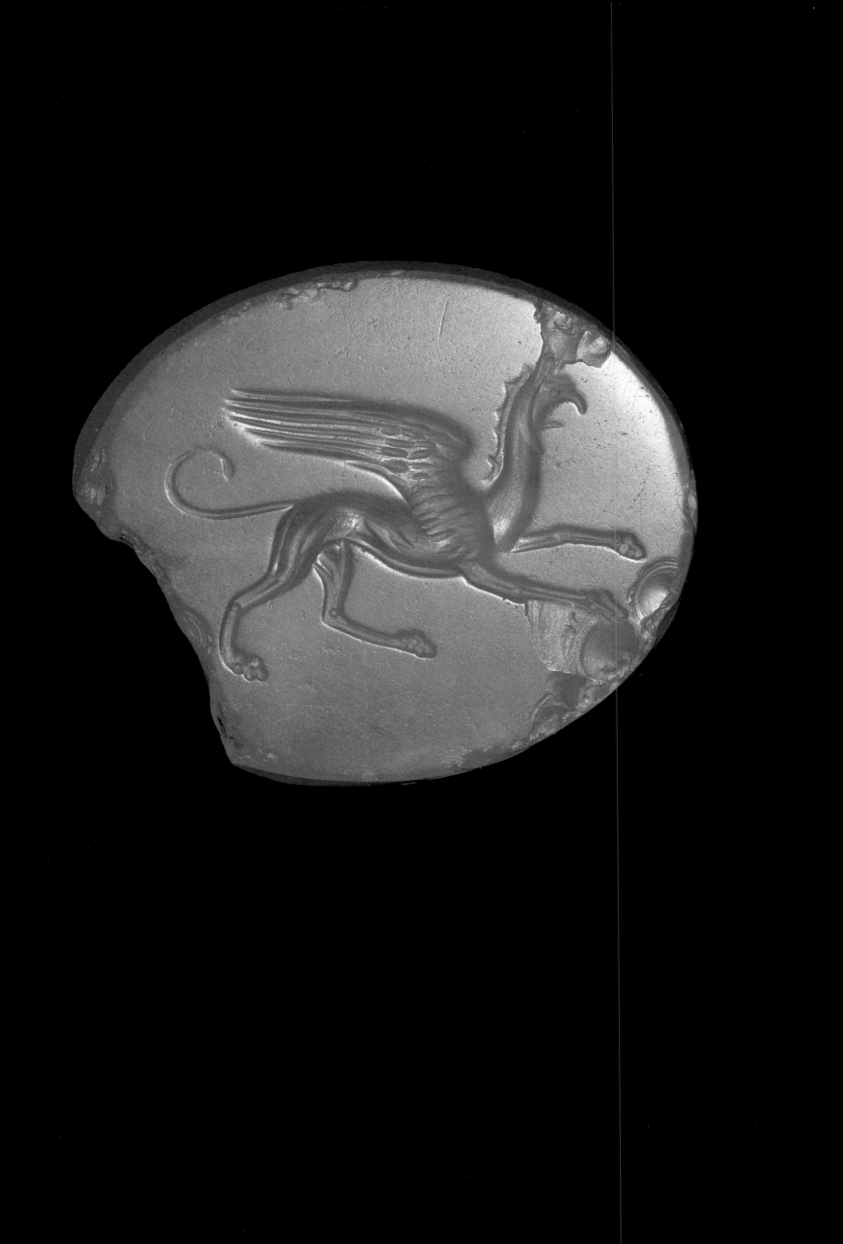

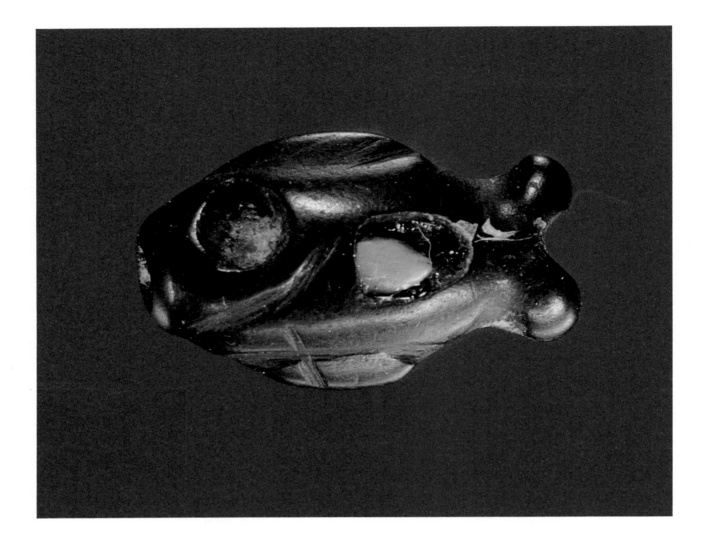

Pendant. Cat. no. 2.14

Lion-shaped pendant. Cat. no. 5.7

132

77–79 →
Clasps with amorous scene. Cat. no. 6.2

136

80
Figurine of the Kushan Aphrodite. Cat. no. 2.6

81
Clasp with representation of warriors. Detail.
Cat. no. 3.1

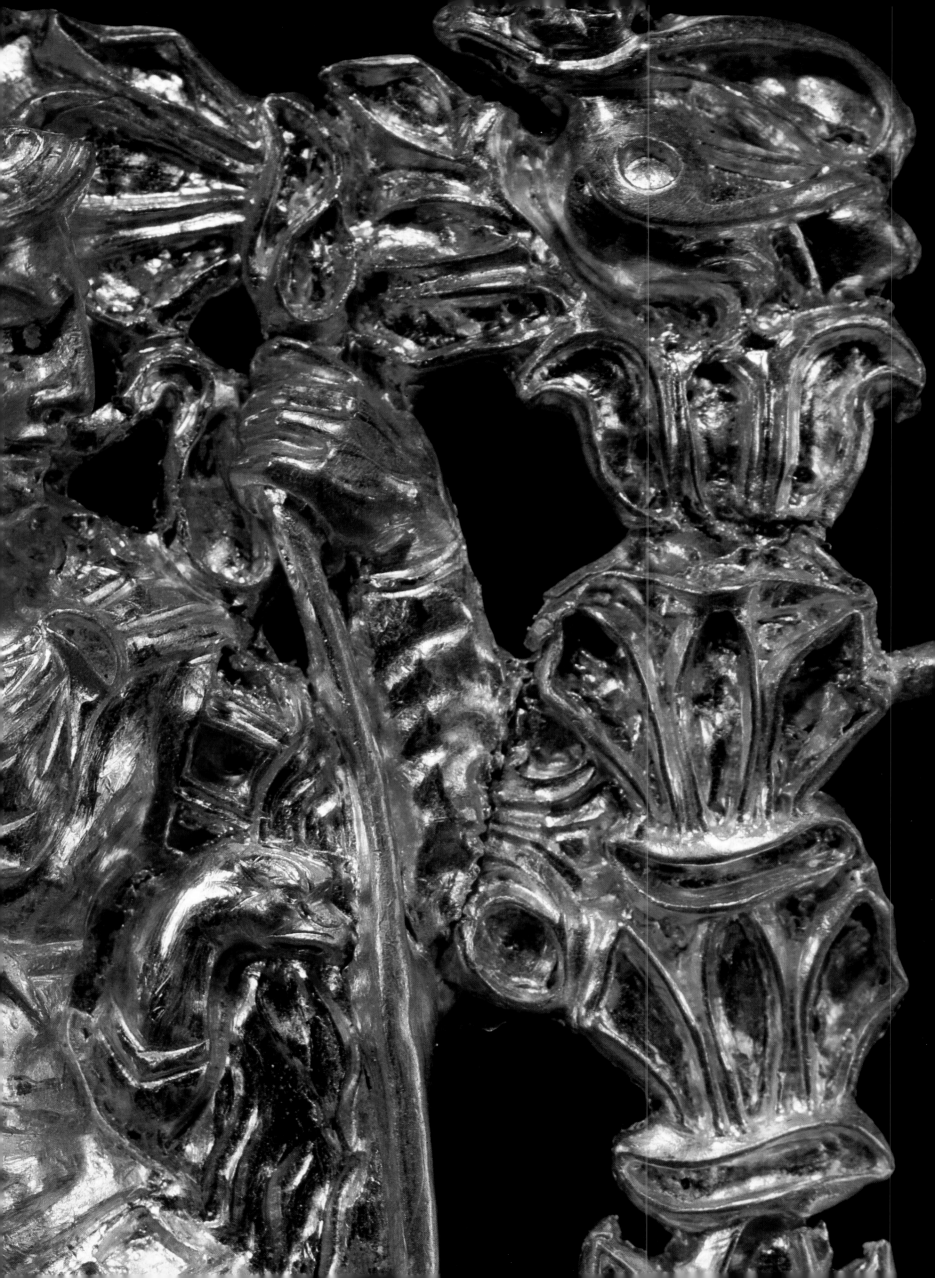

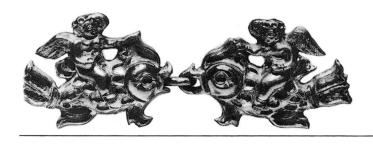

85
"Cupid riding a dolphin" clasps. Cat. no. 2.5

146

86
"Man with a dolphin" plaques. Cat. no. 1.1

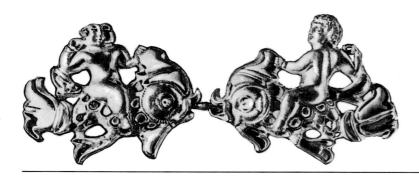

149

"Cupids riding dolphins" clasps. Cat. no. 3.2

88–97 ⇒
Gold belt. Cat. no. 4.2

152

154

Plaques with representations of panthers and of a
dragon. Cat. no. 4.4; no. 4.34

156

Figurine of the Bactrian Aphrodite. Cat. no. 6.3

108
Signet ring with representation of Athena.
Cat. no. 2.1

123
Plaque depicting a panther mauling an antelope.
Cat. no. 4.35

124
Round "dragons chariot" shoe buckles. Cat. no. 4.1

125 ⇒
Hemispherical plaques with raised rims.
Cat. nos. 3.4–6

126 ⇒
Pennant-shaped plaques. Cat. no. 3.43

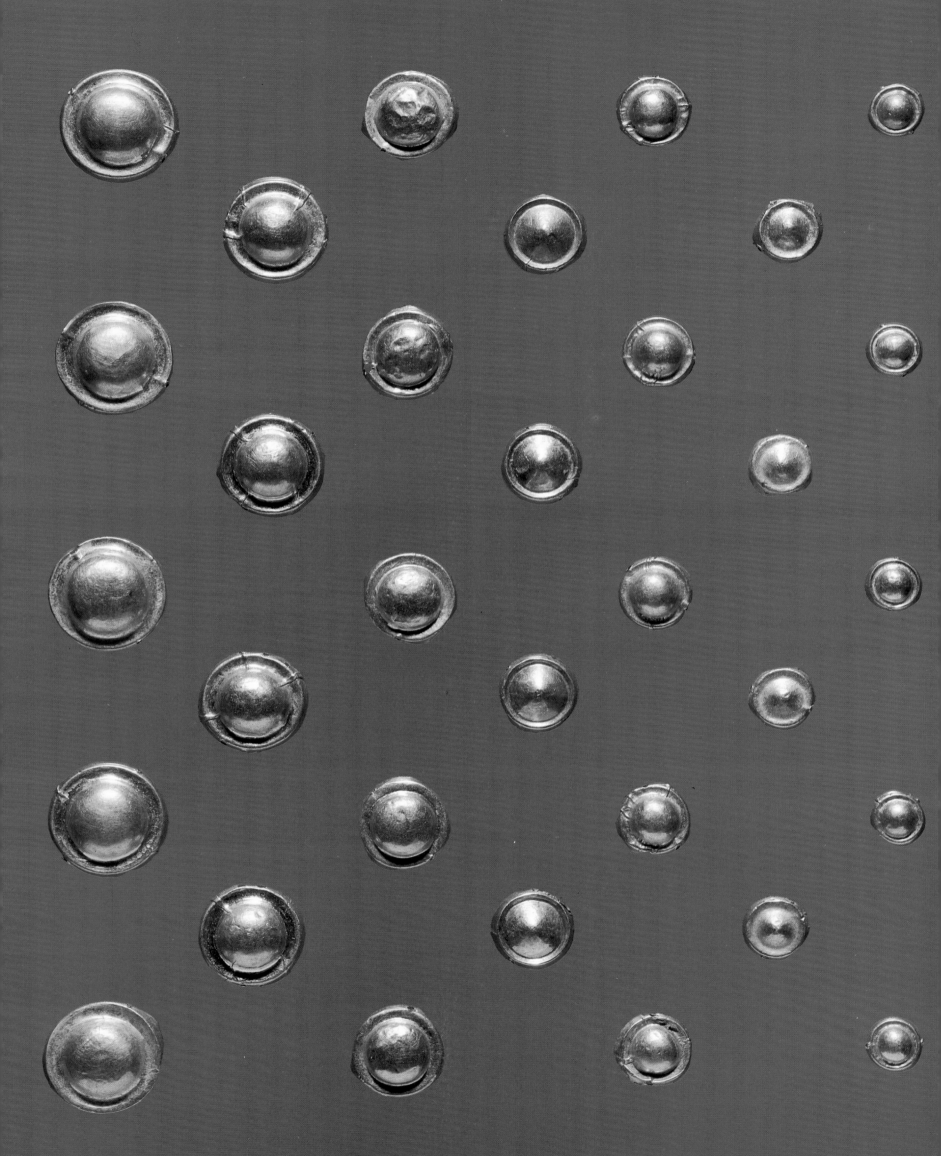

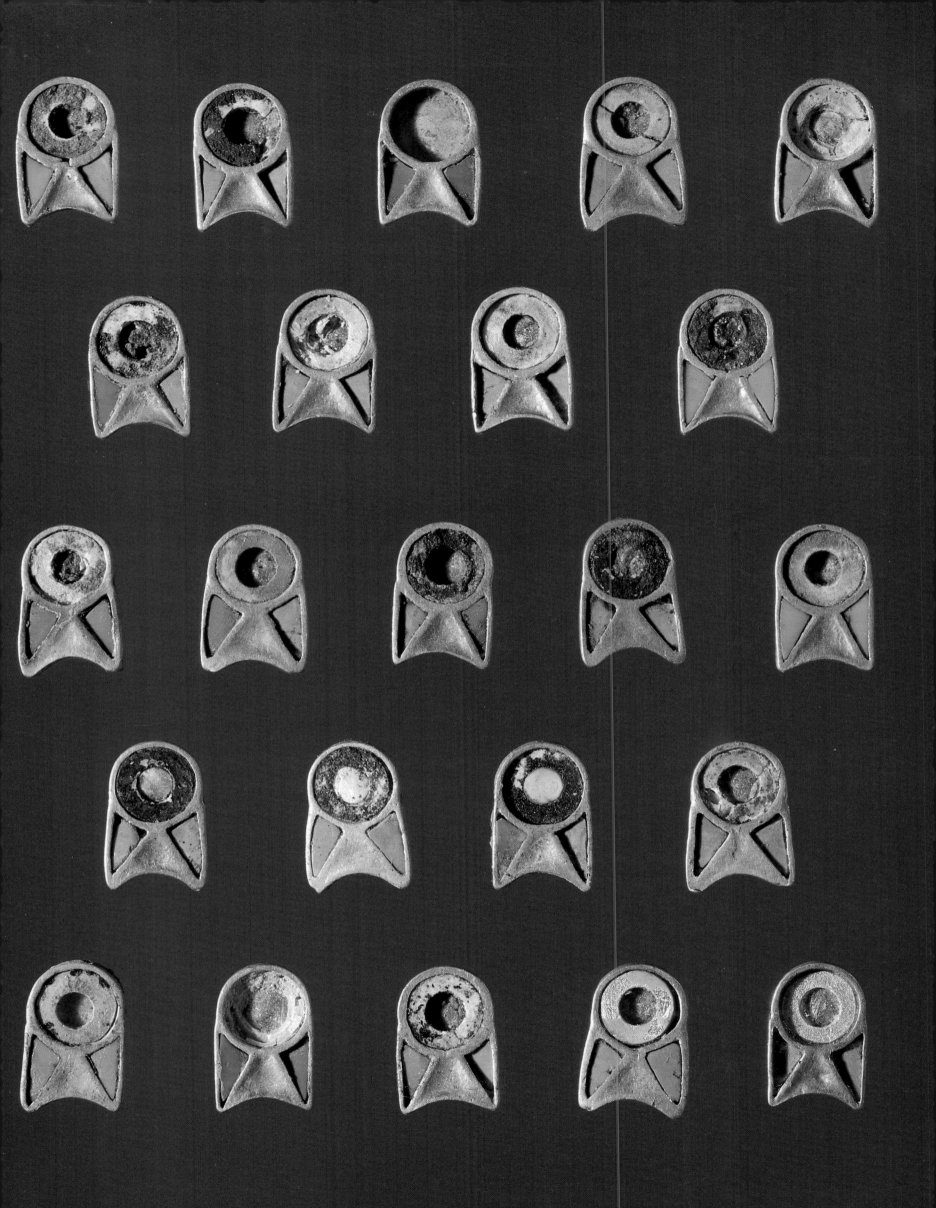

186

127
Silver Parthian coin. Cat. no. 3.48

128
Gold coin. Cat. no. 6.32

129
Silver coin. Cat. no. 6.33

130
Gold Roman coin. Cat. no. 3.47

188

131
Indian coin. Cat. no. 4.25

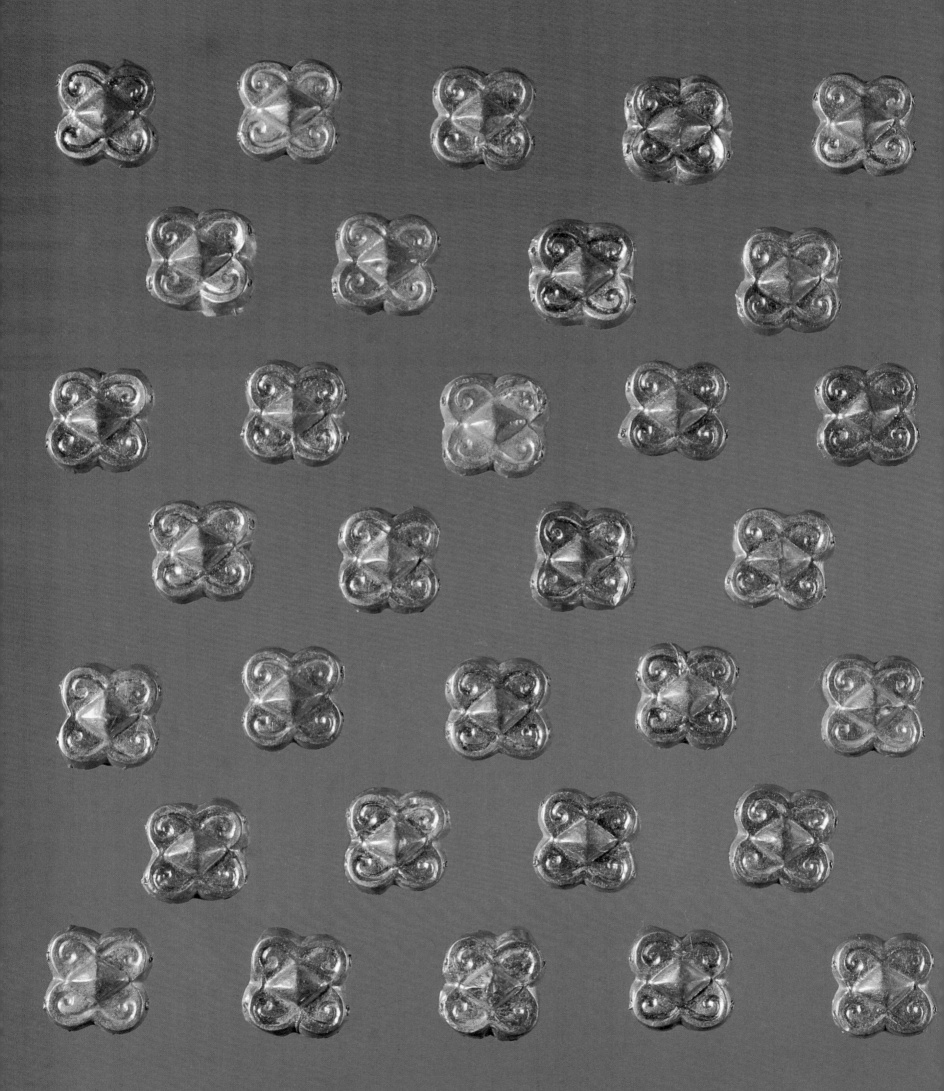

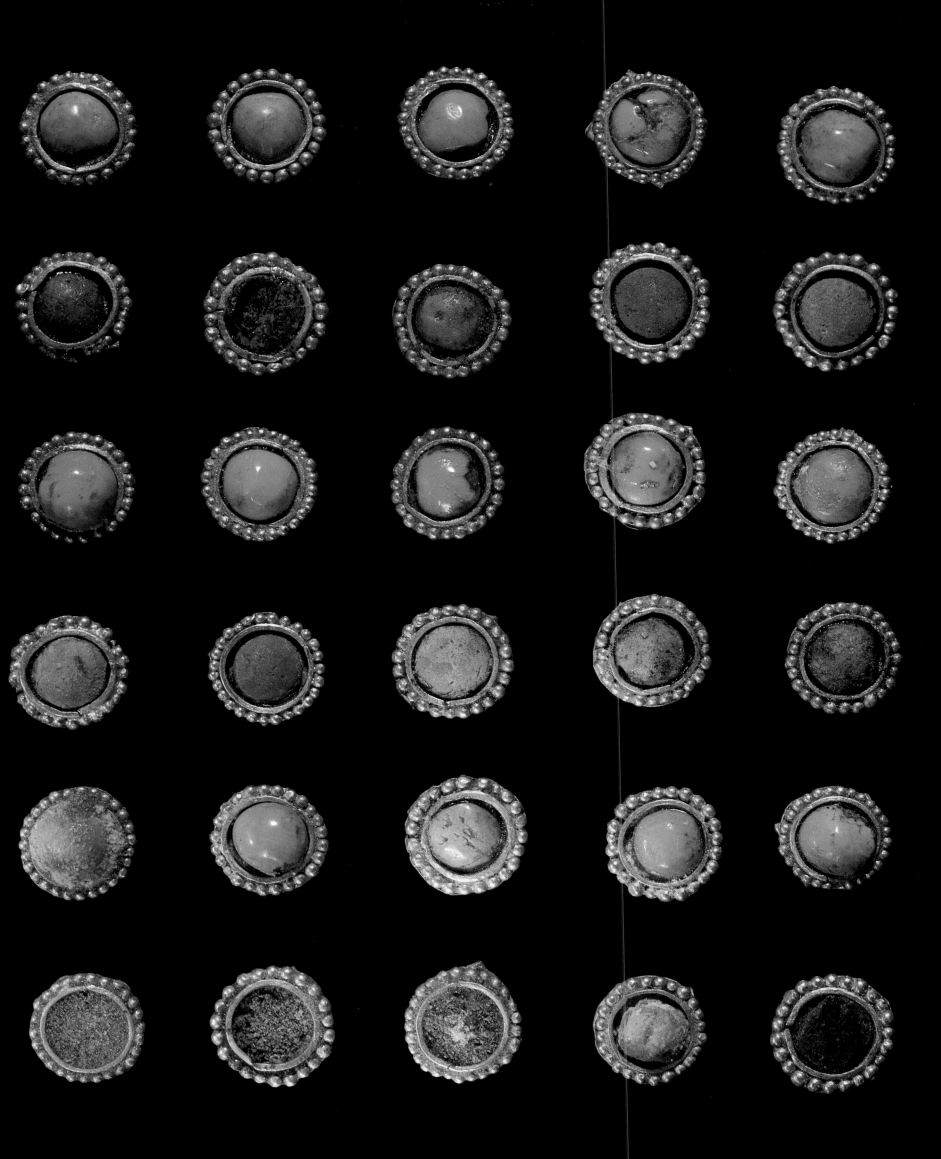

192

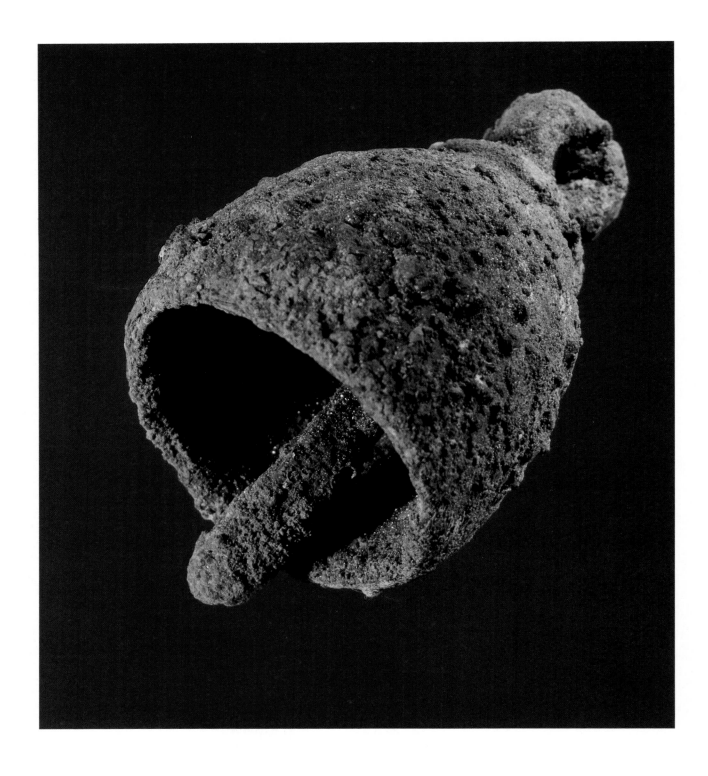

←
132
Plaques with centrally positioned lozenges.
Cat. no. 3.7

←
133
Round plaques with granulation and turquoise
inlays. Cat. no. 3.39

134
Small bell. Cat. no. 5.11

135
Silver bowl. Cat. no. 3.69

136
Basin. Cat. no. 6.28

195

137
Bowl. Cat. no. 5.13

138, 139
Phiale. Cat. no. 4.31

140
Basin. Cat. no. 3.73

141
Lidded pot for cosmetics and vessel with an
inscription in Greek. Cat. no. 3.18; no. 3.41

200

142
Ivory comb. Cat. no. 3.56

143
Mirror. Cat. no. 5.12

202

144
Mirror with handle. Cat. no. 3.71

145
Chinese mirror. Cat. no. 2.34

204

146
Pot for cosmetics. Cat. no. 1.30

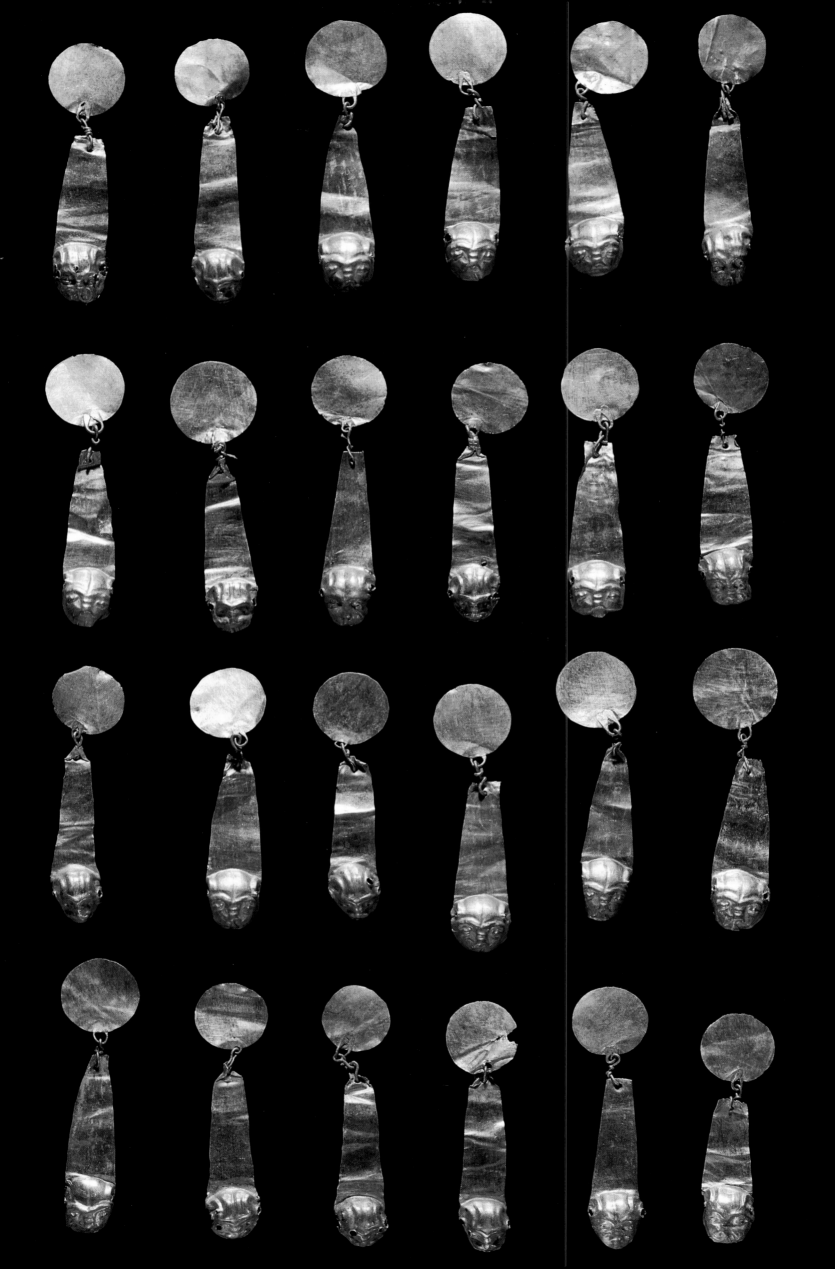

210

←
153
"Ram's heads" plaques. Cat. no. 2.8

←
154
Lion-face pendants. Cat. no. 3.12

155
Quiver top. Cat. no. 4.33

156
Arrowheads. Cat. no. 4.37

160, 161 →
Sheath. Details. Cat. no. 4.8

162, 163
Sheath with scene of two dragons. Cat. no. 4.9

CATALOGUE

All the artifacts listed below were recovered from the Tillya-tepe necropolis incorporating tombs dating from the first century B.C. to the first century A.D., during excavations conducted in 1978–79. The finds described are grouped according to the burial site number. All finds are of gold, with a few exceptions that are specifically indicated. Also indicated are all inset stones. The number of identical copies is designated in parentheses, should there be more than one. Dimensions are in centimeters and the weight, in grams.

The anthropological data were provided by L. Boucher, a staff member of the French National Scientific Research Center, on the basis of the examinations carried out in Kabul in 1982.

Approximate Equivalents
to Metric Measurements

.5 cm = $\frac{3}{16}$″	1 g = $\frac{1}{30}$ oz
1.0 cm = $\frac{3}{8}$″	5 g = $\frac{1}{6}$ oz
1.5 cm = $\frac{9}{16}$″	10 g = $\frac{1}{3}$ oz
2.0 cm = $\frac{3}{4}$″	20 g = $\frac{2}{3}$ oz
2.5 cm = 1″	30 g = 1 oz
3.0 cm = 1 $\frac{3}{16}$″	40 g = 1 $\frac{1}{3}$ oz
3.5 cm = 1 $\frac{3}{8}$″	50 g = 1 $\frac{2}{3}$ oz
4.0 cm = 1 $\frac{9}{16}$″	
4.5 cm = 1 $\frac{3}{4}$″	
5.0 cm = 2″	

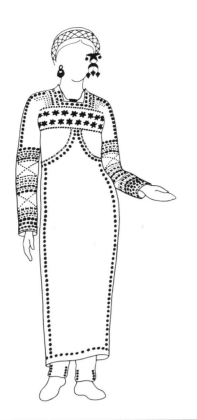

SITE 1

1.1 Ill. 86
"Man with a dolphin" plaques (seven)

The figure of a genuflecting man is depicted. His head is slightly turned, his straight nose has distinctly modeled nostrils and his full lips are curved in a faint smile, emphasized on some plaques by the stressed neck muscles. His hair is rendered by minute dots punched after the figure had been embossed. Only the left ear is visible: it has on its lobe a deeply indented dot, which may serve to symbolize an earring.

The man is holding a dolphin with its head on his left shoulder and its tail on his right one. The dolphin's body is covered with scales from head to tail; the round tail is picked out by minute dots. The man's arms are bent at the elbow and clasp the dolphin's head and tail; his fingers are distinctly delineated. The man is also grasping what is presumably a rudder in his right hand. Behind his shoulders elongated leaves descend

in a garland to the ground. His wasp waist is encircled by a narrow girdle from which a large trefoil with clearly marked veins droops. Two smaller trefoils rise up from winding stems behind the larger trefoil, their tips ending below the man's hands. The larger trefoil is bordered by four curving scrolls below, while still lower down at the base of the plaque there are round cloisons. The man's navel and nipples are indicated by deeply impressed dots. Note that all these details were punched after the figure had been embossed. Writhing snakes serve in place of legs. Several perforations have been made along the rim to enable the plaque to be stitched onto a garment or piece of cloth. Judging by the burrs, they were

made after the plaque had been completed by piercing the metal from the back to produce one perforation—on some plaques, two or three—at each of the four corners.

Dimensions: length 3.1×2.9; rim height 0.3
Weight: plaque no. 1: 4.98; plaque no. 2: 4.45; plaque no. 3: 5.46; plaque no. 4: 4.96; plaque no. 5: 5.54; plaque no. 6: 6.02; plaque no. 7: 5.26
State of preservation: distinct signs of wear

1.2
Clasp disks (two)

Massive convex cast disks, with three massive rings soldered to the back of each for purposes of fastening. Soldered to one is a hook, and to the other, a loop; both terminate in inward-turned scrolls.

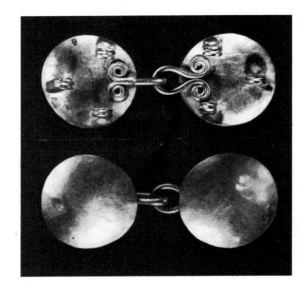

Dimensions: disk diameter 3.3; hook (loop) length 2.0; diameter of fastening rings 0.7
Weight: disk with hook: 16.02; disk with loop 16.2
State of preservation: both hook and loop show heavy signs of wear

1.3 Ill. 18
Hairpin

Shaped as a quatrefoil of thin gold sheet so that two of the lobes are horizontally aligned and the other two are bent down. Centrally positioned on the back is a 1 cm long fitting that was soldered perpendicularly and that has retained traces of iron inside, presumably from the no-longer-extant iron shaft. Soldered to the tips of all four of the quatrefoil's leaves are minute rings through which fine gold wire has been passed. Small disks with soldered-on tiny rings are attached to the two horizontally aligned leaves by the gold wire that has been rather crudely twisted. The two other downward-bent leaves also have wires attached. These wires incline inward toward each other, and their ends are attached to a small, thin, hand-cut crescent-shaped plaque. One of the

wires is threaded with a pearl in a poor state of preservation; it is quite likely that the second wire was also originally threaded with a pearl. Dangling from tiny loops soldered to the crescent are another three wires; attached to the end of each is a stylized leaflet bearing an impressed design that serves to convey the veins. Central in this design is the middle vein from which slender, slightly curved lines radiate in pairs, with the tips of the top pair curved into a semi-spiral.

Dimensions: overall length of the two horizontally aligned leaves 6.5; disk diameter 1.7; crescent length 3.5; leaflets 2.0×1.8; quatrefoil thickness 0.03; thickness of crescent and leaflets roughly 0.05
Weight: 4.72
State of preservation: signs of wear; iron shaft broken off and missing

1.4 Ill. 43
Five-lobed brooch

A massive cast rosette with a centrally inset turquoise head into which a pearl has been mounted. Each of the five heart-shaped lobes is embellished with a pair of pear-shaped turquoise inlays; along the outer rim the lobes are partitioned by small lozenges. The rim is curved in and raised; soldered to the back are four ring-shaped loops by means of which the brooch was sewn onto the garment.

Dimensions: diameter 5.0
Weight: 19.98
State of preservation: faint signs of wear

1.5
Six-petaled rosettes (thirty-two)

Cut—often crudely from sheet gold—with the result that not all petals are identical in shape. The tip of each petal carries a perforation produced in most cases by punching from the back. Centrally positioned on the reverse of each rosette is a loop by which it was stitched onto the garment.

Dimensions: diameter 3.5; thickness 0.03; loop
diameter 0.4
Weight: 60.0
State of preservation: faint signs of wear

1.6
Floret plaques (two)
Identical plaques save for a few minor details. Cut from sheet
gold in the forms of rosettes comprised of four heart-shaped
lobes, each of which, in turn, is impressed with a straight and
deep line down the middle and a curved line along the rim.
The lobes are separated by narrow, elongated petals with a
centrally marked vein. Soldered to the tip of each petal is a
tiny loop through which gold wires are passed; the wires have
disks attached to them. Rising from the center of each rosette
are three wire "stamens" with loops at their ends, from which
heart-shaped petals with a centrally marked vein dangle. In
the case of one rosette one such petal is missing and the stem

sprouts from a cone-shaped boss; on the other no such boss is
in evidence. Soldered to the back of each plaque are two loops
to enable it to be attached.
Dimensions: rosette diameter 4.0; disk
diameter 1.2; thickness 0.03
Weight: 5.6 and 4.6
State of preservation: faint traces of
deformation

1.7 Ill. 32
Earring clip
Thick-walled, hollow, boat-shaped, and comprised of two
soldered halves. The terminals are embellished with an
identical ornamental design: running along the rim are round
grains, followed below by a slim band after which comes

another row of round grains; the whole is sandwiched
between thin, flat strips. The 3 mm space in between is filled
with a stretch of broken lines creating a chain of equilateral
triangles. Still lower down is a chain of lozenges, below which
comes a strip of grains. Finally, beneath this banded design is
a large semicircle with one small roundel on each side; the
entire pattern is of thin smooth wire that has been soldered on
and bordered by granulation on one side. Inscribed within
the large semicircle is a triangle; both terminals of the
semicircle and the apex of the triangle are embellished with
three small arc; slipped over it are one large and two smaller rings. The
smaller rings are solid; one bears traces of a missing fitting;

the other does not manifest such traces, and when it is viewed
through a microscope one sees that its ends were pressed, not
soldered, together. The larger ring is open-ended and its
terminals are much thicker. The second end of the arc freely
penetrates the perforation of the earring itself, inside of which
one can distinctly make out two small gold tubes, whose
significance is somewhat obscure.
Dimensions: height 2.9 (without ring);
width 2.4
Weight: 19.38
State of preservation: faint signs of wear

1.8
Pectoral
A braided chain, the terminals of which are soldered to the
two small cylindrical tubes of the clasp. Each tube has a raised
rim in the form of a band. One tube ends in a massive loop;
the other has two loops at the edge with a gap between to
receive the more massive loop. When brought together and
properly aligned, the loops were secured by means of a gold
pin, whose tip is bent upward toward the head.

Dimensions: overall pectoral length 45.0; tube
length 1.5 and width 0.5
Weight: 16.6
State of preservation: faint signs of wear

1.9 Ill. 22
Triangular plaques (thirty-three)
Each triangle consists of fifteen tiny globules soldered together in such a fashion as to form an equilateral triangle with
five at the base and ranging up to one at the apex. All the
globules are hollow and have perforations by means of which
the plaques were sewn on the various articles of clothing.
Dimensions: height 1.3; width 1.0
Weight: 0.65 (of one of the plaques); 21.8
(of total)
State of preservation: faint signs of wear

1.10
"Bow with bosses" plaques (eight)
Stamped in mold. On the obverse of the wings of the "bow" is
an identical design composed of two bosses and a triangle.
There are six perforations along the rim, with two at the edge
of each wing and another two in the middle.
Dimensions: length 1.1; width 0.7; width at
middle 0.2
Weight: 0.16 (of one); 1.4 (of total)
State of preservation: some plaques are
deformed

1.11
"Inlaid bow" plaques (twenty-two)
The wings of the bow are inlaid with triangular insets of
turquoise, lapis lazuli, garnet, and a dark, near-black gem-
stone. Each plaque has a granulated lozenge-shaped inset on
one side. The reverse carries three small soldered-on tubes for
purposes of attachment.
Dimensions: 0.4×0.35
Weight: 2.71 (of total)
State of preservation: faint signs of wear

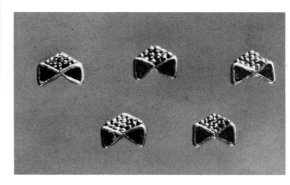

1.12 Ill. 26
"Floret" plaques (seven)
Cast with cloisons. Inset in the central cloison is a polished
light-violet gemstone akin to garnet. The five radiating heart-
shaped cloisons are inlaid with sky-blue turquoise. The
triangular gaps between the lobes are also inset with micro-
scopically minute bits of garnet. Soldered to the back of each
plaque are four small hollow tubes to enable it to be attached.
Dimensions: diameter 1.0; height 0.1
Weight: 3.112 (of total)
State of preservation: many gemstones missing

1.13 Ill. 29
"Face mask" plaques (four)

Cast in the cloisonné technique. In the middle, touching one edge is a raised oval bezel inset with three garnets that together comprise what could be taken for a face mask with holes for the eyes and mouth or nose. The "face mask" is sandwiched between two narrow turquoise inlays from which round turquoise insets rise up in an arch; the tiny

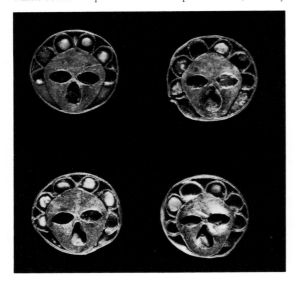

triangular gaps between the round turquoise inlays are inset with cornelian. Each plaque has soldered to the back four small hollow tubes to enable it to be attached.

> Dimensions: diameter 1.0
> Weight: 2.0 (of total)
> State of preservation: many inset stones missing

1.14 Ill. 24
"Eye-pupil" plaques (twenty-nine)

Square and stamped in mold, each has a centrally impressed almond-shaped sunken relief inset with a turquoise bead in the middle, possibly intended to imitate an eye with its pupil. Each square is embellished with bosses, running along the rim in a descending number of six to three per side, thus adding up to a total of eighteen. The opposite corners each have two perforations for purposes of attachment.

> Dimensions: 0.9×0.8; rim height 0.2
> Weight: 7.44 (of total)
> State of preservation: many insets missing

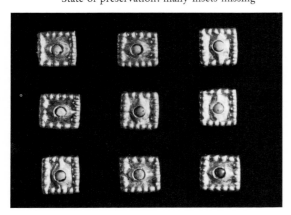

1.15 Ill. 27
Plaques with flowers (six)

Square and stamped, each plaque has a centrally positioned, raised, four-petaled flower with a round turquoise bead set in the middle. Running along the rim are bosses—seven each on two sides and six and five on the other two. Each of the

opposite corners has two perforations by which the item may be fastened.

> Dimensions: 1.0×1.0; rim height 0.2
> Weight: 2.4 (of total)
> State of preservation: some inlays missing

1.16 Ill. 25
Plaques with elongated insets (sixteen)

Oblong and stamped in mold, each has a small rim sandwiching two centrally positioned, elongated parallel cloisons inset with turquoise. Each of the opposite corners has two perforations by which the item may be sewn on.

> Dimensions: 0.9×0.8; rim height 0.2
> Weight: 4.4 (of total)
> State of preservation: some inlays missing

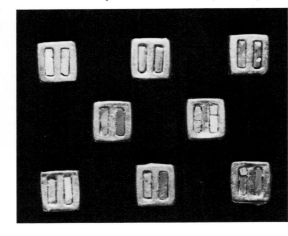

1.17
Plaques with bosses (sixteen)

Square and stamped in mold, each has a slightly raised rim. The obverse carries three rows of five raised hemispherical bosses. Two perforations have been made in each corner for purposes of attachment.

> Dimensions: 0.7×0.7; rim height 0.2
> Weight: 4.7 (of total)
> State of preservation: faint signs of wear

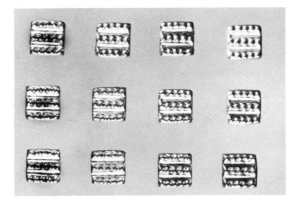

1.18
"Keg" beads (sixty-six)

Cast with longitudinally aligned soldering seams in evidence on both sides and with centrally positioned perforations by which the item may be attached.

> Dimensions: 0.8×0.6; orifice diameter 0.3
> Weight: 23.0 (of total)
> State of preservation: faint signs of wear

1.19 Ill. 9
"Volute" plaques (ninety-five)

Hand-cut from thin sheet gold in the shape of two paired volutes with spirally twisted ends. Soldered to each of the four opposite corners on the back is a minute ring by which the object was attached.

> Average dimensions: 1.1×1.0; thickness 0.1
> Weight: 45.0 (of total)
> State of preservation: some plaques deformed

1.20 Ill. 35
Scarab-type plaques (eighty-five)

Cut from thin sheet gold, with turquoise or lapis lazuli insets in soldered-on cloisons shaped as hearts (in the middle) and as half-moons of which there are four. The rims are edged with grains ranging in number from ninety to one hundred. Soldered to the middle of the back are two small hollow tubes by which the item may be fastened. All plaques are identical except for insignificant differences in dimensions and the fact that on some plaques the turquoise inlays are flat and on others, convex.

> Average dimensions: 1.3×1.1;
> thickness 0.3–0.4
> Weight: 81.0 (of total)
> State of preservation: many insets missing

1.21 Ill. 51
"Inlaid trefoil" plaques (sixty-one)

Each plaque consists of a miniature lozenge sandwiched between two stamped crescents and has cloisons soldered on. The lower, broader sections of the crescents and the lozenges are filled with black paste; the remaining sections of the

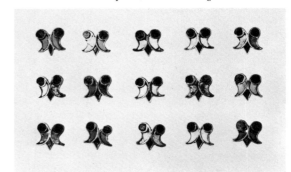

crescents are inlaid with flat turquoise. Soldered to the back of each plaque along the longitudinal axis are two hollow tubes by which the object may be fastened.

    Average dimensions: 0.9×0.9; thickness 0.15
    Weight: 22.0 (of total)
    State of preservation: some turquoise insets missing

1.22
"Twin leaves" plaques (twenty-one)
Consist of two stamped spreading leaves divided at the top by a round boss. On each side of the latter are perforations for purposes of attachment.

    Average dimensions: 0.9×0.7; rim height 0.2
    Weight: 2.81 (of total)
    State of preservation: some items slightly deformed

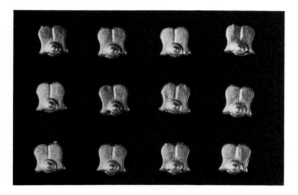

1.23
"Trefoil" plaques (ten)
Molded and stamped, by virtue of which each has a slightly raised rim. The hammered ornamental design on the obverse consists of a trefoil whose central leaf is shaped as a lozenge and whose other two leaves are pointed and curled outward. There are two symmetrically placed perforations along the rim for purposes of attachment.

    Average dimensions: 1.0×0.9; rim height 0.2
    Weight: 1.77 (of total)
    State of preservation: some plaques slightly deformed

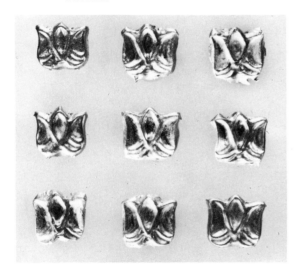

1.24
Round plaques (twelve)
Stamped in mold, with five-lobed rosettes in sunken relief on the obverse. Each lobe is heart-shaped, and there is a round indentation in the middle of each rosette. Two perforations,

one opposite to the other, have been made in the rim for purposes of attachment.

    Dimensions: diameter 0.7; rim height 0.2
    Weight: 1.33 (of total)
    State of preservation: some pieces heavily deformed

1.25
Pendants with central disk (seven)
All are identically shaped, stamped five-lobed rosettes with a centrally positioned convex hemisphere edged at its base with minute granulation. The radiating lobes, which are also convex, consist of two halves and are separated by a perforation. Each central hemisphere is perforated; a gold wire passes through each hole. One end of the wire is a loop fastened within the hemisphere, and the other end protrudes and is bent into a closed loop to which a disk is secured by

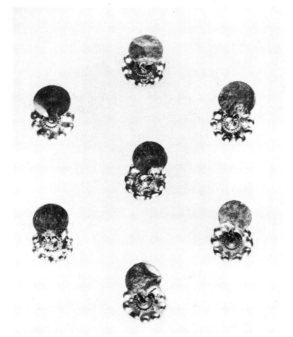

means of a tiny loop soldered to its edge. The pendant was attached using the perforations between the lobes plus the loop enclosed within the hemisphere.

    Dimensions: rosette diameter 1.4; disk diameter 1.2
    Weight: 7.5 (of total)
    State of preservation: some items partly deformed

1.26
Pendants with dangling disks (three)
Both stamping and casting employed. The fourteen-petaled rosette was stamped separately, and a hemisphere was subsequently soldered to its middle. Both the base of the hemi-

sphere and all fourteen petals are edged with microscopic granulation. Soldered to the edge of the back of the rosette is a small loop through which a gold wire holding a disk is passed, so that the disk dangles; further up the back two gold loops were soldered on to allow it to be attached.

    Dimensions: rosette diameter 1.5; disk diameter 1.2
    Weight: 3.7 (of total)
    State of preservation: partly deformed

1.27
Pendants (two)
Though only partly preserved, together they provide a general notion of what this type of pendant originally looked like. The upper section consists of a small cast and perforated sphere to which a square with a smaller square inscribed is attached. The central smaller square is inset with turquoise in one pendant, and with lapis lazuli in the second. In the latter case, the triangles formed within the larger square are also inlaid with lapis lazuli. Small, round loops have been soldered to two corners of the larger square. In the case of the pendant

inset with lapis lazuli, part of which is missing, a pearl and a minute disk are attached to one of the loops by means of thin wire. In the case of the pendant inlaid with turquoise, there dangles from one loop a disk without a pearl; attached to the second loop is a short chain of three links with a hollow, hemispherical pendant. Soldered to the obverse of this pendant is a crescent-shaped cloison evidently intended to be a setting, and dangling from it is another three-link chain. Suspended to the chain is a pearl and a hollow, cone-shaped pendant whose base is embellished with a slender band of tiny grains.

    Average dimensions: length 4.0; length of the side of the larger square 0.7
    Weight: 2.0 (turquoise pendant); 3.3 (of both)
    State of preservation: both damaged

1.28
Drum-shaped pole top (?)
The purpose for which this hollow cylinder was intended is obscure. Symmetrically disposed at both ends are eight crudely perforated holes: four smaller ones of up to 1 mm in diameter were perforated from the outside, while the four larger holes with a diameter of 3 mm were pierced from within before the item was soldered together. The outside is divided into two registers, each of nine hemispherical cloisons; set between the two registers is a row of lozenges. The cloisons are encrusted alternately with garnet and turquoise, and the lozenges are inlaid with pearl or mother-of-pearl. The rims are edged with two granulated bands.

    Dimensions: 1.4×1.1
    Weight: 3.7
    State of preservation: heavily damaged

1.29
Flat bell-shaped plaques (four)
All are hollow, flat, and made of soldered-together thin sheet gold. All have on top soldered-on loops for attachment.
    Dimensions: 1.8×1.8; thickness 0.3 (of the larger item); 1.3×0.8; thickness 0.4 (of three smaller items)
    Weight: 0.6 (of the larger item); 1.8 (of all three smaller items)
    State of preservation: slightly deformed

1.30 Ill. 146
Pot for cosmetics
This miniature silver lidded vessel has a distinctive flat bottom with scratched circles on it and a hemispherical body along whose upper part runs an engraved ornamental band depicting a vine with leaves. The top is slightly recessed to take the lid, which like the body of the pot is also hemispherical in shape, and is ornamented with the same design and has a sculptured handle.
    Dimensions: height 4.7; body diameter 3.0; bottom diameter 1.5
    Weight: 18.0
    State of preservation: traces of deformation

1.31
Small ring
Plain, cast, embellished with an ornament executed in relief, with a circle in the center and pear-shaped pieces on the sides.
    Dimensions: diameter 1.5
    Weight: 1.51

1.32
Gold threads from gold-thread embroidery
Thin, wavy, not smooth

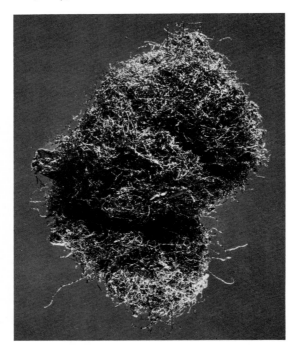

1.33
Pearls from gold-embroidered cloth
All are bored to enable them to be sewn on.
    Average dimensions: 0.2–0.4
    State of preservation: partly fragmented and covered with white film

SITE 2

2.1 Ill. 108
Signet ring with representation of Athena
Massive and hollow with a centrally positioned gold bezel attached by means of a dark-brown adhesive. Engraved in the middle of the bezel is the representation of a seated female in profile, facing to the left. Her head is capped by a Macedonian-type helmet possibly with a plume. Her nose is large, and her neck long, slightly twisted, and bedecked with a necklace; her shoulders face forward. Her breasts are faintly denoted beneath the robe by two circles, and her slender waist is girdled with a double belt from beneath which the garment billows in softly falling folds; a soft fold is set horizontally across her hips. From her waist to her bent knees the garment drops in deeply incised, slanted folds terminating in tiny paired bosses; further down it is articulated into straight, falling folds tracing the outline of the long, lissome legs beneath. The tips of sandals peep out from beneath the flounced hem, which is embellished with two rows of minute dots. Held in her left arm which is bent at the elbow and rests

on an oval shield, and trimmed with sawteeth along the rim, is a long lance or spear. Athena's right arm is also bent and ends in a gracefully outstretched hand with distinctly modeled, straight fingers. Engraved in the field in front of the figure is the mirror image of the Greek name of the goddess. The darker yellow of the mount sharply contrasts with the lighter yellow of the bezel.
    Dimensions: 3.0×2.7 (entire signet); 2.1×1.7 (bezel); height 2.5; setting oval 1.9×1.8

Weight: 25.2
State of preservation: faint signs of wear on the bezel

2.2 Ill. 109
Signet ring with an intaglio
Round, hollow, with the transverse soldering line visible at the neck. Evidently, the upper, broader segment was made first, after which a plate was cut, bent and inserted with its ends joined together at the neck of the mount. Mounted on a dark-brown bezel in the broader, upper segment is an oval turquoise inset carrying the incised representation of a seated female figure. Her tiny head crowned with a wreath or perhaps a calathos is slightly thrown back. Her small torso is crisscrossed by a looped cord and the slender waist is caught

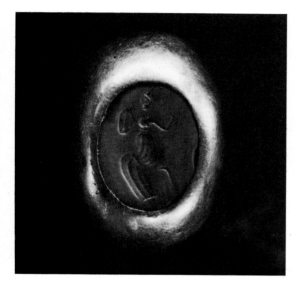

by a girdle high up beneath the breasts. From beneath the girdle long garments trail gently down to the ground, with the folds terminating at the knee in a series of small and shallow indentations. Her left arm is raised to the side, and her right arm carries a round object, presumably a shield. Also depicted is a curved leg of what is apparently a chair.

Dimensions: 1.7×1.2 (bezel); 2.0×1.7 (orifice); 3.0×2.7 (entire ring)
Weight: 22.72
State of preservation: the gemstone bezel shows signs of wear

2.3
Signet ring
Hollow, with a large flat bezel. As far as one can gather from the extant signs, first the outer side was cut out of a thin sheet (the sharp edge is distinctly visible at the neck of the mount) after which the inner section was cut and the ends were joined at the neck. The bezel was then soldered on, with such care that no outer sign of the soldering line is visible. Set in the middle of the bezel is a strongly convex oval garnet, so translucent that the base of the bezel can be glimpsed through it. Disposed around the central gem are twelve smaller beads, mostly of turquoise, lapis lazuli, and garnet.

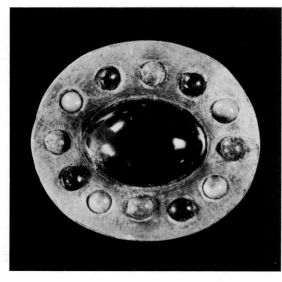

Dimensions: 3.3×3.0 (bezel); 2.5 (height), 2.0×1.8 (hoop)

Weight: 14.1
State of preservation: faint signs of wear

2.4 Ills. 105, 107
Bracelets with antelope terminals (two)
Cast with open-ended terminals, oval in cross section. Both terminals are identically shaped as racing antelopes with their legs fully extended. Set in the corners of their disproportionately large, bulging almond-shaped eyes are tiny turquoise beads that represent the whites of the eyes; the pupils are represented by round pellets of a translucent, yellowish cornelian. Their petal-like ears and coiled horns are encrusted with convex and highly polished turquoise beads. Their muzzles are pressed to the slightly bent outflung legs that end

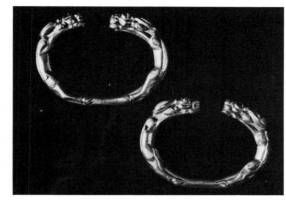

in hooves with pear-shaped turquoise inlays. Special indentations mark the hooves and the pointed knuckle bones are well modeled; the softly bent knees are picked out by slightly raised semi-oval folds. The shins carry slanted incisions that convey the underhair. Set between the hindquarters is a short but broad tail with a herringbone pattern of incisions on top that extends along the back and runs into the tips of the horns. The musculature of the bodies of the racing animals is enhanced by the special large turquoise insets beneath the hooves.

Dimensions: 8.5×6.3
Weight: 254.37 and 253.23
State of preservation: heavy signs of wear
Reference: S. Rudenko, "The Siberian Collection of Peter I," *Reports of the Institute of Archaeology*, Moscow–Leningrad, 1962, table IX, nos. 4–5 [С. И. Руденко, "Сибирская коллекция Петра I," *САИ*, Москва–Ленинград, 1962, табл. IX, № 4–5].

2.5 Ill. 85
"Cupid riding a dolphin" clasps (two)
Hollow, identical copies (for description turn to p. 26). The obverse was molded and is relatively massive. Soldered to the back is a thin sheet cut out to duplicate the outline of the obverse. The reverse also carries four soldered-on loops by which the item could be attached. The significance of the

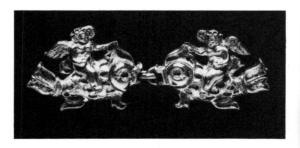

triangular tonguelike perforations on the back is rather obscure. On one clasp the dolphin's mouth ends in a hook; on the other, in a loop. Cloisonné technique.

Dimensions: 4.5×3.0 (each)
Weight: 18.0 and 20.0
Reference: N. Glueck, *Deities and Dolphins*, London, 1965, pls. 17–20.

2.6 Ill. 80
Figurine of the Kushan Aphrodite
The figure of a winged female standing between two columns is represented in high relief; a cupid is shown perched on the column by the left arm (for description turn to pp. 25, 26). The obverse was cast, and the back cut out of sheet gold to

---

duplicate the outline of the obverse and then soldered to the obverse's inward-bent edges. Also, four loops were soldered to the back in pairs to enable it to be attached.

Dimensions: 4.5×2.5; thickness 0.3–0.4
Weight: 14.8
State of preservation: faint signs of wear
References: J. Richter, *Catalogue of Engraved Gems*, Rome, 1956, p. 40, pl. XXVI, nos. 157–59; S. Reinach, *Répertoire de la statuaire grecque et romaine*, vol. 1, Paris, 1897, pl. 632.

2.7 Ills. 44–47
"Ruler and dragons" pendants (two)
These two-sided, specially molded pendants present a king engaged in combat with dragons (for description turn to pp. 24, 25). Attached to the hem of the depicted garment and to the paws of the dragons on each pendant are four loops secured to which are twisted chains serving to create a webbing of triangles and lozenges. At their joints the chains are embellished with tiny roundels inset with garnet. The corners of the webbing have a total of six round plates attached; soldered to each of them are three radiating heart-shaped cloisons, in several cases encrusted with turquoise and lapis lazuli. Suspended to these plates by thin wires are four-segmented florets (a circle and two petals sandwiching an almond-shaped gem) executed in the cloisonné technique and also inlaid with turquoise and lapis lazuli; the rims of the florets are minutely granulated. The webbed design further incorporates a number of tiny flat disks suspended from thin wires at three different levels, that is, from loops on the plaque, on the garnet-inset roundels and on the florets.

Dimensions: 12.5 and 6.5
Weight: 49.27 (fragmented); 53.9 (whole)
State of preservation: the lower segment of one pendant and some insets on both pendants are missing
Reference: S. Rudenko, *The Culture of the Population of the High Altai in the Scythian Period*, Moscow–Leningrad, 1953, fig. 137 [С. И. Руденко, *Культура населения горного Алтая в скифское время*, Москва–Ленинград, 1953, рис. 137].

2.8 Ill. 153
"Ram's heads" plaques (forty-two)
Each item has been cut out of a molded thin gold. The round eyes are inlaid with yellow cornelian and the curled-back horns and ears, with turquoise. The nostrils and half-open mouth are well modeled. There are perforations in the mouth and at the back of the head to enable it to be attached.
Dimensions: 1.5×1.0; thickness 0.1
Weight: 1.2 (one of the plaques); 36.0 (of total)
State of preservation: many insets missing

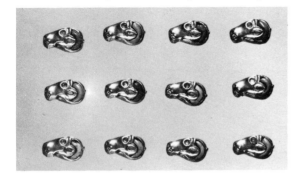

2.9
Ribbed cylinders (fifty-four)
Hollow and constructed of thin strips of sheet gold rolled into small tubes and soldered together. Ornamented with transverse ribbing. Each item has a soldered-on loop in the middle by means of which it was sewn onto the cuffs.

Dimensions: length 0.8–1.0; diameter 0.5, thickness 0.05
Weight: 22.44 (of total)
State of preservation: partly deformed

2.10 Ill. 100
"Little heart" plaques (167)
Molded. The obverse has a heart-shaped indentation to carry a large convex turquoise inlay. Along the longitudinal axis each plaque is perforated on the rim to allow it to be attached.

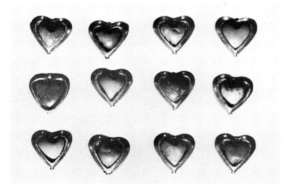

Dimensions: 1.1×1.0; rim height 0.2; thickness 0.05
Weight: 0.3 (one of the plaques); 47.0 (of total)
State of preservation: many insets missing

2.11 Ill. 42
"Dual axhead" plaques (ninety)
Molded and stamped. Shaped as lozenges with identical figures reminiscent of axblades, on two sides.

Dimensions: 1.6×1.1; thickness 0.05
Weight: 0.6 (one of the plaques); 28.2 (of total)
State of preservation: some heavily deformed

2.12 Ill. 11
"Steering wheel" plaques (four)
Three large and one small, all manually cut from thin sheet gold. Centrally positioned is a six-petaled rosette with a tiny turquoise bead rimmed with minute granulation in the middle. The tips of the petals are hemmed by a circle edged by a row of small triangles.
Dimensions: diameter of larger plaques 2.0; diameter of smaller plaque 1.4; thickness 0.05
Weight: 0.8 (one of the large plaques); 0.74 (of small plaque)
State of preservation: in the case of three plaques the triangular teeth along the rim have been partly broken off.

Plaques with small hearts (two)
Cut manually from thin sheet gold, each has a central circle rimmed by five pierced heart-shaped designs. They were used together with the "steering wheel" plaques to ornament a braided basket.
Dimensions: diameter 1.6; thickness 0.05
Weight: 0.35 (one plaque)
State of preservation: faint signs of wear

2.13 Ill. 17
Merlon-shaped plaques (seventy-nine)
Cut by hand from thin sheet gold in the shape of a three-tiered pyramid. Soldered to the back of each are two small tubes at the top and bottom to enable them to be attached.
Dimensions: 1.2×1.0; thickness 0.1
Weight: 39.0 (of total)
State of preservation: signs of wear

2.14 Ills. 54, 75
Teardrop and lozenge-shaped pendants
Chiseled out of turquoise-type gemstones. Both mounted in gold fittings having loops from which they may be suspended.

Dimensions: 1.0×0.3; 1.0×0.5
Weight: 0.4; 0.5
State of preservation: faint signs of wear

Astragal pendants (two)
Carved from turquoise-type gemstones and bored through center.
Dimensions: 0.8×0.5
Weight: 0.57 (one pendant)
State of preservation: faint signs of wear

Garnet pendant
Carved from a semi-translucent round garnet whose upper part is mounted in a gold fitting having a loop from which it can be suspended. To judge by the perforation, the garnet was originally a bead from a necklace.
Dimensions: 1.3×0.7
Weight: 0.85
State of preservation: faint signs of wear

Pomegranate-shaped pendant
Of black paste with three heart-shaped sky-blue turquoise insets. Round with finial comprised of four teeth, which imparts a resemblance to a pomegranate. The finial has a perforation from which it can be suspended.
Dimensions: 1.0×0.6
Weight: 0.18
State of preservation: faint signs of wear

Fish-shaped pendants (two)
Made of black paste. The head bears perforations that resemble eyes and that may have initially been encrusted; the gills are represented by scratches. The bulging sides carry indentations filled with a sky-blue paste. Fins are indicated on back and belly and the broad tail is well modeled. A hole has been bored longitudinally from open mouth to tail to enable the item to be fastened.
Dimensions: 1.1×0.6; 1.0×0.5
Weight: 0.32 (of one pendant)
State of preservation: faint signs of wear

2.15 Ills. 53, 55, 56, 58
Hand-shaped pendants (two)
Carved from a dark-green gemstone and from turquoise; both mounted in gold fittings having loops from which they can be suspended. The fingers are distinctly modeled.

Dimensions: 1.1×0.5 (dark-green gemstone);
1.5×0.6 (turquoise)
Weight: 0.28; 0.91
State of preservation: distinct signs of wear

Foot-shaped pendant
Cast, hollow, with toes distinctly modeled. Provided with a loop on top from which the item may be suspended.
Dimensions: 1.5×0.9
Weight: 0.84
State of preservation: distinct signs of wear

Foot-shaped pendants (two)
Carved from inferior white-streaked lapis lazuli and mounted in a gold fitting provided with a loop from which the item may be suspended. Toes on one pendant are well modeled.
Dimensions: 0.9×0.4; 1.0×0.4
Weight: 0.69
State of preservation: faint signs of wear

2.16
Lozenge-shaped beads (eight)
Cast and flat, with snipped-off points, they are bored along the longitudinal axis for purposes of attachment.
Dimensions: 0.8×0.7
Weight: 4.65 (of total)
State of preservation: faint signs of wear

2.17
Round and elongated beads (twelve)
Carved out of turquoise and other gemstones; all are bored.
Dimensions: 0.8×0.6; 0.6×0.3; 0.5×0.5; 0.5×0.4
State of preservation: faint signs of wear

Flat lozenge-shaped beads (two)
Carved out of a red gemstone, possibly garnet; both are bored along the longitudinal axis.
Dimensions: 1.0×0.8; thickness 0.2
Weight: 0.95
State of preservation: faint signs of wear

Round beads (five)
Of a vitreous paste, bound in the middle by gold wire, and bored.
Dimensions: 0.6×0.4
Weight: 0.97
State of preservation: one bead split into two halves

Round beads (twelve)
Carved out of a red gemstone, possibly garnet, and bored.
Dimensions: diameters (of six) 0.5; (of three) 0.6×0.5; (of another three) 0.7
Weight: respectively 1.65; 1.78; 2.73
State of preservation: heavy signs of wear

Small gold fittings with insets missing (six)
Each has a loop at the top to enable the item to be suspended; one has a sawtooth rim at the bottom.
Average dimensions: 1.8×0.5
Weight: 1.5 (of total)
State of preservation: partly deformed and with signs of wear

Small barrel-shaped beads (eight)
Carved out of turquoise, all bored.
Dimensions: 0.8×0.4 (of the biggest)

Sky-blue beads (two)
Both of paste and bored. One is round, the other pear-shaped.
Dimensions: 0.7×0.4

Hollow beads (twenty-five)
Round, of different sizes, and bored.

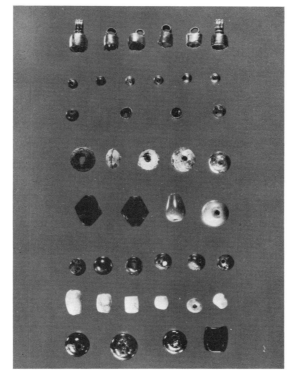

Dimensions: diameter 0.2–0.3
Weight: 1.0 (of total)
State of preservation: some split, where soldered, into two hemispheres

2.18
Paste beads (four)
Round and of black paste, the tops are ornamented with white-striped pentagons. All four are bored.

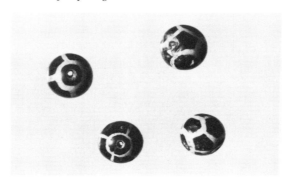

Dimensions: diameter 1.0
Weight: 3.75 (of total)
State of preservation: faint signs of wear

2.19 Ill. 62
Large composite plaques (sixty-six)
Each consists of thirty-four roundels alternating with thirty-two dividers, both of which were molded, have raised rims of 2–2.5 mm in height and are pierced to allow them to be attached. Centrally positioned on the obverse of each roundel is a triangular indentation enclosed by three turquoise-inset cloisons in such a manner as to create a whorl-shaped rosette. The dividers are shaped as two crescents joined back to back; at either end of the joint are stamped heart-shaped indentations inset with turquoise.
Dimensions: roundel diameter 2.0; divider 3.1×2.5

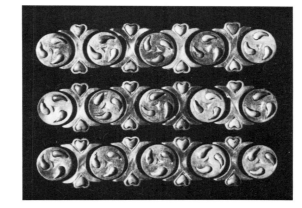

Weight: one roundel 1.4; of total 48.46; one divider 0.7; of total 52.11
State of preservation: partly deformed and with some turquoise insets missing

2.20 Ill. 60
Small composite plaques (twelve)
Composed of roundels alternating with dividers. The roundels are hand-cut from thin sheet gold and have soldered-on cloisons consisting of one tiny centrally positioned round turquoise inset and five radiating heart-shaped turquoise inlays. Each roundel is edged with granulation. The dividers are also cut from thin sheet gold in the shape of crescents joined back to back and have soldered-on heart-shaped cells inset with turquoise at either end of the joint. Each of these cells in turn has a loop through which thin wire is passed and from whose other end a miniature disk dangles. The cusps of the crescents on the two end dividers are spiral-shaped. Each divider has two small tubes soldered to the reverse for purposes of attachment.

Dimensions: roundel diameter 1.5; divider 1.8×1.8
Weight: one roundel 2.0; of total 12.96; one divider 2.7; of total 17.0
State of preservation: partly deformed and with signs of wear

2.21 Ill. 101
"Floret with disk" plaques (fifty)
Four-petaled rosettes with pointed ends and small central prongs cut from thin sheet gold. The prongs are inserted into cone-shaped stems attached to the rosettes by means of thin, jutting loops in the middle of the rosettes. The other ends of the stems are pierced; a wire passes through this perforation and is attached to dangling miniature disks.

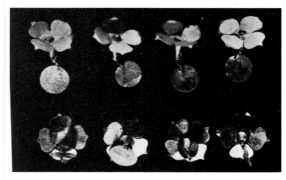

Dimensions: length 2.7; rosette diameter 2.0; disk diameter 1.0
Weight: 1.1 (of one plaque); 59.0 (of total)
State of preservation: partly deformed

2.22
Small tube
Rolled of thin sheet gold with one edge overlapping the other. Not soldered together. One end has been cut longitudinally into eight long strips which have been bent outward to form a brush. Slipped over the tube below the brush are two thin rectangular hand-cut plates with jagged edges and centrally positioned square-shaped holes.
Dimensions: tube length 4.0; diameter 0.7; average strip length 3.5; plates 2.5×2.1 and 2.6×2.2; thickness 0.05

Weight: 4.72
State of preservation: plates and strips partly
deformed

2.23
Hemispherical plaques with raised rim (692)
Mold-stamped and have a raised rim with two opposed
perforations for fastening.

Dimensions: diameter 1.5; height 0.5;
thickness 0.05
Weight: 0.5 (of one plaque); 35.9 (of total)

2.24. Ill. 39
Large pendants with attached disks (156)
Molded, hemispherical convex plaques edged with round
convex bosses. Each has three perforations, two of which are
for purposes of attachment; passed through the third are thin,
crudely twisted wires with dangling plain, flat disks attached
to the end of each.

Dimensions: plaque diameter 1.5; disk diameter
1.0; total length 2.5; thickness 0.05
Weight: 0.6; 81.88 (of total)
State of preservation: partly deformed; disks
missing on some; some have torn edges

2.25
Small pendants with attached disks (142)
Molded hemispherical convex plaques edged with round
convex bosses and having five perforations of which two pairs
are for purposes of attachment; passed through the fifth is a

fine, crudely twisted gold wire to whose ends the loops of
flat, plain disks are soldered.
Dimensions: diameter 1.0–1.2; length 2.5
Weight: 70.0 (of total)
State of preservation: slightly deformed

2.26
Hemispherical plaques with round tops (145)
Stamp-molded, with paired perforations for attachment.

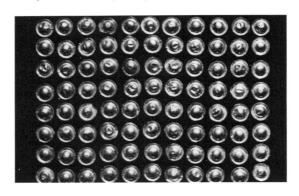

Dimensions: diameter 1.4
Weight: 78.6 (of total)
State of preservation: partly deformed

2.27
Pear-shaped plaques (seventy-one)
Hollow, molded, and convex.

Dimensions: 0.8×0.5; thickness 0.03
Weight: 2.0 (of total)
State of preservation: partly deformed

2.28
Ribbed keg-shaped beads (ten)
Hollow, with perforations. Were made by rolling ribbed gold
sheeting into keg-shaped tubes; the protruding ends are
covered with minute incisions.
Dimensions: 1.3×0.6; thickness 0.02
Weight: 5.0 (of total)
State of preservation: faint signs of wear

2.29 Ill. 59
Figurines of musicians (two)
Hollow, the obverse of each figurine was molded; the back
consists of a flat plate cut to shape and soldered to the
obverse. The face is round with large, protruding eyes and
faintly marked nose and mouth. Traces of hair are visible. At
the top of the head is a raised circle denoting the beginning of
a hole that goes right through to end in a similar raised ring
between the feet (this perforation served for purposes of
attachment). The figures have hardly any neck, their torsos
are broad, and their arms are bent, clasping stringed lyre-like
musical instruments to their breasts. Their legs are crossed
and their long trousers are caught at the ankles by laces.

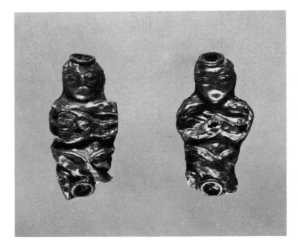

Dimensions: 2.3×1.2; thickness 0.03
Weight: 1.16
State of preservation: greatly deformed, signs
of wear with cavities in places

2.30 Ill. 63
Banded beads (four)
Presumably made of ivory and painted black, the beads
consist of two hemispheres edged at the base with thin gold
wire. Each hemisphere has a slight central indentation from
which broad incised lines radiate in such a manner as to form a
six-lobed rosette. The halves are firmly joined together by a
light-toned adhesive mass, to produce a black, carved, slightly flattened hexagonal sphere girdled by two bands of gold
wire. Inserted into the perforation piercing the middle is a
bronze prong having two loops by means of which the beads
were threaded onto the necklace.
Dimensions: diameter 2.0; height 1.8; gold
wire thickness 0.05; band width 0.2
Weight: 9.0 (of one bead); 27.87 (of total)
State of preservation: wire loops partly broken

Granulated beads (six)
Hollow and formed of two hemispheres soldered together
with the joint carefully smoothed. Each bead consists of an

indented six-lobed rosette, with the facets of all the lobes embellished with two rows of granulation. The grains were soldered on after the two hemispheres comprising the bead had been firmly soldered together. The beads were threaded onto the necklace through perforations.

Dimensions: 2.4×2.0
Weight: 72.84 (of total)
State of preservation: distinct signs of wear

Plain beads (five)
Hollow, slightly flattened spheres consisting of two hexagonal hemispheres carefully soldered together and with the soldering line smoothed. The surface of each hemisphere carries indentations in the shape of a six-lobed rosette.

Dimensions: 2.2×1.8; thickness 0.05
Weight: 26.56 (of total)
State of preservation: distinct signs of wear

Cone-shaped clasps (two)
Hollow, made by rolling thin sheet gold into the shape of a cone and carefully soldering the edges together. Additionally secured by three slender horizontally placed bands, one at the tip, one in the middle, and the third at the base. The last also served to attach to the flat end of a separate hemisphere shaped as a rosette with six indented lobes, its jutting edges embellished with two rows of minute soldered-on grains. The cone as such has a hexagonal surface and is embellished with granulation; a row of six triangles descends from the tip. Lower down are two rows of pyramids each comprised of three grains supporting a top, fourth, grain. Fanning out from the central joint are rows of triangles, their apexes pointed in opposite directions and comprised of minute grains in a descending order of five down to one. The next row of granulated triangles is bordered by the third band which is at the tube's widest point. Soldered to each facet of the tube and between two rows of triangles with their apexes facing each other are pairs of tiny pyramids consisting of three grains supporting a top, fourth, grain. At both ends the clasps have small perforations to enable them to be threaded onto a necklace, which they comprised along with the afore-described beads.

Dimensions: length 5.3; width at tip 0.5; width at base 2.5
Weight: 38.86 (of pair)
State of preservation: faint signs of wear

2.31 Ill. 20
Hairpins (two)
Identical and possessing bronze shafts with gold finials. The finials consist of disks from the middle of which project multi-faceted cones with a turquoise bead on each tip, the whole reminiscent of a flower bud. Attached to the edge of the disks are gold wires threaded with pearls. Dangling from wires attached to each finial is a crescent embellished with flat, plain disks.

Dimensions: disk finial diameter 2.7; plain disk diameter 1.5; pin length 4.5
Weight: 50.3 (of one)
State of preservation: disks slightly deformed, bronze shaft heavily corroded

2.32
Five-lobed brooch
A round cast plaque with a raised rim. Radiating out from the centrally positioned raised circlet are five lobes with slightly overlapping ends. On the back is a round loop for purposes of attachment.

Dimensions: diameter 3.1; overall height 0.5; rim height 0.2
Weight: 9.99
State of preservation: heavy signs of wear

2.33
Open-ended anklets (two)
Cast, with heavily thickened ends.

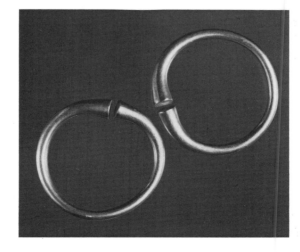

Dimensions: (of one) 9.5×9.0; thicknesses at narrow and wider parts respectively, 0.7 and 1.4; (of second) 9.2×9.0; thicknesses at narrow and wider parts respectively, 0.7 and 1.5
Weight: 623.9 (of pair)
State of preservation: heavy signs of wear especially on the inside

2.34 Ill. 145
Chinese mirror
Of silver with smooth obverse. On the back, at the center, is a horizontally perforated, convex handle embellished all around with a raised design of circlets enclosed in an annular strip of vertical lines. This, in turn, is encircled by an eight-petaled rosette which is rimmed by a circular inscription in Chinese characters. The broad, raised outer rim completes the overall design.

Dimensions: diameter 17.5; handle diameter 2.4; rim thickness 0.6
State of preservation: heavily patinaed

2.35
Silver vessel
Flat-bottomed and pot-shaped, with a heavily flared lip, on a low stand.

Dimensions: lip diameter 20.5; height 9.5; bottom diameter 10.5; stand height 0.8
State of preservation: heavily patinaed, fragment of side missing

2.36
Heart-shaped plaques (ninety-two)
Molded. On the obverse are heart-shaped cells, possibly intended for inlay. The bases and tips are perforated for purposes of attachment.

Dimensions: 1.0×1.0
Weight: 21.1
State of preservation: partly deformed

235

2.37 Ill. 21
Hemispherical plaques (363)
Stamped as ordinary hemispheres with perforations opposite each other for fastening.

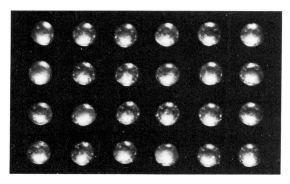

Dimensions: diameter 0.9; height 0.4
Weight: 65.0
State of preservation: good

SITE 3

3.1 Ills. 81–84
Clasps with representations of warriors (two)
The obverse is cast in pierced high relief. Thin plates cast and pierced in the same places as the obverse have been soldered to the back in such a manner as to produce hollow, open-worked clasps, which have occasional cavities due to the use of very thin sheet gold. Both clasps carry identical representations of warriors with the sole difference that on one of the pair the warrior is shown in profile facing the left-hand side, while on the other the profile faces the right-hand side (for description turn to pp. 30, 31). The figure is framed in a rectangular cartouche with a broad band of three stripes forming the base, and what are either columns or trees consisting of four large trefoils, bound at their bases by ribbons with slightly curved ends forming the sides. Perched on top are figures of birds of prey that hold in their beaks fluttering ribbons whose ends curl behind their backs. Along the tops of the pair of clasps are two facing pairs of trefoils bound by vertically curling ribbons. Rings have been soldered to the four corners of the back of each of the pair for purposes of attachment. The long hooks by which the clasps are fastened together have been split into two strips at one end, twisted into spirals, and firmly soldered to the back. Evidently, right after casting the backs cracked in two places, as they have patches soldered over them. The significance of the tongue-shaped perforations in the middle and at either edge of the back plates is somewhat obscure.

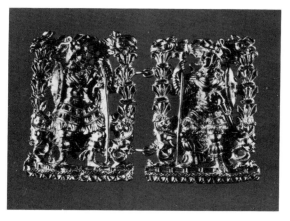

Dimensions: 9.0×6.3 (of each)
Weight: clasp with loops 37.85; clasp with hook 41.0
State of preservation: cavities

3.2 Ill. 87
"Cupids riding dolphins" clasps (two)
Hollow, cast in pierced high relief. The representations are similar, with the cupid on one of the pair facing the viewer, and the cupid on the other clasp having his back turned. On the first the dolphin has a hook protruding from its mouth; on the other a ring protrudes; by this means the pair are fastened (for description turn to p. 29). Note that the dolphin's crest, tail, and fins are picked out by turquoise inlays. The backs of the clasps consist of thin, pierced plates faithfully duplicating the front and soldered to it. Also soldered to the backs are loops for purposes of attachment. The fastenings are of gold wire, with the hook having one end splayed, coiled into two spirals, and soldered firmly together.

Dimensions: 4.2×4.9 (of each)
Weight: 16.0 (one clasp); 33.0 (pair)
State of preservation: some turquoise inlays missing
Reference: S. Reinach, *Répertoire de la statuaire grecque et romaine*, vol. 4, Paris, 1910, p. 288.

3.3
Garnet pendants (eleven)
The finial of each pendant is cast in the shape of a hollow sphere two hemispheres soldered together. The short necks are joined to oval bezels set with highly polished, translucent crimson hemispherical garnets. The bezels are edged with minute granulation; soldered to their lower parts are small loops through which thin wires have been passed. On each pendant the wire passes through the perforations pierced in either a small disk or a heart-shaped piece. The smallest pendant is almond-shaped.

Dimensions: pendant length 1.8 (without disk); bezel width 1.0; disk diameter 0.9
Weight: 14.5 (of one)
State of preservation: one garnet and disks on five pendants missing

3.4–6 Ill. 125
Hemispherical plaques with raised rims: large (415); medium (313), and small (447)
Molded from thin sheet gold, the convex obverse has a raised rim pierced twice for purposes of attachment.

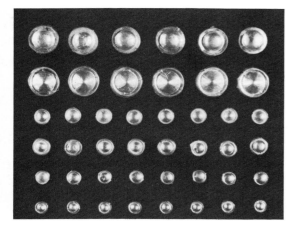

Dimensions: large—diameter 1.5; height 0.4; medium—diameter 1.4; height 0.3; small—diameter 0.6–0.8
Weight: respectively 146.12; 46.77; 28.33 (total)
State of preservation: partly deformed

3.7 Ill. 132
Plaques with centrally positioned lozenges (243)
Centrally positioned on the obverse of each plaque is a convex lozenge edged by an impressed design of volutes. Perforated twice on each of two sides for purposes of attachment.

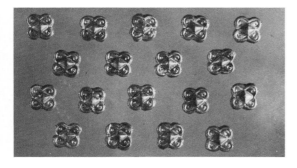

Dimensions: 1.0×1.0; height 0.3
Weight: 35.0 (of total)
State of preservation: slightly deformed

3.8 Ill. 34
Five-circlet plaques (205)
Stamped in mold. The obverse carries a convex design of five circlets with one disposed in the middle and the other four in the corners. Perforated twice on each of two sides for purposes of attachment.

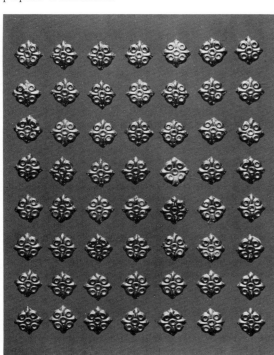

Dimensions: width 1.1; height 0.1
Weight: 27.81 (of total)
State of preservation: slightly deformed

3.9
Convex heart-shaped plaques (294)
Stamped in mold and perforated once on each of two sides for purposes of attachment.
Dimensions: 0.8×0.7
Weight: 21.25 (of total)
State of preservation: slightly deformed

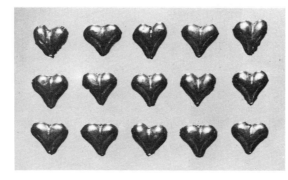

3.10 Ill. 52
Ribbed heart-shaped plaques (seventy)
Stamped in mold in the shape of a heart with a rib running down the middle. Perforated at the edges for purposes of attachment.
Dimensions: 0.8×0.8
Weight: 9.27 (of total)
State of preservation: deformed

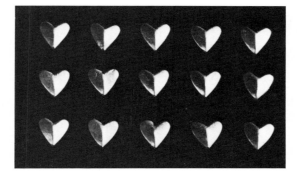

3.11 Ill. 23
Trident-shaped plaques with circlets (twenty-seven)
Cast in mold in the shape of a heart with three teeth; the two edge teeth terminate in tiny circles. Inlaid with turquoise. Two small tubes have been soldered to the back for purposes of attachment.
Dimensions: 0.8×0.6
Weight: 6.123 (of total)
State of preservation: many insets missing

3.12 Ill. 154
Lion-face pendants (fifty-two)
Comprised of a disk and a long strip of thin sheet gold flaring out into a convex lion's face that was stamped in the mold. Its forehead is divided down the middle; its half-round ears are laid back; its eyes, with dots for pupils, gleam from beneath heavy arched ridges of brows; and its nostrils are conspicuously distended. At the narrow end the strip of sheet gold has a perforation through which a wire is passed to secure the disk to the pendant.
Dimensions: length 4.3 (without disk); disk diameter 1.2
Weight: 40.0 (of total)
State of preservation: partly deformed, four items are fragmented

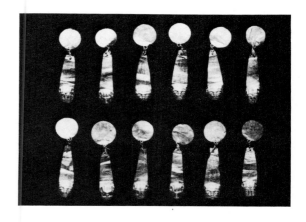

3.13
Pan-shaped plaques: large (150); medium (twenty-seven); and small (850)
Molded in the shape of circles having low rims, with two perforations for purposes of attachment.

Dimensions: large—diameter 1.0–1.2; rim height 0.2; medium—diameter 0.8–0.9; rim height 0.2; small—diameter 0.7–0.8; rim height 0.2
Weight: respectively 10.0; 5.0; 40.0 (of total)
State of preservation: the large plaques are partly deformed, the medium and small items are heavily deformed.

3.14 Ill. 7
Four-petaled rosettes (fifteen)
Manually cut and hence of varying size. Each has a loop soldered to the middle of the back for purposes of attachment.
Dimensions: width 2.3–2.0
Weight: 5.46 (of total)
State of preservation: the petals are heavily deformed and on three items partly fragmented.

237

3.15 Ill. 38
Medallions with busts (four)
Hollow round medallions with pendant disks attached to the sides. The convex obverse has been molded. The minute granulation along the rim encloses a circle composed of slightly inward-curved rectangles that surround a bust given in full face (for description turn to pp. 31, 32). Soldered to the reverse are round plates with four loops to allow it to be attached. The medallions also possess soldered-on side loops, secured to which are twisted wires with disks attached to their ends. The better-preserved specimen also has a third pendant in the shape of a cut-out leaf, from which it may be deduced tentatively that all four medallions originally had three pendants each.

> Dimensions: medallion diameter 2.6; disk diameter 1.6; length with pendant 4.0
> Weight: 21.0 (of total)
> State of preservation: some pendants missing

3.16
Torque
Cast in the shape of an open hoop with heavily flared ends.
> Dimensions: overall length 64.0; diameter of cross section at neck of hoop 0.5; diameter of cross section of flared terminals 2.0
> Weight: 765.18
> State of preservation: signs of wear

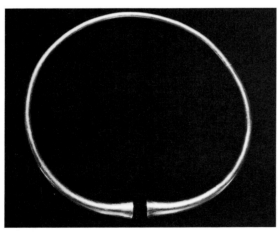

3.17
Bracelets (two)
Cast in the shape of an oval with open-ended, heavily flared ends.

Dimensions: overall length 23.1; diameter of cross section at neck of hoop 0.7; diameter of cross section of flared terminals 2.0
Weight: 290.0 (of one)
State of preservation: faint signs of wear

3.18 Ill. 141
Lidded pot for cosmetics
This cast flat-bottomed pot with an upright lip carries two loops soldered to its shoulders—one on either side—of twisted wire with coiled ends. Passed through both loops are two chains that are attached to the soldered-on ring-shaped handle of the pot's flat lid.

Dimensions: bottom diameter 1.2; body diameter 2.0; lip and lid diameter 1.5
Weight: 7.94
State of preservation: good

3.19
Three-pendant crescent
Attached to the cusps and center of the crescent, which was cut out of thin sheet gold, are open-worked pendants also of thin sheet gold. Part of the central pendant is missing; two of the pierced rays hemming the pierced figure have been broken off. This central pendant is secured to the crescent by a thin, braided chain, whose two ends are passed through the loops soldered to it and the crescent. The remaining rays have loops

with bits of gold chain at their tips, to which apparently more pendants had been fastened. Suspended from the cusps by thin wires passed through soldered-on loops and also through a loop soldered to the central pendant, are three more pendants of identical design; to judge by the smooth edges, these were punched out by a special die. Each has a pierced central lozenge sandwiched between two pairs of scrolls and, at the tip, a triangle with a pierced heart-shaped figure. The top of the crescent carries two soldered-on loops by means of which the entire piece was suspended.

Dimensions: crescent 5.8×1.6; thickness 0.03; overall height with pendants 7.3
Weight: 5.46
State of preservation: pendants are deformed and fragmented.

3.20
Crescent pendants (eight)
The knobs are cast, hollow and perforated, and are joined to the cast crescent-shaped pendant by a round neck-shaped piece. The crescent has indentations contoured by granulation and partly retaining insets of paste or turquoise. Soldered to the downward-curved cusps are loops through which spirally twisted wire has been passed to carry freely rotating miniature disks at the end.

Dimensions: crescent 1.8×1.9; overall height with disks 3.5
Weight: 9.78 (of one)
State of preservation: disks on three items and many insets missing

3.21
Looped disks (152)
Hand-cut from thin sheet gold. The soldered-on side loop enabled the disk to be attached to funerary garments.

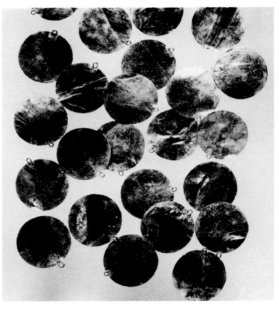

Average dimensions: diameter 3.0; thickness 0.2
Weight: 120.7 (of total)
State of preservation: many disks heavily deformed

3.22
Bowl
Cast of thin sheet gold and subsequently embossed, as is indicated by the traces of partially smoothed, hammered circles. The bottom of the bowl is strongly concave.
> Dimensions: diameter at the widest point 19.7; diameter of bottom 10.5; depth of hemispherical bottom 2.5
> Weight: 305.0

State of preservation: in the process of
hammering, cracks developed and in one place
a bit broke off; it was patched over by
soldering of thin sheet gold.

3.23
Chin stay
A long strip hand-cut from thin sheet gold. Broad at the
middle, it narrows toward both ends, each of which has four
perforations for purposes of attachment.
> Dimensions: length 36.3; width at center 4.0;
> at narrow ends 3.0; thickness 0.03
> Weight: 27.7
> State of preservation: partly deformed

3.24
Five-segmented crown
This open-worked crown, made from thin sheet gold, consists of five segments, each evenly pierced with rows of small
squares. Four are identically sized squares, and each bears
nine pierced squares. The fifth segment has fourteen rows of
three pierced squares each. The edges of all five segments
carry tiny perforations which may have also served to attach
pendants to the crown.

> Dimensions: large segment 33.0×8.2; thickness
> 0.03; small segment (the sole whole one)
> 8.3×8.0; thickness 0.03
> Weight: 76.5 (of total)
> State of preservation: only one segment is
> intact, the other four have been heavily gnawed
> by rodents.
> Reference: I. Rosenfield, *The Dynastic Arts of
> the Kushans*, Berkeley–Los Angeles, 1967,
> fig. 151.

3.25
Square plaques (fifty-four)
Stamped with raised rims and having two perforations at
opposite corners for purposes of attachment.
> Dimensions: 0.5×0.5; rim height 0.2
> Weight: 4.35 (of total)
> State of preservation: partly deformed

3.26
Triangular plaques with circlets (forty)
Stamped out of thin sheet gold with raised rims. Each has two
perforations for purposes of attachment. The apex of each
equilateral triangle carries an impressed convex circlet.
> Dimensions: side length 1.1; rim height 0.25
> Weight: 4.0 (of total)
> State of preservation: good

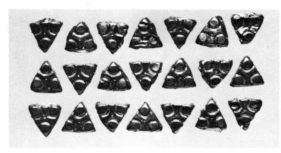

3.27 Ill. 8
"Volute" plaques (twenty-nine)
Stamped from thin sheet gold with perforations at the bases
for purposes of attachment.
> Dimensions: 0.9×0.9
> Weight: 0.77 (of total)
> State of preservation: some specimens heavily
> deformed

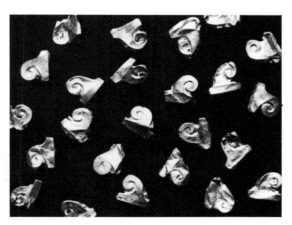

3.28
Large "butterfly" plaques (twenty-one)
Stamped in the shape of two symmetrically disposed pairs of
convex hemispheres with raised rims. Divided by a transversely ribbed central cylinder having perforations at either
end for purposes of attachment.
> Dimensions: 1.4×1.1
> Weight: 3.21 (of total)
> State of preservation: in places, cavities at the
> top of the hemispheres and on the cylinders

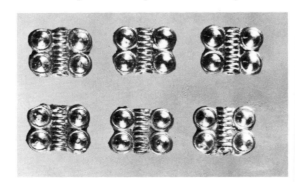

3.29
Small "butterfly" plaques (twenty-three)
Stamped in the shape of two symmetrically disposed pairs of
convex hemispheres divided by cylinders with transverse
ribbing. Each item has paired perforations for purposes of
attachment.
> Dimensions: 0.8×0.7
> Weight: 2.35 (of total)
> State of preservation: some specimens heavily
> deformed

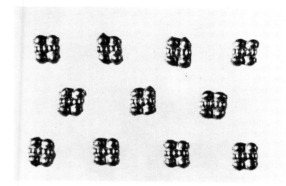

3.30
Large horned plaques (thirty-nine)
Cast in the shape of curved horns with two raised vertical
transversely incised stripes on the front. The rim has been
perforated twice on either side in complete longitudinal
opposition for purposes of attachment.
> Dimensions: 2.2×1.1; rim height 0.2
> Weight: 3.0 (of total)
> State of preservation: good

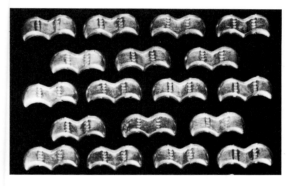

3.31
Small horned plaques (fifty-one)
Stamped in the shape of curved horns with two vertical
unornamented raised stripes on the front. The rim has been
perforated twice on either side in complete longitudinal
opposition for purposes of attachment.
> Dimensions: 1.1×0.4; rim height 0.15
> Weight: 2.93 (of total)
> State of preservation: good

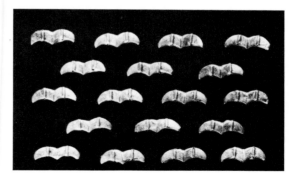

3.32
Fillets (ten) **and disks** (eighteen)
Of varying dimensions, hand-cut from thin sheet gold. The
fillets have rounded ends and are perforated for purposes of
attachment; only one is fully intact. Some disks still have
soldered-on loops with bits of wire attached.
> Dimensions: fillet (intact) 4.6×0.7;
> thickness 0.3; diameter of disks 1.0–1.5
> Weight: respectively of fillets and disks 4.2 and
> 3.8 (of total)
> State of preservation: heavily deformed and
> partly fragmented

239

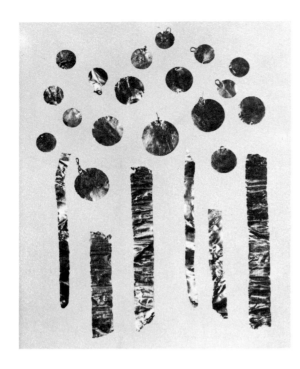

positioned on each rosette is a raised circle rimmed by minute granulation. A disk is attached by wire to the loop soldered to the tip of one of the five petals of each rosette. On the back are two tubes for purposes of attachment soldered on in such a manner as to be at right angles to the dangling disk.

Dimensions: length 3.0; rosette diameter 1.5; disk diameter 1.1
Weight: 13.39
State of preservation: partly deformed

3.38
Hemispherical plaques (500)
Die-stamped in molds in the shape of a hemisphere. All have two perforations at the edges for purposes of attachment.

Dimensions: diameter 0.8–0.7; height 0.3
Weight: 28.0 (of total)
State of preservation: partly deformed

3.33
Cinquefoil rosettes with bosses (two)
Hand-cut from thin sheet gold. Each petal is heart-shaped and has an impressed pair of bosses at its tip. Soldered to the middle of each rosette is a small circlet edged by minute granulation. Also soldered to two opposite petals are eyelets with small, freely rotating disks attached to them by gold wire bent at the ends. Soldered to the back of each rosette are two tubes to allow it to be attached.

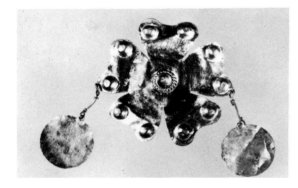

3.35, 36
Cones with disks (forty-one large and eighteen small)
Each stamped cone has at its apex a soldered-on loop to which a freely rotating disk is attached by a thin wire bent at each end.

Dimensions: large cones—overall length 3.0; cone diameter 1.4; average disk diameter 1.2 (2.0 for largest specimen); small cones—overall length 2.1; cone diameter 1.1; average disk diameter 0.9
Weight: respectively 52.0 and 7.3 (of total)
State of preservation: partly deformed

3.39 Ill. 133
Round plaques with granulation and turquoise inlays (fifty-two)
Each is cast in the form of a small roundel rimmed by a soldered-on ring edged with minute granulation. Set within each ring is a convex hemispherical turquoise bead; in some specimens the cells still contain a black-paste inlay. Soldered to the backs are two tubes for purposes of attachment. Fourteen plaques are inlaid with turquoise, eighteen with paste, and the remainder with an as yet undefined material.

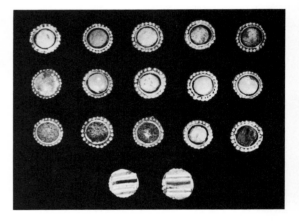

Dimensions: diameter of petal 4.4; diameter of disk 1.7
Weight: 12.65
State of preservation: partly deformed petals

Dimensions: diameter 0.6
Weight: 0.5 (one of the items); 14.66 (of total)
State of preservation: some insets missing

3.34
Cinquefoil rosettes with disks (twenty)
Hand-cut from thin sheet gold. Each petal is heart-shaped and has a pair of grains soldered to its tips. Centrally

3.37
Large cones with raised rims and disks (eighty)
Stamped and edged by raised rims at the bases. At the tips both outside and inside are soldered-on loops. Attached to the outside loops are freely rotating disks, each having a soldered-on eyelet.

Average dimensions: cone diameter 1.2; height with loop 0.8; disk diameter 1.0
Weight: 1.6 (one of the items); 70.0 (of total)
State of preservation: partly deformed

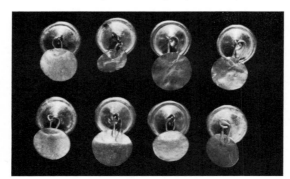

3.40
Two shoe soles
Hand-cut from thin gold sheet. The toe has one perforation and the heel two perforations for purposes of attachment.

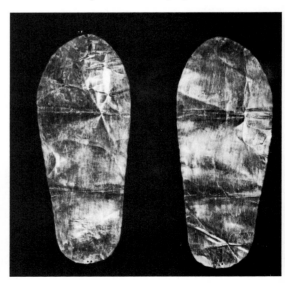

Dimensions: 22.5×8.7
Weight: 47.0 (of total)
State of preservation: good

3.41 Ill. 141
Vessel with an inscription in Greek

Comprised of three segments: bottom, cylindrical body, and lid with handle. The body is whole-cast and is embellished around the middle with a raised horizontal band of laurels, each of which is bound at the base by a curved thong. Rising out of each trefoil is a pair of tendrils that terminate in circles. The separately cast bottom has been soldered to the body, as evidenced by the horizontal stripe along the soldering line. On the bottom are three concentric circles: toward the edge is an inscription in Greek of small dots made by a punch. The inscription reads, "CTAETB," which most likely designates the vessel's weight of "five staters and two drachmae." As the stater tips the scales at just over half an ounce (approximately 17.5 g), this adds up to about three ounces (86.0 g). The lid is embellished with the same ornamental design as the body of the vessel. The protruding handle is topped by a finial or pommel whose shape is reminiscent of a pomegranate; it

carries an embossed ornamental design along the rim. The round loops, one of which is soldered to the lid and the other to the body, are linked by a braided gold chain.

Dimensions: height 5.5; diameter 5.6
Weight: 86.0
State of preservation: faint signs of wear
Reference: E. Saclio, *Dictionnaire des antiquités grecques et romaines*, vol. II, Paris, 1926, no. 7145

3.42
Flat bells (six)

Arc-shaped and cut from thin gold sheet. Each bell is hollow and is comprised of two plates that have been soldered together. Inside is a transverse prong from which a small clapper freely rotates. At the top of each item is a soldered-on loop in the form of a circle with a "foot" for purposes of attachment. Both planes carry an impressed design that is S-shaped on one and crescent-shaped on the other.

Dimensions: 1.6×1.0×0.5
Weight: 9.89 (of total)
State of preservation: partly deformed

3.43 Ill. 126
Pennant-shaped plaques (twenty-five)

Each is cast and consists of an indented circle and two triangles. The circle has a raised rim encrusted with a white paste over which black paste has been superimposed, leaving a white eye in the middle. On two plaques the triangles have been inlaid with turquoise. All insets have been mounted with the aid of an adhesive mass, as is indicated by the remaining traces of some red substance. Soldered to each plaque along the longitudinal axis are two tubes to enable it to be attached.

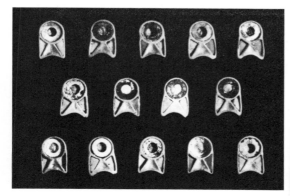

Dimensions: 1.4×0.9
Weight: 34.33 (of total)
State of preservation: partly crumbled encrustation

3.44
Six-pointed star

Hand-cut from thin gold sheet, with a hole punched through its middle. Along its rim perforations have been pierced for purposes of attachment. The tips of the points are slightly curved.

Dimensions: star diameter 5.0; hole diameter 1.2
Weight: 1.68
State of preservation: partly deformed

3.45
Pair of carrot-shaped clasps

Identically shaped and contoured by minute granulation. Inset in the middle are two round and one triangular turquoise inlays. Soldered to one clasp is a hook, and to the other a loop, by means of which the pair were fastened. Also soldered to the back of each clasp are three loops for purposes of attachment.

Dimensions: length 2.2
Weight: 3.86 (of pair)
State of preservation: faint signs of wear

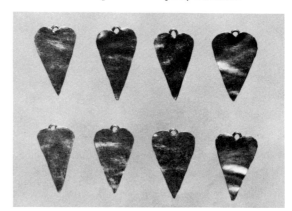

3.46
Heart-shaped pendants (eight)

Hand-cut from thin gold sheet in the shape of an elongated heart, soldered to whose base is a loop for purposes of attachment.

Dimensions: 1.8×1.0
Weight: 3.11 (of total)
State of preservation: partly deformed

3.47 Ill. 130
Gold Roman coin

The obverse bears the profile of the wreathed head of Tiberius facing right; in the field is an inscription in Latin which reads in translation: "Caesar Tiberius son of the Divine Augustus." On the reverse is a draped, seated female figure in profile facing right; in her right hand she holds a scepter and in her left hand a branch; the inscription in Latin in the field reads: "Great Pontifex."

Dimensions: diameter 1.9; thickness 0.25
Weight: 7.77
State of preservation: good

3.48 Ill. 127
Silver Parthian coin

The obverse carries the head of a bearded man in profile facing left; he wears a diadem that is indicated by a circlet of dots. Shown on the reverse is an enthroned figure holding a bow in the right outstretched hand; around the rim is an inscription in Greek.

Dimensions: diameter 2.2; thickness 0.2
Weight: 3.46
State of preservation: good
Reference: V. Sarianidi, G. Koshelenko, "Coins from the Excavations of the Necropolis on the Tillya-Tepe Site," *Ancient India. Historical and Cultural Relations*, Moscow, 1982
[В. Сарианиди, Г. Кошеленко, "Монеты из раскопок некрополя, расположенного на городище Тилля-Тепе," в кн.: *Древняя Индия. Историко-культурные связи*, Москва, 1982].

3.49
Gold-mounted iron dagger handle

The smaller of the two cast gold mounts or fittings is a truncated hollow cone, the surface of which is embellished with two horizontal registers. The upper one is composed of turquoise-inlaid triangles with facing apexes; the lower one is formed of a chain of turquoise-inset semi-ovals separated by small triangles inlaid with lapis lazuli. The second fitting is cylinder-shaped and its surface is embellished with three horizontal registers. The upper one consists of a series of turquoise-inset triangles with facing apexes, each of which is bisected by a horizontally positioned wire; the central register is formed of turquoise-inlaid heart-shaped cloisons separated by small triangles encrusted with lapis lazuli; the third, lowest, register is comprised of a chain of semi-ovals inlaid with turquoise and separated by small triangles inlaid with lapis lazuli. This second fitting also has a perforation in the shape of an elongated triangle with one extremely sharp angle that had apparently been made to take the dagger's iron blade. It was also set on an iron tang carrying traces of wood, and, together with the smaller mount, had evidently served to embellish the iron dagger handle.

Dimensions: smaller fitting 1.2×0.8; diameters 1.2 and 0.8; larger fitting—height 1.5; diameters 1.3 and 1.2
Weight: 10.00 (together with iron haft)
State of preservation: iron rusted and some insets missing

3.50 Ills. 40, 41
Temple pendant with protomas of a horse

Cast, with a raised front and with turquoise and paste inlays. The compositional arrangement is pivoted around two horse protomas, one the mirror image of the other (for description turn to pp. 28, 29). On its upper part the pendant has a groove along its outer rim. So that it can be suspended the ring is mounted on a foot embellished at either end with two circlets of minute granulation. The foot is soldered to a triangle of three cells for inlaying; however, only one of the insets, a gemstone of a dark brown, is extant. On its back the pendant has five soldered-on eyelets at the bottom; attached to them are chains terminating in twisted wire from which tiny disks dangle. Another two chains, each made of three linked heart-shaped figures, droop from the horses' noses and end in hand-cut sculptured leaves. The back of the pendant consists of a thin plate cut in such a manner as to duplicate the outline of the front; the back and front are soldered together.

Dimensions: 8.6×4.6
Weight: 23.0
State of preservation: signs of wear on the back

3.51 Ill. 19
Hairpins (two)

The hairpins are identical and have gold finials atop shafts of silver. The finials are shaped like large twelve-petaled rosettes comprised of an alternating design of six plain leaves that end in loops and six raised leaves whose tips are slightly bent inward. Within the large rosette is a smaller six-petaled one, which also has curled-in tips and raised veins on each petal. In turn, this rosette has inscribed within it a tiny, raised, also six-petaled rosette, again with inward-bent tips marked by tiny perforations. Finally we come to an indented circle at the middle, which is edged by a miniature five-lobed rosette. The loops along the finial's perimeter still have bits of twisted gold wire from which, apparently, small disks had originally been suspended.

Dimensions: diameter 7.5; extant shaft length 4.5
Weight: 50.69 (of both)
State of preservation: silver shafts are partly broken off.

3.52
Lyre-shaped clasps (two)

Both are cast, plain, and have four loops soldered to their backs for purposes of attachment. Also, each has a larger loop whose ends have been twisted into a spiral and soldered to the back.

Dimensions: 4.2×3.8; thickness 0.1
Weight: 27.75 (of pair)
State of preservation: signs of wear on the face and partly deformed

3.53
Finger ring

Cast, plain, and embellished with a punched design comprised of a circle with a centrally positioned dot that is sandwiched between two pear-shaped figures with a series of straight short lines down the middle.

Dimensions: outer diameter 1.6; inner diameter 1.4
Weight: 3.48
State of preservation: strong signs of wear

3.54
Round buckles (two)

Cast rings with jutting mushroom-shaped prongs.
Dimensions: diameter 1.9; thicknesses 0.4 and 0.2 at wider and narrower worn ends; height of prong together with ring 0.9
Weight: 20.87 (of both)

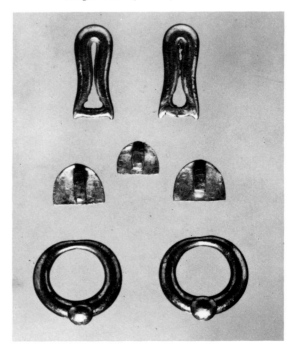

State of preservation: the narrower sections show signs of heavy wear.

Buckle details (three)
Cast, flat, semicircular, with rectangular loops on the back.
Dimensions: 1.1×0.9×0.6
Weight: 5.0 (of three)
State of preservation: signs of wear

Pair of buckles
Cast, elongated, and round at one end. Each has a pair of spikes at the other end.
Dimensions: 2.1×0.8×0.5
Weight: 14.0 (of both)
State of preservation: ends show signs of wear.

3.55
Rectangular plaques with round tops (three)
Cast in the form of elongated rectangular cloisons inlaid with black paste, with a hollow hemisphere at one end and an indented side at the other. Four tubes have been soldered to the back for purposes of attachment.
Dimensions: 1.6×0.5×0.3
Weight: 2.94 (of three)
State of preservation: almost entire paste inlay missing

3.56 Ill. 142
Ivory comb (five fragments)
Only two fragments can be fitted together. Of the apparently five original teeth, only one has retained its initial shape with a broad flat and pointed end. Both sides are finely engraved, with the distinctly marked half-length figure of a human being (for description turn to p. 33) on one side. Otherwise the entire design is so extensively fragmented on both sides that it is hard to decipher.
Dimensions: length 5.0; thickness 0.4
State of preservation: fragmented with segments missing
References: G. Pugachenkova, *Dalverzin-tepe, a Kushan City in South Uzbekistan*, Tashkent, 1978, fig. 154 [Г. Пугаченкова, *Дальверзин Тепе—Кушанский город на юге Узбекистана*, Ташкент, 1978, рис. 154]; I. Hacin, *Nouvelles recherches archéologiques à Beagram*, Paris, 1954.

3.57 Ill. 57
One-loop fittings (seventeen)
Of varied form, all are cast, and each has a soldered-on loop. In some cases the mounted gemstones are extant, including one that is translucent and of a pale violet in color—either an amethyst or garnet. Nearly all, whether oval, round, lozenge, or triangular in shape, show heavy signs of wear. Conspicuous among the fittings is a large one with a sawtooth edging that is inset with a white gemstone perforated in the middle and filled with a splinter of the same type of stone.
Dimensions: varied
Weight: varied
State of preservation: distinct signs of wear

3.58
Two-loop fittings (eleven) **and one-loop fittings** (ten)
All are cast and the loops are soldered on. Most are of a hollow cylindrical shape often with a sealed end. One is marked by three triangular perforations down the side, another is in the shape of a lozenge pendant with an iron core inside.
Dimensions: varied, 1.1 to 1.6
Weight: varied
State of preservation: signs of wear with many insets missing

3.59
Beads with oval insets (five)
All are cast and hollow and have holes bored along the longitudinal axis for thread to pass through. All are inset with large gemstones, except for one which is inset with a lump of iron.

Dimensions: (with green stone inset) 2.2×1.6×1.1; (with brown shale inset) 2.2×1.6×0.9; (with brown stone inset) 2.2×1.7×1.0; (with iron inset) 2.2×1.5×1.3; (with dark-green vitreous inset) 2.2×1.7×0.9
State of preservation: heavy signs of wear

3.60 Ill. 111
Signet ring with the engraved figure of a priest
Hollow with a bezel presumably of turquoise that carries an engraved human figure draped in folds (for description turn to p. 32).
Dimensions: 2.3×2.0; of bezel 1.6×1.1
Weight: 10.14
State of preservation: heavy signs of wear on gemstone bezel
Reference: H. B. Walters, *Catalogue of the Engraved Gems and Cameos, Greek, Etruscan and Roman, in the British Museum*, London, 1926, pl. XXIII, no. 1726.

3.61
Signet ring with inset vitreous mass
Hollow. The engraving on the small convex bezel cannot be deciphered because of strong iridescence.
Dimensions: 2.2×2.2; of bezel 1.2×0.9
Weight: 7.92

3.62 Ill. 70
Zebu intaglio
Carved from a semi-translucent light-brown gemstone in the shape of a hemisphere and bored along the longitudinal axis. Incised on the flat, oval side is a humped zebu with its right forepaw raised in profile facing left.

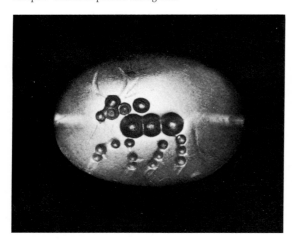

Dimensions: 2.1×1.6×1.0
Weight: 4.58
State of preservation: signs of heavy wear on front

3.63
Etched cornelian bead
Carved from a reddish cornelian in the form of an elongated octagon. Each facet is lozenge-shaped and bored along the longitudinal axis for future threading. The bead is etched with a geometrical design composed of symmetrically disposed rings alternating with zigzags. The central part of the design consists of two rows of rectangles incised with large Xs.
Dimensions: 3.7×1.2
State of preservation: signs of wear

Etched cornelian bead
The waist is girdled by six lozenge-shaped facets followed at each end by six more triangular facets, all edged with white lines, the whole sandwiched between two rings at either end.
Dimensions: 1.7×1.0
State of preservation: signs of wear

Etched cylindrical cornelian beads (two)
Both are bored along the longitudinal axis for future threading and are etched with a design of concentric circular stripes.
Dimensions: 1.8×0.8 and 1.2×0.7
State of preservation: signs of wear

3.64
Beads and pendants (ten)
Carved from diverse gemstones, mostly turquoise and cornelian, all are bored for threading. One, of faience (?), is cylindrical and has been bored along the longitudinal axis. The surface bears the imprints of cloth.
Dimensions: varied, 0.6 to 1.5
State of preservation: signs of wear

Dimensions: diameter 0.6 (of each)
Three hard-stone ornaments and one lead item
Dimensions: varied, 0.9 to 1.9
State of preservation: signs of wear

3.65
Beads, pendants, and astragal (eleven)
Of diverse shape and form and carved from diverse hard stones. Among them one is ax-shaped and of turquoise, another is in the form of an astragal. All are bored along the longitudinal axis for threading.
Dimensions: varied, 0.5 to 1.7
State of preservation: good

3.66
Four small turquoise beads
Round, flat, and pierced through the middle.

3.67
Pins (two)
One has a silver shaft with a round cross section and a partly preserved round head coated with gold foil with three soldered-on eyelets. The second also has a silver shaft but of a rectangular cross section, and a round iron head coated with gold foil. The two pins shown on the right were recovered from Burial Site 6.

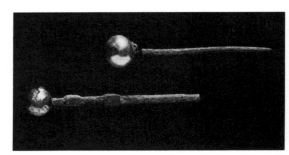

Dimensions: length of first pin 6.0; diameter of head 1.1; length of second pin 5.7; diameter of head 1.2
Weight: 7.8 (of both)

3.68
Gold-mounted tusks (two)
Presumably boar tusks, they are of a dark brown and are well polished; the broad bases are mounted in gold fittings having soldered-on loops on top for purposes of attachment; the tips are slightly bent.

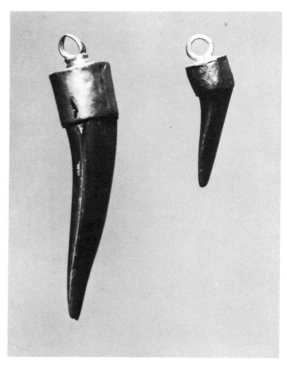

Dimensions: 5.1×1.1 and 2.7×0.7
Weight: 7.55 (of both)
State of preservation: the tip of one tusk is broken off.

3.69 Ill. 135
Silver bowl
Hemispherical, of an inferior grade of silver. The lip, which has been pressed in, has had a scalloped edging of high-grade silver ornamented with a design of elongated hemispheres turned upside down hammered onto it.
Dimensions: diameter 12.0; height 7.4
Weight: 140.0
State of preservation: bottom missing and covered with a green patina

3.70
Chinese mirror

Round and of an inferior grade of silver. The front is flat, the back has a raised rim and a centrally positioned hemispherical pierced handle. The central eight-pointed star is bordered by a circular band carrying an inscription in Chinese characters.

Dimensions: diameter 18.0; rim thickness 0.6
State of preservation: covered with a green patina

3.71 Ill. 144
Mirror with handle

Disk-shaped with a side shaft that widens toward the end. Traces of the nails employed to secure a massive ivory handle have been preserved. The front is flat, and the back has a broad, raised rim and a massive, hemispherical applied blob. The handle has two annular incisions at the top and bottom and a broad end.

Dimensions: mirror diameter 12.3; shaft length 4.5; rim height 1.2
State of preservation: demolished handle

3.72 Ill. 61
Rimmed beads (four)

Of faience and rimmed in the middle by a band composed of two gold wires sandwiching—on two—a series of triangles and—on the other two—a series of rectangles picked out by gold wire and inlaid with turquoise. All four are bored in the middle; set in the perforations are the remnants of fragmented small bronze tubes that were meant for future threading.

Dimensions: 2.3×2.1; band width 0.4; tube diameter 0.5

Plain gold beads (five)

Cast, hollow, and bored for threading.

Dimensions: 2.1×1.9
Weight: 47.0 (of total)
State of preservation: signs of wear

Beads with granulation (eight)

Hollow and slightly flattened at either end. The surfaces are covered with minute grains of gold to create a webbed netting. All are bored for threading.

Dimensions: 1.9×1.6
Weight: 91.36 (of total)
State of preservation: signs of wear

Pair of cone-shaped clasps

Hollow with surface ornamentation. Toward the base is a band of minute but deep indentations. Next, higher up, comes a series of large triangles originally embellished with minute bosses that have been almost completely erased due to use. Meeting these triangles is a series of smaller triangles with spear-shaped apexes pointing downward. Still further up, toward the tip, is another row of even smaller triangles, also with spear-shaped apexes and covered with tiny bosses. The top row is of tiny triangles as well, with apexes pointed down and separated from the previous series of triangles by raised bosses. Both clasps are bored along the longitudinal axis for purposes of attachment.

Dimensions: length 4.0; diameter at tip 0.5; diameter at base 1.8
Weight: 34.0 (of pair)
State of preservation: strong signs of wear
All the above items initially comprised one necklace.

3.73 Ill. 140
Basin

A large utensil of an inferior grade of silver on a tall base with a round body and an upright rim. A broad, flat lip with its edges turned down is soldered to the rim.

Dimensions: lip diameter 22.5, height 13.5, base diameter 13.5; base height 1.2
State of preservation: covered with a green patina

3.74
Two-handled jug

Ceramic, with a wide throat and a conspicuous lip. The body broadens out to the middle, and the bottom is flat. Beneath one handle is the impression of a bust-length human figure.

Dimensions: lip diameter 12.0, height 39.0; bottom diameter 12.5; handle width 3.0
State of preservation: good

3.75 Ill. 31
Round objects with flared ends (two)

Shaped as small bracelets, whose designation is obscure. The flared ends and narrow loops show signs of wear, which implies that they may have been employed as buckles.

Dimensions: length 7.0; terminal cross section diameter 1.1; loop cross section diameter 0.5
Weight: 65.0 (of both)

3.76
Button-shaped plaques (eighteen)

Hollow spheres contrived of two hemispheres soldered together. Some loops are soldered to a "foot," by means of which the plaques were sewn on.

Dimensions: diameter 0.8; height 1.1
Weight: 11.0 (of total)
State of preservation: partly deformed

3.77
Minute spherical plaques (sixty)
A tiny loop is soldered to a "foot" of each hollow ball and serves for purposes of attachment.

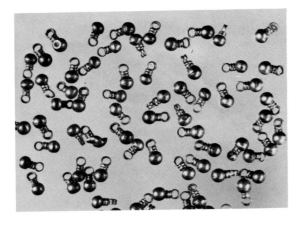

Dimensions: diameter 0.4; height 0.7
Weight: 14.5 (of total)
State of preservation: good

3.78 Ill. 73
Pendant with representation of Athena
A massive cast oval, carrying on the back four loops for purposes of attachment. The obverse depicts a draped standing female figure holding a shield and a spear. In the field is the mirror image of the goddess' name in Greek.

Dimensions: 1.6×1.2×0.6
Weight: 8.0
State of preservation: the obverse shows heavy signs of wear.

3.79
Lidded silver pot
Flat-bottomed, of a cylindrical shape slightly tapering toward the top. The lid is embellished in the middle with a tall, sculptured handle.

Dimensions: height 10.0; bottom diameter 6.3
State of preservation: heavily deformed when found; shown after restoration.

SITE 4

4.1 Ill. 124
Round "dragons chariot" shoe buckles (two)
Cast openwork with the design on one of the pair a mirror image of the other. The raised rim is encrusted with two rows of convex, almond-shaped turquoise beads mounted in a herringbone pattern. Sandwiched between them is a narrow strip of gold. Protruding from the rim is a mushroom-shaped prong on whose shaft the leather straps that were used have left signs of wear. Depicted within the circle is a man driving a chariot to which dragons have been harnessed (for description turn to pp. 41, 42). Still visible on the back is the imprint of the cloth employed in the casting process, which recalls similar traces on some of the items in the Siberian collection of Peter the Great to be seen in the Hermitage, Leningrad. Also on the back are four tall loops that served to attach the buckles to the footwear.

Dimensions: diameter 5.5; height 1.1
Weight: 125.16 and 125.9
State of preservation: distinct signs of wear on the front
Reference: *Cultural Monuments of Ancient China*, Peking, 1962, fig. 226 (in Chinese).

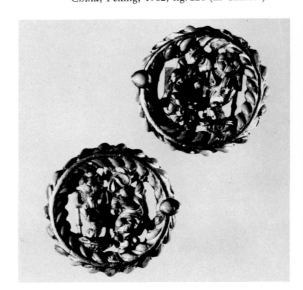

4.2 Ills. 88–97
Gold belt
Braided of gold thread in eight rows and comprised of eight segments linked together by nine hollow plaques cast in almost round high relief. The plain rim of each plaque has on top a ring of minute granulation, contoured by two concen-

246

tric circles of semi-oval cells, but with no inlays. They in turn enclose the basic ornamental design which is the same for all nine plaques, that depicts a female figure riding a lion (for description turn to p. 38). The two end plaques, which serve as clasps, present the design in its mirror image, while the other seven must have been cast separately, as each representation is given at a slightly different angle. Soldered to either edge of each plaque are hollow rectangular fittings into which the braided segments comprising the belt have been firmly imbedded; however, one of the plaques has in place of one such fittings a hollow, ornamented protuberance with five loops inside; inserted through these is a prong by means of which the end plaques were buckled by a special strap.

Dimensions: length 97.6; width 2.0; plaque diameter 4.0
Weight: 840.0
State of preservation: faint signs of wear
References: K. Akishev, *The Issyk Barrow*, Moscow, 1978 [К. Акишев, *Курган Иссык*, Москва, 1978]; I. Rosenfield, *The Dynastic Arts of the Kushans*, Berkeley–Los Angeles, 1967, p. 910.

4.3 Ill. 112–120
Figurine of an ibex
Hollow cast. The animal is depicted standing on all four legs with its front legs straight and its hind legs slightly bent. Its head, with its well-marked web of bulging veins, is crowned by a pair of coiled, knobby horns thrown backward. Its muzzle is slightly pointed, its small eyeballs protrude, its nostrils are splayed, and the mouth is half-open. The entire body is covered with fine indentations intended to represent the fleece; a gently curling, long, thick beard descends down the front of its neck. The well-modeled hooves rest on rings by which the figurine was attached; between the horns is a tall, hollow tube into which the prong or tang of some other item may have been inserted.
Dimensions: height 5.2; length 4.0
Weight: 18.1
State of preservation: good
Reference: I. Tolstoi, N. Kondakov, *Russian Antiquities in Art Relics*, St Petersburg, 1890, issue 3, figs. 152, 153 [И. Толстой, Н. Кондаков, *Русские древности в памятниках искусства*, С.-Петербург, 1890, вып. 3, рис. 152, 153].

4.4 Ill. 98
Plaques with representations of panthers (two)
Flat, cast, slightly tapering towards one rounded end. The other end is hollow and has a transversely disposed prong inside for purposes of attachment. The back is flat. Portrayed in relief on the front is a crouching predator, presumably a panther, with an elongated head, open jaws, and flattened-back ears. The front legs are stretched out and lie under the head; the hindquarters are unnaturally contorted. The long tail is compressed beneath the belly. On both the front and back the wider end terminates in square cells inset with square plates that hide the aforementioned prong.

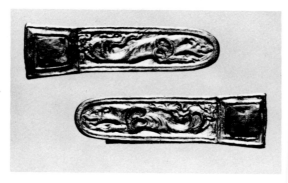

Dimensions: (of both) length 4.0; end widths 1.2 and 0.8
Weight: 10.35 and 14.47
State of preservation: obverses show heavy signs of wear.
Reference: S. Rudenko, *The Culture of the Population of the High Altai in the Scythian Period*, Moscow–Leningrad, 1953, table IV, nos. 8–9 [С. И. Руденко, *Культура населения горного Алтая в скифское время*, Москва–Ленинград, 1953, табл. IV, № 8–9].

4.5 Ill. 148
Phalera with representation of a beast biting its tail
A hemispherical cast plaque with a transverse prong with a flat cross section used for fastening, within remnants of well-preserved leather. Depicted in high relief is a fantastic winged creature coiled into a ring and biting its own tail. Its eyes stare menacingly, its jaws are spread wide open, and its thick, wrinkled nose displays distinctly modeled nostrils. Two taloned paws protrude from beneath its neck. Stretching from its tangled mane is a sharply bent wing with well-articulated plumage that has a round turquoise inset at the base. The sinuous body is coiled into a ring, as was noted, with its tail thrust between its hind legs and ending in the beast's jaws.
Dimensions: diameter 2.6; height 1.2
Weight: 7.65
State of preservation: heavy signs of wear
Reference: S. Rudenko, "The Siberian Collection of Peter I," *Reports of the Institute of Archaeology*, Moscow–Leningrad, 1962, table XXIII, nos. 23–25 [С. И. Руденко, *Сибирская коллекция Петра I, САИ*, Москва–Ленинград, 1962, табл. XXIII, № 23–25].

4.6 Ills. 149, 150
Phalerae with representations of a beast coiled into a circle (three)
Almost round, cast, with a transversely disposed prong soldered to the middle, and with remnants of leather inside. The fantastic creature is of the eagle-griffin type. The visage displays a vulpine curved beak, bulging, knobby brows, and laid-back ears. Running down its spine is a raised stripe denoting the crest; the toothed edging beneath the belly serves to convey the cropped underhair. The cells on the flanks, which were most likely designed to be inset with turquoise, denote a pair of wings laid flat together along the back; the front legs with their unsheathed, curled claws are thrust forward. The hind legs are tucked in under the belly, and the furry tail is concealed between the paws also under the belly.

Dimensions: diameter 1.8; orifice diameter 1.2
Weight: 47.7 (of all three)
State of preservation: heavy signs of wear
Reference: A. Mantsevich, "Find in the Zaporozhye Barrow," *The Scytho-Siberian Animal Style in the Art of the Peoples of Eurasia*, Moscow, 1976, pp. 182–187 [А. П. Манцевич, "Находка в Запорожском кургане," в сб.: *Скифо-сибирский звериный стиль в искусстве народов Евразии*, Москва, 1976, с. 182–187].

4.7 Ills. 151, 152
Phalerae depicting a beast biting its paw (two)
Both cast in the round and in relief in the form of a coiled beast of prey with snarling jaws, wrinkled nostrils, and laid-back ears. Wings sprout from its back, the unsheathed three talons on its paws are tense, and the sinuous tail curls into a loop at the tip. Its long body, embellished with deeply indented cells possibly intended to hold inlays, is contorted; its front legs are thrust out. Its right hind leg is compressed under its belly, while its left hind paw is stretched back and inserted between the creature's jaws. One can gather from minor details that the two phalerae were cast in different molds.

Dimensions: diameters 2.2 and 2.1; heights 1.8 and 1.7; orifice diameters 1.1 and 1.4
Weight: 14.0 (of both)
State of preservation: worn down to cavities

4.8 Ills. 157–161
Gold-handled dagger and sheath ornamented with scenes of the mauling of animals
The iron double-edged blade, lozenge-shaped in cross section—which has a gold-mounted hilt—was found in a wooden scabbard covered with leather, of which the obverse was also embellished with a gold plating. The scabbard has two pairs of plates with "snap-on buttons" in the form of a

disk-shaped head with two wires attached. Passed through the plates and leather casing, the wires were bent aside to thus secure the gold plating to the scabbard. The plating itself is cast in high relief and is edged with a plant design consisting of meandering tendrils encrusted with small turquoise beads. Enclosed between this frame, which runs along the entire length of the sheath, is the basic composition depicting five beasts mauling one another (for description turn to pp. 38, 39). The composition is carried over onto the gold plating of the hilt which has a plain cross guard, a rather long grip, and a round pommel. Like the sheath, the hilt is encrusted with turquoise beads that are round on the grip and almond-shaped on the pommel; the ornament depicts two beasts mauling one another and, separately, a bear holding a vine (for description turn to p. 39).

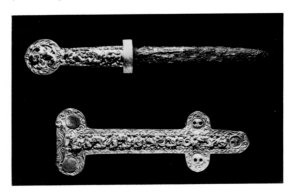

Dimensions: overall length 37.5
Weight: sheath 188.1; dagger 245.85
State of preservation: some turquoise insets missing; only two of the original five "snap-on buttons" extant
References: M. Artamonov, *Treasures of the Sakas*, Moscow, 1973, fig. 213
[М. И. Артамонов, *Сокровища саков*, Москва, 1973, рис. 213]; R. Ghirshman, *Iran, Parthes et Sassanides*, Paris, 1962, figs. 78–80.

4.9 Ills. 162–166
Sheath with scene of two dragons
The sheath has an elongated bronze plate with rounded ends—one broad, the other narrower—and two side attachments. Inserted into the central convex portion is the iron blade of a dagger possessing a carved ivory hilt with two transverse gold mounts; the dagger's tip is further secured in the sheath by a smaller bronze plate set crosswise to the other. On the front of the scabbard's bronze base is a gold mount, one of whose plates has still retained its fastening. The gold mount is cast and embellished along the entire border—

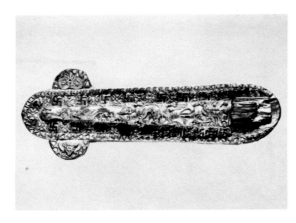

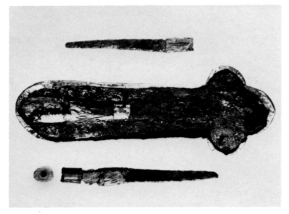

except for the top of the ivory hilt—with convex heart-shaped turquoise inlays set in deeply indented cells. The sides of the convex central part are ornamented with a design of swastikas alternating with quatrefoil rosettes. Also to be found here—executed in high relief along the longitudinal axis—is the scene of two fantastic creatures mauling one another (for description turn to pp. 39, 40). Besides the main one-edged dagger, another two smaller daggers could be inserted into the leather sheathing on the back of the scabbard (for description turn to pp. 40, 41).

Dimensions: scabbard length 26.0; scabbard widths 5.0 and 6.0 (at either end); dagger overall length 23.0; haft length 11.0; widths of haft fittings 1.8 (lower) and 2.8 (upper)
Weight: 196.5 (of dagger, scabbard, and bronze plating)
State of preservation: some turquoise insets missing
Dimensions of small daggers: overall lengths 20.5 and 25.0; haft lengths 5.0 and 10.0
State of preservation: heavily corroded blades and damaged ivory hilts

4.10 Ills. 68, 69
Pectoral with cameo
Contrived of two thick gold wires interlaced to form a series of irregular loops that have been soldered together where the wires intersect. From the two miniature loops on the ends, which were fastened at the nape of the neck by means of a bent pin, the loops gradually expand in size toward the middle where, by means of small loops and gold prongs, they are linked to the center cameo set in an oval gold mount contoured by two rows of minute granulation. As the cameo is secured to the chain in such a manner as to present the engraved image sideways, this would seem to suggest that the cameo had originally been worn differently. The cameo itself is of two-layered stone with the image carved in brown on a white ground (for description turn to pp. 37, 38). Soldered to the back of the gold mount is a plate cut so as to duplicate the outline of the front.

Dimensions: total length 65.0; diameter 21.0; cameo 4.0×3.5×0.7
Weight: 165.5
State of preservation: cameo mount deformed
Reference: G. Pugachenkova, *The Art Treasures of Dalverzin-tepe*, Leningrad, 1978, tables 78, 79 [Г. А. Пугаченкова, *Художественные сокровища Дальверзин-тепе*, Ленинград, 1978, табл. 78, 79]

4.11 Ill. 2
Sewn-on tubes (508)
Rolled of thin sheet gold and carefully soldered together.
Dimensions: average length 1.1; diameter 0.2
Weight: 69.49 (of total)
State of preservation: good

4.12 Ill. 1
Eight-lobed rosettes (555)
Stamped, with a central convex hemisphere and two perforations pierced on opposite sides of the rim for purposes of attachment.

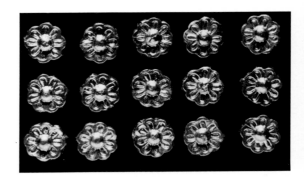

Dimensions: diameter 1.3; height 0.15
Weight: 86.0 (of total)
State of preservation: signs of wear in places

4.13 Ill. 6
Square plaques with hearts design (454)
Stamped in the form of squares; inscribed in relief is a rosette consisting of four heart-shaped petals divided by straight lines. Perforations have been pierced in the corners along the edge for purposes of attachment.

Dimensions: 1.4×1.4; rim height 0.2
Weight: 90.0 (of total)
State of preservation: some pieces are deformed

4.14 Ill. 30
Square plaques with central circlets (158)
Stamped in the form of squares; inscribed in relief is a four-lobed rosette comprised of a central circlet and paired semi-ovals; the square as such is diagonally intersected by a straight line. Two pairs of perforations have been pierced on opposite sides for purposes of attachment.
Dimensions: 1.0×1.0; rim height 0.2
Weight: 23.0 (of total)
State of preservation: faint signs of wear

4.15 Ill. 4
Disks (fifty)
Hand-cut from thin sheet gold and perforated on one side for purposes of attachment.
Dimensions: diameter 3.6–3.8
Weight: 56.28 (of total)
State of preservation: partly deformed

4.16 Ill. 5
"Butterfly" plaques (676)
Stamped in the form of two pairs of raised circlets divided down the middle by a raised double row of minute squares. Perforations have been made in all four corners for purposes of attachment.

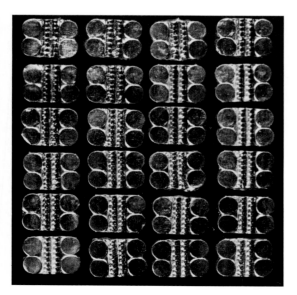

Dimensions: 1.9×1.3×0.2
Weight: 183.8 (of total)
State of preservation: faint signs of wear

4.17
Pan-shaped plaques (368)
Stamped in mold with the rim perforated in two places for purposes of attachment.
Dimensions: diameter 1.1; rim height 0.2
Weight: 48.82 (of total)
State of preservation: partly deformed

4.18
Hemispherical plaquettes (392)
Stamped in mold with two perforations opposite each other along the edge for purposes of attachment.
Dimensions: diameter 1.0; height 0.4
Weight: 126.0 (of total)
State of preservation: partly deformed

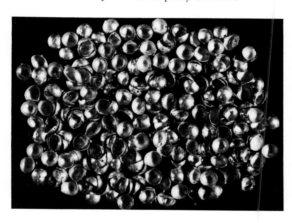

4.19
Hemispherical plaquettes with inner loops (257)
Stamped in mold with loops soldered to the inside for purposes of attachment.
Dimensions: diameter 0.5; height 0.25
Weight: 32.15 (of total)
State of preservation: partly deformed

4.20 Ill. 3
Hemispherical plaques with raised rims (2,630)
Stamped in mold with two perforations in the rim for purposes of attachment.
Dimensions: diameter 1.0–0.8; height 0.2–0.3
Weight: 247.44 (of total)
State of preservation: partly deformed

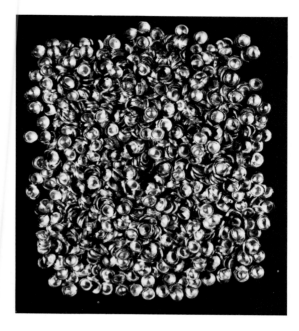

4.21
Two armlets
Cast with slightly flared open-ended terminals. Rectangular in cross section.
Dimensions: total length 21.0; end width 1.1; width 0.5
Weight: 126.45 (of both)
State of preservation: signs of wear

4.22 Ill. 37
Cinquefoil plaques (two)
Cast, with heart- and almond-shaped cells inlaid with turquoise. The design consists of two heart-shaped cells placed back to back down the middle and sandwiched between four almond-shaped insets radiating in four different directions, all interspersed with double volutes. Soldered to the back of each plaque are three long loops for purposes of attachment.
Dimensions: 2.5×2.7
Weight: 16.0 (of both)
State of preservation: faint signs of wear

4.23
Chin stays (two)

Hand-cut from thin sheet gold. One is larger, one smaller, but both taper slightly toward the end, in which several perforations have been made for purposes of attachment. The larger of the two is noticeably broader and has eight perforations at one end and ten at the other; the smaller displays a hardly discernible bulge in the middle and has four perforations at one end and seven at the other.

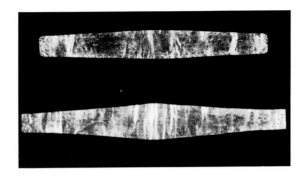

Dimensions: length 36.3 and 31.7; central width 5.3 and 4.1; end width 2.7 and 3.0
Weight: 65.37 (of both)
State of preservation: slightly deformed with some perforations torn

4.24
Buttons (two)

Round, hollow, and comprised of two hemispheres soldered together, with loop soldered to the top for purposes of attachment.

Dimensions: diameter 2.4; height 3.1
Weight: 27.93 (of both)
State of preservation: good

4.25 Ill. 131
Indian coin

The obverse depicts a naked male figure in profile facing right, resting on the Wheel of Dharma, plus an inscription in Kharoshthi, one of the Prakrit languages, which reads: "The turn of the Wheel of Dharma." The reverse depicts a lion with its front paw raised, and in the field the Pandipada symbol and the legend "As fearless as a lion."
Dimensions: diameter 1.6
Weight: 4.33
State of preservation: good

References: V. Sarianidi, G. Koshelenko, "Coins from the Excavation of the Necropolis on the Tillya-tepe Site," *Ancient India. Historical and Cultural Relations*, Moscow, 1982, fig. 1, no. 5 [В. Сарианиди, Г. Кошеленко, "Монеты из раскопок некрополя, расположенного на городище Тилля-тепе," в сб.: *Древняя Индия. Историко-культурные связи*, Москва, 1982, рис. 1, №5].

4.26
"Flower-stem" tube

A hollow tube rolled of thin sheet gold that broadens out toward one end where it terminates in fourteen long petals with pointed tips.
Dimensions: length 13.0; end diameters 0.6 and 1.6
Weight: 12.0
State of preservation: petals partly deformed

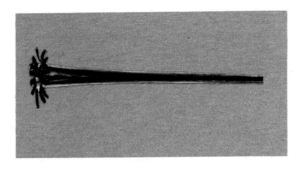

4.27 Ill. 71
Plaque with the Heraclidae

Oval, rimmed by minute granulation. At the center is a two-layered intaglio, with the top layer brown and the lower layer white. It depicts three male figures of the Heraclidae drawing lots (for description turn to p. 44). Soldered to the back of the mount is a gold tube by means of which the intaglio was threaded or attached to a garment.

Dimensions: 1.8×1.3×0.6
Weight: 2.6
State of preservation: heavy iridescence
Reference: O. Neverov, "Italic Carved Gems from the Necropolises of North Pontic Cities," *From the History of the Northern Pontic Lands*, Leningrad, 1979, fig. 5 [О. Я. Неверов, "Италийские геммы в некрополях северопонтийских городов," в сб.: *Из истории Северного Причерноморья*, Ленинград, 1979, рис. 5].

4.28 Ill. 121
Scale model of a tree

Consists of a long, hammered shaft (trunk) with thin wires (branches) soldered to it. Dangling from the wires are disks and pearls designating leaves and fruit (for description turn to pp. 36, 37).

Dimensions: height 9.0
Weight: 16.46
State of preservation: some disks deformed
Reference: M. Artamonov, *Treasures of the Sakas*, Moscow, 1973, fig. 275 [М. И. Артамонов, *Сокровища саков*, Москва, 1973, рис. 275].

4.29
Clasp

Cast in the form of a hollow tube of a semi-oval cross section, topped by a round finial. The front has three indented rectangles bordered by granulation; the finial has two pear-shaped indentations linked by a half-moon cell and also contoured by minute granulation.
Dimensions: length 2.6; tube width 0.9; finial diameter 1.2
Weight: 4.5
State of preservation: good

4.30
Tube with finial

Hollow. At one end two small set-apart disks are soldered on, the top one crowned by a cone.
Dimensions: tube length 15.3; diameter 0.7; disk diameter 1.5
Weight: 16.62
State of preservation: good

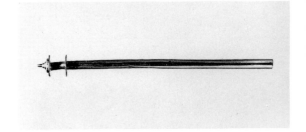

4.31 Ills. 138, 139
Phiale
A cast dish or salver fluted with thirty-two grooves fanning out from the central circlet. Punched on the outer side is the stippled inscription in Greek: "CTAMA."

Dimensions: diameter 23.0; height 4.0; bottom diameter 7.5
Weight: 638.0
State of preservation: good

4.32
Quiver mounts (four)
Hand-cut from thin sheet gold, rolled, and secured where the ends overlap by small gold nails with bent tips. There are large round perforations along one edge.

Dimensions: diameter 7.5 and 7.0; height 5.0
Weight: 124.13 (of total)
State of preservation: partly deformed

4.33 Ill. 155
Quiver top
A massive cast-silver object embossed with a plant design with gilt ribbons in the shape of florets along the upper edge and of vines along the middle. A band of semi-ovals is embossed along the lower edge. Soldered to the middle of the blank top end is a loop set upon a raised four-lobed rosette.
Dimensions: height 11.0; diameter 7.5; loop diameter 1.7
Weight: 304.98
State of preservation: heavily patinaed

4.34 Ill. 98
Plaque with representation of a dragon
Rectangular and flat, rounded at one end and with a rectangular slot at the other end. The back is unornamented, the front carries a finely engraved design (for description turn to p. 42).

Dimensions: 3.5×0.8
Weight: 7.92
State of preservation: signs of wear
Reference: A. Bernstam, "The Gold Diadem from the Shaman Burial on the River Karagalinka," *Reports of the Institute of the History of Material Culture*, Moscow–Leningrad, 1940, issue 5, fig. 2
[А. Н. Бернштам, "Золотая диадема из шаманского погребения на р. Карагалинке," *КСИИМК*, Москва–Ленинград, 1940, вып. 5, рис. 2].

4.35 Ill. 123
Plaque depicting a panther mauling an antelope
Cast in the form of a shield with a mauling scene executed in relief on the obverse (for description turn to p. 43). The reverse is furnished with five hooks which, along with the two perforations in the bottom corners, served to enable it to be attached.

Dimensions: 4.7×3.6×0.5
Weight: 18.6
State of preservation: good
Reference: M. Artamonov, *The Treasures of the Scythian Barrows*, Prague, 1966, table 116
[М. И. Артамонов, *Сокровища скифских курганов*, Прага, 1966, табл. 116].

4.36 Ill. 122
Plaque depicting predators savaging a horse
Cast in the form of a shield contoured at the rim by turquoise mainly pear-shaped insets, except for heart shapes at the corners and tip. Inscribed within is the scene in high relief that is described on pp. 43, 44. On the back the edges have been bent in and have retained traces of powdery dust, thus supporting the assumption that initially the plaque had served as mount for a wooden object.
Dimensions: 5.1×4.3×0.7
Weight: 11.79

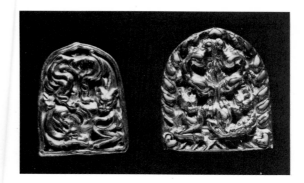

State of preservation: some turquoise insets missing
Reference: M. Artamonov, *ibid*, figs. 133 and 134.

4.37 Ill. 156
Arrowheads (ten)
Of iron, pronged, and trilobed.
State of preservation: rusted

4.38
Overall view of plaque design. This arrangement of various types of gold spangles on the back of the deceased was found as had been initially sewn onto the funerary attire.

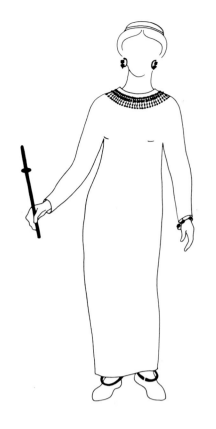

SITE 5

Dimensions: fittings with insets as listed above: 1.2×0.9; 1.2×0.9; 1.3×1.0; 1.1×1.1; 1.4×1.1; bracelet diameter 6.7; thickness 0.2
Weight: 15.65
State of preservation: one fitting missing
Reference: G. Pugachenkova, *Art Treasures of Dalverzin-tepe*, Leningrad, 1978, table 73 [Г. А. Пугаченкова, *Художественные сокровища Дальверзин-тепе*, Ленинград, 1978, табл. 73].

5.2 Ill. 33
Earring clips (two)
Two identical cast oval rings with open ends. Soldered to one end is a bezel in the shape of a heart topped with an oval, both inlaid with turquoise. The ends are blunt and of a round cross section.

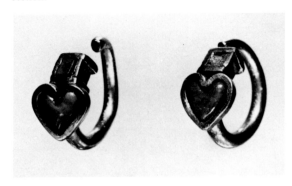

Dimensions: overall length 7.2
Weight: 26.0 (of both)
State of preservation: good

State of preservation: disk missing on one pendant
Reference: I. Marshall, *Taxila*, vol. 3, Cambridge, 1951, pl. 193, nos. 56–58.

5.4
Anklets (two)
Cast, oval-shaped, and open-ended with flared terminals.

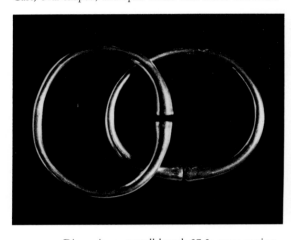

Dimensions: overall length 27.0; cross section 0.5; terminal cross section 1.0
Weight: 306.78 (of both)
State of preservation: inside faint signs of wear from use

5.5
Chin stay
Hand-cut from thin sheet gold and tapering at both ends, each of which has a perforation for purposes of attachment.

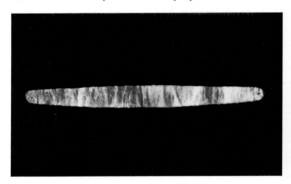

Dimensions: length 32.0; widths 3.0 and 1.5
Weight: 22.95
State of preservation: slightly deformed

5.1 Ills. 102, 103
Expandable bracelet
Consists of a thin gold wire to which seven mounts with insets are soldered. The ends, coiling on each other, are twisted into spirals to allow the bracelet to be gently expanded to the required size. The first fitting, oval in shape, is inset with an amber-type resin of local origin that is contoured with granulation; on the back the mount has two loops for purposes of attachment, which indicates that it had been employed in a different context before. The next fitting, evidently lost in antiquity, is missing; all that remains of it are two loops serving for purposes of attachment. The third mount in the row, contoured with minute granulation, is oval in form and is inset with an intaglio, a sky-blue gemstone carrying the deeply incised representation of a standing female figure, most likely the goddess Athena. She is garbed in a long robe; her left arm is raised and rests on a spear, and in her right hand she holds a shield. The fourth mount is also oval in form, contoured with granulation, and inset with a white gemstone. The fifth mount, a miniature gold pendant, is shaped like an ax with a hole in the middle. The sixth fitting is square-shaped and is inset with a white gemstone and edged with a slender half-erased ornamental design of ovals with tiny bosses, evidently intended to represent a vine. The top is also contoured with granulation. The last mount is in the form of an oblong inset with a black-colored inlay and rimmed with an ornamental design composed of a solid chain of tiny circles plus two rows of granulation.

5.3 Ills. 64, 65
Necklace
Composed of two types of quadripartite pendants. One, a hollow ball bored so that it could be threaded, has a narrow neck with a soldered-on circlet inset with either a bright red gemstone akin to garnet or with turquoise, the whole contoured by granulation. Soldered to the back of the circlet is a tube for purposes of attachment. Attached by gold wire to this part of the pendant are, first, a dangling teardrop inset with a dark stone and also edged with granulation, and, second, a tiny disk. The other pendant type, which alternates on the necklace with the one described above, consists of a broad ring covered with rather large granulation. Firmly attached to it is a flat figure shaped like two crescents joined back to back. This figure also has a horizontally soldered-on tube for purposes of attachment on the back. Secured by a long wire, a dangling teardrop inset with a dark gemstone and edged with granulation comes next, and still lower down, another dangling disk. The first type of pendant with garnet and turquoise insets also alternates. At either end of the necklace is a cone-shaped clasp ornamented with triangles of minute soldered-on grains; at the top the apexes point down, and at the base up, while along the middle the triangles point either up or down.

Dimensions: pendant length 4.1; clasp length 3.6
Weight: 112.23 (of total inclusive of 41 pendants)

5.6
Astragals (three)
One is carved from lapis lazuli and is fitted around the longitudinal axis with a gold mount having sawtooth edges and a top loop for purposes of attachment. Another is of a very soft black medium, possibly paste; it is also fitted along the longitudinal axis with a gold mount with sawtooth edges and is transversely perforated to allow it to be attached. The

last is of a very light flecked yellowish medium akin to amber and is transversely perforated for purposes of attachment.
Dimensions: (in the order listed) 2.0×1.0×1.0; 1.6×1.2×1.0; 1.7×1.0×0.8
State of preservation: distinct signs of wear

5.7 Ill. 76
Lion-shaped pendant

Carved from a very light, flecked brown medium akin to amber. Depicted is a seated lion. Its visage is barely delineated, and its eyes are denoted by round orifices topped by scratched semicircular brows; its mouth is represented by a straight line, its nostrils by two dots, and its tail is pressed to its back. Between the paws there is a perforation along the longitudinal axis and in the middle of the body another transverse perforation, both serving for purposes of attachment.

Dimensions: 2.6×2.2×1.0
Weight: 3.4
State of preservation: faint signs of wear

5.8 Ill. 74
Intaglio with representation of a griffin

Carved of translucent, milky-white chalcedony. The oval bezel carries a meticulously executed deeply incised griffin with a small head and wide-open beak. Bored along the longitudinal axis for purposes of threading.

Dimensions: length 3.1; width 2.8; height 1.2
Weight: 114.36
State of preservation: edge broken off in antiquity

5.9
Gold-mounted tusk

Probably a boar tusk with a sharpened tip set in a gold mount supplied with a loop for purposes of attachment.

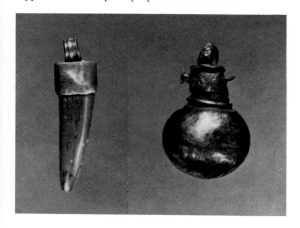

Dimensions: 3.0×0.8
Weight: 1.89
State of preservation: signs of wear on mount
Reference: S. Rudenko, "The Siberian Collection of Peter I," *Reports of the Institute of Archaeology*, Moscow–Leningrad, 1962, table XXI, no. 41 [С. И. Руденко, "Сибирская коллекция Петра I," *САИ*, Москва–Ленинград, 1962, табл. XXI, №41].

Ball-shaped pendant

A miniature, hollow round-bodied object with a tall neck and lid pierced horizontally by a gold nail with a head. On top lies a loop to allow it to be attached.

Dimensions: height 2.7; diameter 1.7
Weight: 4.4
State of preservation: slightly deformed body

5.10 Ill. 72
Plaque with representation of Nike

A round intaglio gemstone (for description of composition turn to p. 46), set in a silver mount having on its back a loop for purposes of attachment.

Dimensions: diameter 1.0; overall height with loop 0.8
Weight: 0.85
State of preservation: cracked mount

5.11 Ill. 134
Small bell

Bronze. Cone-shaped, with a thick top terminating in round loop, and with a freely rotating clapper suspended from the inside loop.

Dimensions: diameter 2.5; height 3.1; clapper protrudes 0.5
Weight: 28.5
State of preservation: heavily patinaed

5.12 Ill. 143
Mirror

Round, with raised rim and central cone-shaped bulge. The handle-stand is hollow and embellished with vertical ribbing

---

and two wide rings around the top. Possibly of an inferior grade of silver.

Dimensions: overall height 25.0; disk diameter 15.0; rim width 3.0; handle height 10.0; handle diameter 8.0
Weight: 630.0
State of preservation: covered with a green patina

5.13 Ill. 137
Bowl

With a flat, unmarked bottom, low, round body, and strongly thrust-out lip. Made of an inferior grade of silver.

Dimensions: lip diameter 17.0; height 10.0; body diameter 16.5; wall thickness 0.05
State of preservation: covered with a green patina, cavity in side

5.14
Lidded pot

Silver, with a hemispherical body on a faintly marked bottom and a slightly indented rim; the lid has a tall cone-topped handle in the middle.

Dimensions: body diameter 7.0; bottom diameter 6.5; height 8.0
Weight: 184.0
State of preservation: heavily deformed

5.15
Gold-embroidered case (?)
Remnant of what is probably a mirror case with some amount of preserved gold-and-pearl embroidery.

State of preservation: in bits and pieces

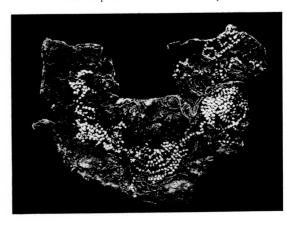

5.16
Beads and pendants (sixteen)
Of diverse shape and form, carved from turquoise, cornelian, garnet, and what is probably agate.

Dimensions: diverse
State of preservation: good

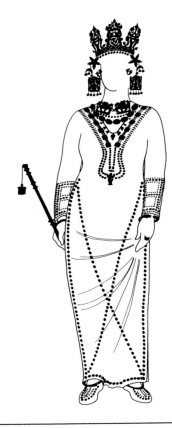

SITE 6

6.1 Ills. 12–15
Crown
Consists of a fillet-base and five attached palmettes. All segments are hand-cut from thin sheet gold. Soldered to the ends of the fillet are two cast loops that are linked together by laces. On the obverse the fillet is embellished with twenty hand-cut six-petaled gold rosettes; a miniature disk is attached to each petal by a wire passed through a perforation at its tip. Each flower has a central soldered-on round cell, contoured by granulation and inset with turquoise. Each flower is secured to the fillet by means of a gold loop passed through a perforation. Vertically soldered to the back of the fillet are tubes that hold the palmettes, which are designed in the form of stylized trees (for a full description turn to pp. 47, 48).

Dimensions: fillet length 45.0; fillet width 2.3; palmette height 13.0; palmette width 7.5; height of central palmette 13.0; width of central palmette 8.0
Weight: 214.14
State of preservation: flowers partly deformed
Reference: G. Borovka, *Female Headgear from the Chertomlyk Barrow*, Petrograd, 1921 [Г. И. Боровка, *Женские головные уборы Чертомлыцкого кургана*, Петроград, 1921].

6.2 Ills. 77–79
Clasps with amorous scene (two)
Oblong, cast, and open-worked in high relief. The scene on one is the mirror image of the other (for description turn to pp. 50–52). Soldered to the back of each clasp is a flat plate duplicating the obverse in outline. Further, soldered to each of the four corners of the base plate are loops; in the middle are two pierced perforations of a triangular cross section with small projections or flaps. The hook on one of the pair of clasps and the loop on the other have two split hammered ends that are coiled into spirals and soldered on fast. The clasps buckle together by means of hook and loop.

Dimensions: height 6.5; length 7.0; thickness 0.8
Weight: 97.27 (of both)
State of preservation: faint signs of wear and one inset missing
Reference: S. Reinach, *Répertoire des reliefs*, Paris, 1909, 1, fig. 75, no. 2.

6.3 Ill. 99
Figurine of the Bactrian Aphrodite
A cast, hollow, high-relief representation of a winged female deity (for description turn to pp. 49, 50). Soldered to the back is a base plate which duplicates the outline of the obverse. Soldered to it, in turn, are three loops, one at the top and two at the bottom, by means of which the figurine was attached. Also in the middle of the back is a perforation of a triangular cross section, with a protruding flap.

Dimensions: height 5.0; width 2.6; thickness 0.6
Weight: 14.0
State of preservation: signs of wear on the obverse

6.4 Ills. 48–50
Temple pendants depicting the Great Goddess among animals (two)
Cast, hollow, open-worked in high relief, and encrusted. The identical scene is on both of these oblong pierced plates (described on pp. 48, 49). Soldered to the back is a flat base plate hand-cut in such a manner as to duplicate the outline of the obverse. Soldered to it, in turn, level with the heads of the birds and at a point halfway up the columns on the obverse, are two pairs of loops to which disks are secured. Another seven loops, likewise for securing disks, were soldered to the bottom of the base plate.

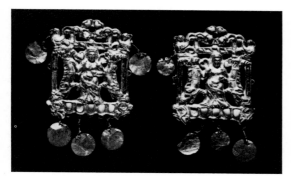

Dimensions: height 5.8; width 4.6;
thickness 0.5
Weight: 31.58 (of both)
State of preservation: faint signs of wear and
paste inlays partially crumbled

6.5 Ill. 36
**Earring clips with representations
of cupids** (two)
Identically shaped, cast in the form of open-ended rings; one
end is intensely flared and is embellished with a disk having a
ribbed ornamental design that has been slipped on over it.
The other end is decorated with the sculptured representation
of a winged cupid with a pierced crescent on the forehead.
    Dimensions: overall length 7.0; width 1.5
    Weight: 43.65
State of preservation: heavy signs of wear,
especially on the hoop

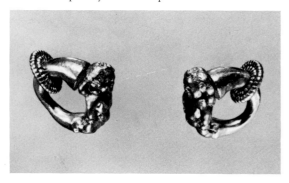

6.6 Ill. 110
Signet ring with an intaglio
Oval bezel inset with a dark cherry-red gemstone, presumably a garnet, carrying a deeply incised profile of a male head
turned to the right.
    Dimensions: 2.0×1.7; hoop diameter 1.3;
    intaglio 1.1×0.9
    Weight: 3.8
    State of preservation: good

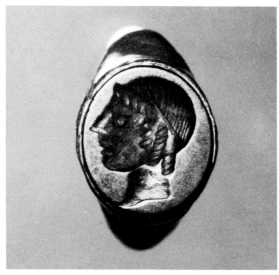

6.7
Bell-shaped object
Cast, hollow, in the shape of a cylinder with an indrawn
waist, and embellished with a slightly curved fluting having
rounded ends. The object has a significance that is still rather
obscure. The broad bottom end is filled by a soldered-on

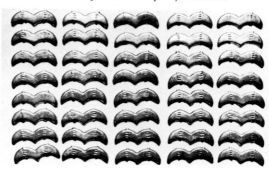

depressed roundel with an impressed cinquefoil rosette that
has a small hole in the middle and sixteen minor perforations
along the outer rim. The shoulders at the top are embellished
with turquoise inlays and are surmounted by a tall annular
projection with a wide hole in the middle.
    Dimensions: height 2.9; diameters 2.9 and 1.5
    Weight: 13.25
    State of preservation: good

6.8–10
Pan-shaped plaques (598) and large (555) and
small (224) plaques
Molded, each with two perforations opposite each other
along the bottom of the rim for purposes of attachment.
    Dimensions: diameters 1.5, 0.9–1.0, and 0.7;
    rim heights 0.2 and 0.1
    Weight: 198.0, 37.1, and 35.31 (of total in all
    three cases)
    State of preservation: pan-shaped plaques and
    large plaques partly deformed, small plaques in
    good condition

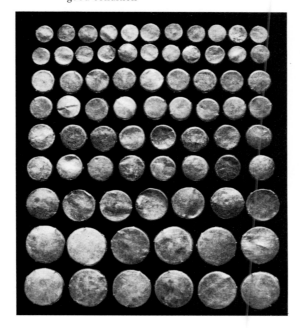

6.11
Rimmed hemispherical spangles (313)
Molded, each with two perforations opposite each other
along the base of the rim for purposes of attachment.

Dimensions: diameter 1.5, height 0.4
Weight: 59.1 (of total)
State of preservation: partly deformed

6.12
Horn-shaped plaques (seventy-six)
Cast in the form of a jointed pair of horns, ornamented with
short, impressed lines and each having two diametrically
opposed perforations along the base of the rim for purposes
of attachment.
    Dimensions: length 1.7; width 0.7; height 0.25
    Weight: 32.74 (of total)
    State of preservation: partly deformed

6.13
Large disks (forty-eight)
Hand-cut from thin sheet gold and perforated on one side for
purposes of attachment.
    Dimensions: diameter 2.6–2.9
    Weight: 30.13 (of total)
    State of preservation: heavily deformed

6.14
Bell-shaped ornaments (three)
Cast and conical in shape, with the bottom and top edged
with rings of minute granulation. On the outside a ring has
been soldered to the short neck at the apex to enable the object
to be suspended; a smaller loop has been soldered on inside,
also at the top of the cone.

Dimensions: height 1.5; diameter 1.7
Weight: 12.11 (of three)
State of preservation: partly deformed

6.15 Ills. 104, 106
Armlets (two)
Cast, oval, with ends in the shape of hollow heads of fantastic horned lions (for description turn to p. 52).
Dimensions: overall length 18.5; hoop thickness 0.5; head thickness 1.4
Weight: 150.0 (of both)
State of preservation: signs of wear, with one head having a jagged cavity
References: Ye. Zeimal, *The Amu Darya Treasure*, Leningrad, 1979, fig. 131 [Е. В. Зеймаль, *Амударьинский клад*, Ленинград, 1979, рис. 131]; I. Marshall, *Taxila*, vol. 3, Cambridge, 1951, pl. 195, nos. 133–136.

6.16
Anklets (two)
Cast, with open-ended flared terminals embellished with turquoise teardrop insets.

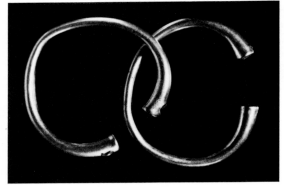

Dimensions: overall length 21.2; hoop thickness 0.5; terminal thickness 1.1
Weight: 243.3 (of both)
State of preservation: heavy signs of wear

6.17 Ill. 16
Hairpins (two)
Both consist of silver shafts topped by identical gold finials in the form of large five-petaled rosettes hand-cut from thin sheet gold. Soldered to the middle of each rosette is a roundel contoured by minute granulation. Gold disks dangle from wires attached to two of the petals, each of which is perforated close to the tip. Two other petals are linked by a piece of wire, from which a large crescent dangles on another piece of wire. Three disks dangle from wires attached to the middle and cusps of the crescent. Some of the wires still retain the

pearls initially threaded on them. On the center of the back of each rosette is a short, gold tube-like fitting into which the sharp end of the silver shaft is inserted. A petal on one of the rosettes, fragmented in antiquity, was patched together by two rivets.
Dimensions: shaft length 6.5; rosette diameter 7.0; disk diameter 1.8; crescent length 4.0
Weight: 36.74 (of both)

6.18
Cylinder with sawtooth petals
The significance of this object is obscure. It was hand-cut from thin sheet gold and soldered together along the vertical axis. The top edge is cut into sawtooth petals; soldered to it at the other end is a disk with protruding rims and a short jutting tube in the middle. It is suggested that the object may have dangled on a thong from a wand or scepter.
Dimensions: cylinder diameter 3.0; disk diameter 3.5; height 3.8; tube length 1.3; tube diameter 0.5
Weight: 6.4
State of preservation: partly deformed

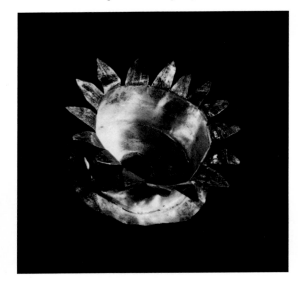

6.19
"Scepter"
This takes the form of a pipe, one end of which is rounded and slightly flattened and has three indentations on top. The other end is pierced in the middle; from this point radiate four indentations, possibly in the shape of originally inlaid petals. The pipe has four ribbed rings at one end and two at the other. Made of almost foil-thin sheet gold.

Dimensions: length 35.0; diameter 1.5; end diameters 1.9; ribbed ring diameters 2.0
Weight: 42.75
State of preservation: poor

6.20 Ills. 66, 67
Necklace of gold beads
Originally threaded together of hollow, slightly elongated beads and secured by a pair of cone-shaped clasps. The beads are bored along the longitudinal axis. The surface of each bead is articulated into eight facets, with the ribs marked by minute granulation. Four facets are plain, the others have soldered-on rosettes of thin wire in the middle and are contoured with granulation, whose heart-shaped lobes are inlaid with turquoise. The plain and ornamented facets alternate, as they do also on the cone-shaped clasps, on which the facets are similar. Each clasp is also edged by two transverse bands of

granulation. At the base each clasp has a perforation for threading, which is edged with granulation, and at the tip an ornamental design in the form of a trefoil.
Dimensions: bead 2.8×2.5, clasps 5.0×2.2
Weight: of bead and entire necklace respectively 14.0 and 154.19
State of preservation: heavy signs of wear

6.21
Cinquefoils (two)
Hand-cut from thin sheet gold with heart-shaped petals and a centrally soldered-on roundel contoured with granulation. Disks dangle from pearl-threaded wires secured to two of the petals. Three loops have been soldered to the back of each rosette to enable them to be attached.

Dimensions: rosette diameter 3.0; overall length with disks 5.7
Weight: 6.8 (of both)

6.22
Round encrusted plaques with dividers (six)
Each plaque carries on the obverse indented quatrefoil rosettes encrusted with heart-shaped turquoise beads each with a central soldered-on boss. Two of the plaques, each of which has two soldered-on tubes on the reverse to enable them to be attached, have each a flat disk secured by wire. Each divider consists of two crescents joined back-to-back and inlaid with heart-shaped turquoise beads at the joints. Soldered to each

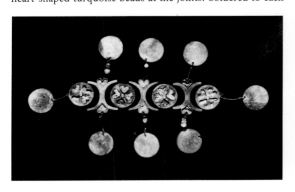

heart-shaped turquoise bead is a loop to which a plain disk is secured by a piece of wire. Soldered to the back of each divider are tubes enabling them to be attached.

Dimensions: plaque diameter 1.7; length with pendant disk 4.6; length of joined crescents with two pendant disks—8.2; crescent height 2.6; plain disk diameter 1.7

Weight: plaques 11.5; dividers 34.78 (of total in both cases)

State of preservation: several plain disks and most turquoise inlays missing

6.23
Various ornaments

Hand-shaped pendant. Roughly carved from turquoise and mounted in a gold fitting with sawtooth edges and a loop on top.

Dimensions: length 1.3; width 0.7

State of preservation: faint signs of wear

Plain pendant

Carved from a white gemstone in the form of a spatula with one end inserted into a gold fitting that is provided with a loop.

Dimensions: length 1.3; width 0.5

State of preservation: faint signs of wear

Empty mount

Gold, with sawtooth edges and a loop on top.

Dimensions: diameter 0.6; length 1.0

State of preservation: faint signs of wear

Ax-shaped pendant

Carved of a hard stone in the form of a minute ax and perforated at the narrow end to take a thong.

Dimensions: length 1.2; blade width 0.5

State of preservation: good

Fragment of a gold object in the shape of a ring soldered to a thin broken plate

Dimensions: diameter 0.5

State of preservation: faint signs of wear

Two encrusted spangles

Both are oval and inlaid with a vitreous mass, one black, the other coffee-colored and both have loops soldered to the middle of their backs to enable them to be attached.

Dimensions: 1.3×1.1 (black), 1.4×1.0 (coffee-colored)

State of preservation: heavily deformed

White-inset spangle

A tiny oval inset with white soft stone or paste and with two soldered-on loops on its back to enable it to be attached.

Dimensions: length 0.9; width 0.6

State of preservation: signs of wear

Two disks

Segments of larger ornaments, the smaller having a bit of gold wire attached.

Dimensions: diameters 1.5 and 0.7; thickness 0.1

State of preservation: signs of wear

Hard stone pendant fitted in a gold mount with scalloped edges and a loop on top

Dimensions: length 1.7; width 0.5

State of preservation: hard stone severely cracked

Silver fitting of a hemispherical shape

Possibly part of a larger ornament.

Dimensions: diameter 1.3; thickness 0.2

State of preservation: patinaed

Three mounts

One holds a small cylinder of a black vitreous paste, another a small cylinder of a pale-blue color that may be turquoise. Both fittings have scalloped edges and a ring-shaped loop on top. The third mount consists of a pair of tubes soldered together, one of which holds the vestiges of a black vitreous paste inlay.

Dimensions: 1.2×0.4; 1.0×0.5; 0.7×0.7

State of preservation: heavy signs of wear

6.24
Trident-shaped pendants (four)

Cast in the form of a crescent with an extra, third tooth in the middle. The crescents are inlaid with a vitreous paste that is of a sky-blue tint on two items and of a dark blue on the other two. The extra tooth on all four is also inlaid with a vitreous paste of a sky-blue color. Each pendant is contoured with minute granulation and has a ring on top.

Dimensions: height 1.5; width 1.0

Weight: 3.5 (of total)

State of preservation: inlays partly crumbled

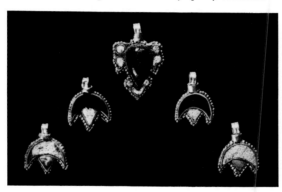

Leaf-shaped pendant

Cast in cloisonné with a centrally-positioned convex paste inlay sandwiched between turquoise insets, contoured with granulation. A ring has been soldered on top to enable it to be attached.

Dimensions: length 2.0; width 1.4

Weight: 1.52

State of preservation: good

6.25 Ill. 10
Ribbed tubes (153)

Hollow, resemble jelled pellets, of three each in most cases.

Dimensions: length 0.5–1.0; diameter 0.1

Weight: 6.22 (of total)

State of preservation: some pieces deformed

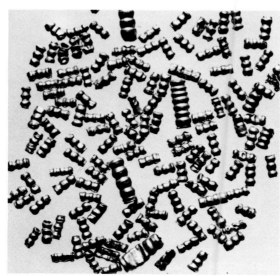

6.26 Ill. 28
Oblong plaques (twelve)

Massive and cast in the form of an oval. Consists of two middle rows of convex hemispheres of five each, sandwiched between two outer rows of cells of five each inset with black

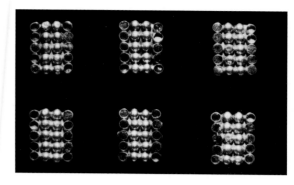

paste. On the back four tubes have been soldered on transversely to enable them to be attached.

Dimensions: 2.0×1.7

Weight: 57.7 (of total)

State of preservation: some paste insets partly missing

6.27
Cinquefoil rosette

Cast and round, with five radiating petals partly overlapping one another. Inscribed within the rosette is a five-pointed star whose rays are shaped as veined leaves; a round turquoise is inset in the middle. A thin disk is soldered to the back in such

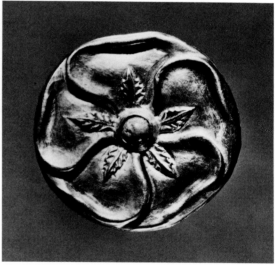

a manner as to leave a hollow in between. Soldered to the middle of the back is a ring-shaped loop to enable it to be attached.

Dimensions: diameter 3.2; thickness 0.3

Weight: 6.4

State of preservation: good

6.28 Ill. 136
Basin

Large, squat, round, with a distinctly marked base and concave bottom. The clearly silhouetted neck flows into a strongly protruding lip. Made of an inferior grade of silver with thin walls.

257

Dimensions: lip diameter 18.0; bottom
diameter 13.0; height 9.0; wall thickness 0.1
State of preservation: covered with a green
patina, with broken-off base

Dimensions: diameter 2.0
Weight: 2.77
State of preservation: good
Reference: V. Sarianidi, G. Koshelenko, *ibid.*

6.29
Dish
Small, rounded, with round bottom and flattened simple lip
slightly bent out. Made of an inferior grade of silver.

Dimensions: diameter 22.0; height 3.5; lip
width 0.4
State of preservation: partly covered with a
green patina

Dimensions: diameter 17.0
State of preservation: heavily oxidized

6.34
Lidded boxes for cosmetics (two)
Round and carved of ivory. The lid of one of the two has a
sculptured handle and a raised design of circles.

6.30
Mirror with an ivory handle
The obverse is plain and smooth except for the slightly raised
edge. On the back there is a broad, slightly sharpened bulge,
bordered along the rim by a round, convex bulge terminating
in a short pointed tang with an implanted ivory handle. The
latter is carved in the form of a pillar with a distinctly marked
flat base; halfway up and at the top the handle is embellished

6.32 Ill. 128
Gold coin
The obverse carries the left-turned profile of a bearded king
wearing a tiara, in front of which in the field is an unknown
symbol. Behind the head is a countermark in the form of a
full-fronted face. On the reverse is the figure of an enthroned
archer presented in profile turned right, and in the field is an
illegible inscription in Greek.

Dimensions: diameters 8.5 and 6.2; heights 6.5
and 5.3
State of preservation: poor, heavily damaged

6.35
Knife handle
Ivory, oval in cross section, and covered with an engraved
design of small scrolls. At the ends and around the middle, the
handle is fitted with gold mounts. At one end is a bronze ring
plated with sheet gold, at the other, the broken-off top of the
iron blade.

with two broad, protruding annular bands. Made of an
inferior grade of silver.
    Dimensions: diameter 14.5; hem width 2.0;
    handle length 5.0; handle width 2.0; handle
    height 9.0; handle base diameter 8.0; handle
    base height 2.5; width of annular band halfway
    up handle 2.0; width of top handle band 1.5;
    overall height 24.0
    State of preservation: heavily patinaed and
    damaged handle
    Reference: I. Marshall, *Taxila*, vol. 3,
    Cambridge, 1951, pl. 182, no. 21.

Dimensions: diameter 1.8
Weight: 3.35
State of preservation: fair
Reference: V. Sarianidi, G. Koshelenko, "Coins
from the Excavations of the Necropolis on the
Tillya-tepe Site," *Ancient India. Historical and
Cultural Relations*, Moscow, 1982
[В. Сарианиди, Г. Кошеленко, "Монеты из
раскопок некрополя, расположенного на
городище Тилля-тепе," в сб.: *Древняя Индия.
Историко-культурные связи*, Москва, 1982].

Dimensions: length 15.0
State of preservation: shown here after
restoration

6.31
Chinese mirror
Plain in front, it is ornamented on the back with a design
bordered by a circular inscription in Chinese characters. In
the middle is a convex handle with a perforation. Probably
made of an inferior grade of silver.

6.33 Ill. 129
Silver coin
The obverse carries the head of a king wearing a diadem, in a
left-turned profile. A countermark beneath is in the form of a
man wearing a Macedonian-type helmet, again in profile but
turned right. On the reverse is the figure of an enthroned
archer turned right in profile and in the field is a practically
illegible inscription in Greek. Of an inferior grade of silver.

6.36
Lidded pot with spatula
Silver, cylindrical in form with a tiny looped handle by the
upper rim. The cone-shaped lid has a sculptured handle in the
middle. Found inside was a small spatula that was definitely
used for cosmetic purposes.

Dimensions: height 8.0; diameter 5.0; spatula
length 6.5
State of preservation: poor, shown here after
restoration

6.37
Silver bowl with upper marked rim
Dimensions: height 5.3, lip diameter 5.0
State of preservation: poor, shown here after
restoration

6.39
Earthenware vase
Round, with a smooth out-turned lip of red clay; decorated
with a dark-red slip and partly burnished.
Dimensions: height 7.0; bottom diameter 3.5;
lip diameter 5.8
State of preservation: fair

6.40
Pins (two)
Silver, with round, hollow heads in the form of pomegran-
ates, covered with gold foil. The upper parts of the shafts have
a four-sided bulge decorated with incised lines.

Dimensions: extant length 5.0;
head diameter 1.0
State of preservation: shaft ends broken off

6.38 Ill. 147
Glass bottles (two)
The larger of the two, with a round body and long neck, was
made in the *millefiori* technique of differently colored—
white, pale-blue, and yellowish—glass rods. The smaller
bottle is sky-blue in color and is pear-shaped with a straight
neck and protruding lip.
Dimensions: height 10 and 5.0; bottom
diameter 3.0 and 2.0; lip diameter 2.0 and 1.7
State of preservation: poor, shown here after
restoration

ЗОЛОТО БАКТРИИ

Альбом (на английском языке)

Издательство „Аврора". Ленинград. 1985
Изд. № 1116

Printed and bound in Austria by Globus, Vienna